NEVER PLEAD GUILTY

NEVER PLEAD GUILTY

The Story of Jake Ehrlich

John Wesley Noble

Bernard Averbuch

Farrar, Straus

and Cudahy

New York

CONTENTS

Part Three: **THE CASE-BOOK**
   The Shooting Never Stopped

Part Four: **THE FRIEND**

PREFACE

SOME of America's best legends have blossomed in the gossipy atmosphere of such criminal court habitats as the battered old pressroom in San Francisco's Hall of Justice. How many times, after murder trials, its telephones have announced: "Not guilty!" "Acquitted!" "The Master walked 'em out again!"

The man they call "The Master" is the criminal lawyer, Jake Ehrlich.

Three decades of reporters have debated the Ehrlich story, sitting out "death watches" while his juries deliberated. A fat dossier of Ehrlichiana has accumulated and there have often been rumors that someone was putting it into a book.

"It would make great reading," people said, *"if it could all be told."* But that, they thought, Jake would never permit.

When Bernie Averbuch came on the police beat, he listened through many a night to the Ehrlich tales of his colleagues, Hank Peters, Jimmy Leonard, Harvey Wing, Neil Hitt, Jimmy McFadden, and Eddie Ammer. He was enormously impressed.

Finally he went to the newspaper files and read the daily story of San Francisco back into the twenties. Jake was omnipresent in it. He appeared to have played a more significant role than even the pressroom realized.

Bernie brought the idea to me. I had once been a newspaperman too. I considered the obvious questions. Would a successful lawyer, at the peak of his career, permit *all* of his story to be told? Could we really get behind the scenes? What did he have in mind during this big case? What did he actually do in preparation for that one? What strategy defeated a certain tough prosecutor and set a murderess free? The daily reports often miss the deep, hidden drama of the courtroom.

We went to see Jake. We talked it all over and he decided to let us write the book. The average successful lawyer will not permit his story to be told while he is still alive and practicing. It might involve judges before whom he must appear again; prosecutors, too, who perhaps had not shown too brilliantly against him in the past but might have become judges since. Other lawyers would learn from the book about the adroit methods that had beaten them and, next time, be prepared. All this I laid before Ehrlich.

With the same confidence he brought to San Francisco originally, Jake decided he still could win for his clients, no matter what the book disclosed. The book, in fact, would prove his point that he never uses the same maneuvers in any two trials.

"Jake," I warned him, "a book about you would be fascinating, but it would involve a colossal invasion of privacy—your own."

He nodded. "It wouldn't be worth a damn if it wasn't honest."

I believed him. So Bernie and I set out to backtrack the legend to its beginnings. We found the record wonderfully documented. Trial transcripts were available. There were files of clippings in the libraries of five metropolitan newspapers. On many Ehrlich trials there had been staffs of reporters and sob sisters to record the utterances of all the dramatis personæ.

In a city as cohesive as San Francisco most of the principals were still available and easy to locate, some of them in nearby prisons. Jake's memory was uncanny. Other people corroborated the details.

"Talk to everyone who has any story about Jake Ehrlich," I told Bernie. "Write down the unfavorable as well as the favorable reports. No man is a saint. This man doesn't claim to be one. We will write him as he is."

We have done that. We have not even changed any names.

Jake came to San Francisco an unknown, when it was still relatively small, just fourteen years after its catastrophic earthquake. He believes that he has grown with the city.

We had liked Jake Ehrlich as we saw him through press-room eyes. We know him better now, and like him more. We can comprehend his personal philosophies though we don't agree with them all. We are different men, by temperament, experience, training and outlook. But we can respect one another's abilities and ideas. In our private ledgers that is the vital thing.

J. W. N.

Part One: **THE LEGEND**

FIRST THINGS

APRIL wind was hounding torn newspapers off the walk as a natty little man of fifty-four with gray in his black wavy hair and a big accordion-board briefcase under his arm turned in at the alley. He skirted the police cars parked there, passed the Coroner's door, and ducked in at the basement entrance to the Hall of Justice.

Probably ten thousand times, in thirty-three years of law practice, Jake Ehrlich had come this way—up Montgomery from the financial district, up Merchant and into the drab gray edifice facing on Portsmouth Square where the accused of San Francisco are tried and convicted or set free. But this was big—his fifty-sixth murder trial as counsel for the defense. Up to now no client of Jake's had ever paid the extreme penalty.

The crux of the case was as obvious to him as Coit Tower up on the hill. But how make the jurors see it? Several trials back, arguing with the court, Jake had tried to hammer home a similar idea. Waving impatiently, the judge had chided: "Go on with your evidence. The jury knows what murder in the second degree is."

Jake had cocked his head and fixed the bench with half-lidded eyes. "Judge," he said icily, "I'm certain the jury knows

what murder in the second degree is, but I am going to repeat it so you and I will know."

The judge had flushed, cleared his throat ominously, and
then settled back in the big chair. "You may proceed, Mr.
Ehrlich."

So he had, and won the case.

Now crowds were streaming along Kearny Street; drama
was building, and Jake liked that. It usually helps the defense.
He didn't smile—for there are no laughs in murder—but he
felt good. It was spring, and the jury panel was new again.

In San Francisco spring can be exhilarating when raw
scouring winds raise up out of the Pacific to put sparkle on
the grand old city where legends grow. A freighter wallowing
home from the Orient pitches sluggishly near Mile Rock,
turning up an underbelly that is red as the arching span of
the Gate Bridge. The wind, like a giddy charwoman done up
in dust cloths of cumulus, pushes back the furniture and
sweeps behind the hills. The Top of the Mark glitters on the
skyline—sharp as Jake's crisp white cuffs and the starch-stiff
handkerchief at the breast pocket of his proper, tailored funereal suit. Good clothes and snowy linen are his trade mark.

Up in Chinatown, beyond the Square, windy white wings
are fetching off the strange Cathay odors. And over in North
Beach the paisanos will be pelting dialects across fences the
length of the block. The cloistering drapery would be drawn
for sunning at St. Francis Wood, brightening spirits there and
in the unexclusive Mission, and Butchertown as well.

A happy day. In all the big city one mortal alone must put
up his life as forfeit against the sobering charge of murder.
In Union Square the pigeons would be busy. Market Street
would be swept clean. There would be throngs at the beach,
the Cliff House, at Seals Stadium for baseball, and tourists
everywhere.

Jake could feel the sap rising, though not because of spring.

Inside, as always, he himself was being the man accused. To save the other—a bartender this time—he must save himself first. That is the strange game Ehrlich always plays with himself, and invariably it succeeds.

It is April. Jake likes to try his murder cases in April—or in July, if necessary, or October or January—the months when new jury panels are sworn. In April honest citizens are quickening to life. They are fresh. They form a new panel which hasn't sat too long. That, in Jake's phrase, is "Before the district attorney has educated them to hate."

A good jury must always be that small group of men or women who can feel themselves inside another mortal in given circumstances, capable of any act—including murder.

Now, at the Hall of Justice, the basement door clattered open and a gargoyle little man in uniform looked at Jake and giggled: "You gonna walk 'im out like usual, Mr. Ehrlich?"

2

In San Francisco they like to believe that all criminal cases defended by Jake Ehrlich are walkaways. "If you're in trouble," they say, "get Jake."

The legend has fattened on brilliant performance in a score of sensational cases, and elevated the banty plantation-born ex-cavalryman, harvest hand, ex-pugilist and one-time process server to the ranks of the nation's great mouthpieces. People who never heard of William Fallon, Earl Rogers, Clarence Darrow or Samuel Leibowitz get Jake and sleep easier. For years he has been the Northern California columinary of Jerry Giesler, the noted Los Angeles barrister who keeps Hollywood stars lustrous in their appearances at the bar. Headline-watchers, the ordinary folk from whom juries are chosen, nod wisely: "Get Jake and you're safe."

Not long ago a beautiful young model stopped off at a young man's apartment in the early hours of the morning—for a cup of coffee, she said. Some time later she screamed for police and claimed she had been assaulted. The young man, scion of a prominent family, got Jake. Overnight the story took on a different color. There were chuckles between the newspaper lines, and householders raised titillated eyebrows. Alert to the public interest of the moment, a Market Street store took advertising space in the *Examiner* to offer used office furniture under a heading: THESE "MODELS" HAVE *REALLY* BEEN BEATEN UP! And the Grand Jury decided not to return criminal charges.

"That Jake!" chortled the townspeople.

To describe Ehrlich, reporters have used the full thesaurus: cynical, steely, brilliant, impudent, grasping, boisterous, maudlin, urchin, cocky, generous, sly, shrewd, ruthless, profane, flamboyant, gregarious, sentimental, egotistical and tender. All are probably correct, at times and in degree. Jake has many moods. He has even been called a Christian, mistakenly. He is a Jew. People have said Jake will spit in a judge's eye, which is not quite true, and that Joan of Arc would never have paid with her life had gallant Jake been there to defend her.

One day on his restless rounds of the Hall of Justice, he stepped into Women's Court on a routine matter. Nodding to the bored reporters and policemen, he scanned the spectators and was leaving when he noticed the defendant. She was a straw-haired girl, scarcely seventeen, with sullen, downcast eyes. "What's she up for?" he asked.

"Vagrancy," said the lady prosecutor, a middle-aged protector of virtue. Jake noticed that the girl's lips were quivering. Policemen had found her in a cheap hotel with two sailors. She would be sent to quarantine, like any prostitute, and then to the county jail. Jake moved toward her.

"She isn't your client!" protested the lady prosecutor. "Will the court please remind Mr. Ehrlich that he is not involved in this case?"

"He is now," said Jake.

He spoke gently to the girl, urging her not to be frightened. Suddenly tearful, she blurted out her story. She had run away from Montana when her parents died. Wandering broke and alone, she had made her way to San Francisco, where she met the sailors. They gave her a place to stay. That was all there was to it.

"If Your Honor please," said Jake, "this little lady will plead not guilty." He shushed the prosecutor's objections with an airy wave of his hand—the left hand, on which a diamond ring flashes like a sheriff's badge. Then he spent five minutes rephrasing the girl's story and launched into his unrehearsed argument.

"From my own experience—which the court will agree has been extensive in these matters—I tell you that the City and County of San Francisco is preparing to make a prostitute of this frightened little girl. Put her through the humiliating police procedure, throw her in with those you have convicted of the oldest profession, and you can make of her, too, a woman of the streets. She should be returned to her home."

"There is no fund for sending her home, Mr. Ehrlich," droned the judge.

"There is now," Jake said, and reached for his wallet. Released to his custody, the girl boarded a northbound train that evening, newly outfitted and with money in her purse. Six years later Ehrlich heard from her again in a letter addressed simply: "To Lawyer Jake—San Francisco." She was happily married to a young rancher and had just given birth to their first son. "His name is Jacob, for you," she wrote. "I didn't learn your last name, but if it hadn't been for you I would not be here—and neither would he."

3

Jake was the lawyer whom influential friends called when Madge Bellamy, the movie beauty, tried to shoot up San Francisco and one of its prominent nabobs. Howard Hughes got Jake to defend *The Outlaw,* the movie that introduced a star named Jane Russell, when it encountered trouble with the censors. Sally Rand came to him, sans fans, when police harassed her swishing performances. Billie Holiday, the blues singer, called for Jake when narcotics agents arrested her. There were also two well-known local women, Madames Dolly Fine and Sally Stanford, both adept at entertaining men but shy before the law.

And there were nobodies, as panic-stricken as any celebrity when the long arm reached out for them: Alfred Cline, the man of silence, who steadfastly refused to talk about the murder charge or even converse with Ehrlich after engaging him to defend him. Gertrude Morris, a jittery housewife who cracked—as murderers invariably do—but picked the worst possible moment. Jake had her on the stand in her own defense when she exploded like a firecracker in his hands. And there was a pathetic little whore named Jean Collins who became world-famous overnight because Jake believed her story and set out to save her life.

Thirty years ago, when the legend began, Jerry Giesler sent for Jake to help defend Alexander Pantages, the theatre magnate, accused by a schemingly pretty girl. The boy who once yearned to be a lawyer while he washed dishes in the old Imperial Hotel has laundered a lot of soiled linen since then. In San Francisco courtrooms, flicking his spotless cuffs, Ehrlich represents an assortment of people. Abroad, Jake represents San Francisco.

Perhaps it is because the man, like the city, is a cosmopolitan swashbuckler. Both snort at pretense. Both are honest sophisticates. They recognize that the rich man's dollar breaks easily into grimy dimes that buy Skid Row muscatel or a flop on Howard Street. Both work hard to create illusions. Neither suffers delusions. It was Jake's pixie pal, William Saroyan, who wrote of San Francisco: "It is an unreasonable city. It makes friends of thieves and opens its heart to saints. But only for a moment. It soon returns to the thieves and abandons the saints."

Jake likes to hear himself touted as a shrewd, high-priced lawyer who billed one client $500,000 for a divorce, and he loves to flash the gold cuff links blessed by Pope Pius XII. But he also likes to dun glowering Superior Judge George Schoenfeld for $1 allegedly owed him for thirty years—since the days when His Honor was a struggling lawyer and Jake, struggling harder, served legal papers at a dollar a throw. Always the judge grumbles: "That debt has been outlawed by the statute of limitations. Now proceed with the matter at hand—*Mister* Ehrlich."

When he isn't neck-deep in murder, Jake is good for laughs. Once when Dorothy Lamour complained to a columnist that she was getting no sleep because the bedsprings at the St. Francis Hotel creaked, Jake chortled with glee. That evening, as the glamorous actress dined in the haughty Mural Room, the maître d'hôtel staggered in under a huge, expensive, gift-wrapped mattress. A gift from Jake.

On another occasion a letter came to his office from out of town. "Please advise," it said, "how long a woman, under California law, needs to live with a man to be able to claim him as a common-law husband. Does the fact that he brought her pork chops which she cooked for him in her domicile affect the case?" Jake dropped everything to reply: "It all depends on what was cooking besides the pork chops."

He also has dropped high-fee work to represent judges in

their own difficulties, and he has defended more policemen
than any other attorney in town, for little or no fee. When the
telephone rings in the still of the night and a terrified voice
cries out for Jake, he drops big-wig clients and listens. "Their
cries," he notes, "are wails of human despair."

These are the cases—though they represent only 3 per cent
of his practice—which have made him the famous mouthpiece. The other 97 per cent, which are civil matters, have
made him money. Ehrlich is known as "the man who makes
the case big automatically" when he adds his name to it. In
April, 1954, the box score read:

> *Murder cases tried* 55
> *Outright acquittals* 41
> *Clients convicted of manslaughter only* 12
> *Clients convicted of murder, second degree* .. 2

There *was* one first-degree conviction, which calls for the gas
chamber in California. It was reversed overnight by the judge,
and made to stand at simple manslaughter. One jury was out
only thirteen minutes before it brought back an acquittal.
Another took four minutes—time only to name its foreman
and poll itself—and the verdict was not guilty.

Jake swears there are no tricks in his repertoire. Tricks
are for almost-successful lawyers. Jake hears them in the
courtroom, the young weisenheimers: "Ehrlich used that in
the Borelli case. It worked fine."

But "The cases are never the same," Jake explains over and
over to his office staff. "You must understand that, once it has
happened this way, the format changes. If we have successfully defended a prostitute who killed her man with his own
gun, there won't be another case quite like it for a long time.
For one thing, the pimps will get scared and hide their guns.

"You never sit down to a murder case as if it were a formula
story and say, 'All right, we'll insert Trick Number Eight in

here.' Because you are not Galileo figuring an abstraction.
Two plus two simply don't add up to four in a sociological
problem."

When Jake defended Jean Collins, the prostitute who shot
her man, he was determined that the jury should comprehend
one proposition. He hammered at it over and over, for failure
to make it clear could mean the dread verdict: Guilty. Did
the jurors believe, wrongly, that a prostitute, because of the
nature of her occupation, could more easily commit murder
than another woman? Could they understand, as he would
prove, that this prostitute too was a woman inside? That this
man she loved meant everything to her? That she felt everything that a normal and good housewife feels and accepts
when, trustingly, she falls asleep in the arms of her husband?
To murder him she must destroy the one thing in life she
has loved. Jean Collins did that, says Jake, and it broke her
at the peak of the trial. In effect, from that moment on, he
was defending a woman already dead.

"Every person who kills," Jake says, "comes to a point
where it stalks him. Some last longer than others. But after a
while the tension is so great they can't control it. It is like trying to lift a load that is beyond your strength. You heave three
times and then put all you have into it. But you sense the
absolute futility of your position. You snap. That's when a
trial lawyer is in trouble."

4

Once a friend asked Ehrlich his average fee for defending
a murder suspect. Jake eyed him defiantly and spelled it out.
"E-v-e-r-y-t-h-i-n-g."

"You mean everything the accused person owns?"

Jake spelled it again, louder. "E-V-E-R-Y-T-H-I-N-G."

"But," protested the friend, "a doctor with equally great skill and experience operates on a person who is deathly sick, saves a life and never thinks of asking all that patient's worldly goods."

"When a doctor walks into surgery," said Jake deliberately, "everyone in the building is alerted to help him. The room is prepared for his skill and convenience. Nurses hold his gown for him. A trained assistant stands at his elbow. Everyone else is barred. Even the business office downstairs has completed each minor detail to make this come off successfully. The doctor doesn't need to give a damn whether it is a man or a woman on the table. He doesn't even have to look at the face. No one is going to yell suddenly that this person was once a jailbird. There is only one problem, a physical one.

"Now think of the courtroom, a scene of struggle. Every eye is turned on my client. There are emotions, interruptions, tensions, interpretations and misinterpretations. There are jurors who have their own everyday complaints. Yet, somehow, they must be made to *feel* as the defendant does. Did you ever feel the other guy's toothache when your own tooth wasn't aching?

"On the day the jury goes out, invariably, four jurors have had fights with their wives. One is failing in business. One gal is three days late, she thinks she's pregnant, and she hates the world. And the judge has an attack of piles.

"The judge must be objective and cautious, for a life rides on each decision he makes, on every objection he sustains or overrules. But he doesn't need to be sympathetic with the accused. The prosecution is steadily springing traps to convict the defendant. Only your Uncle Jake is living the life of that poor person."

By this time in a trial, usually, Jake has put himself through the accused's entire daily routine. He has finally convinced himself that he *is* the other person. Says Ehrlich: "Eating, sleeping and living the case brings you to see hallways, doors and windows, all beginning to open. You lead the jury to see the light as you open them. When you see the heads go down —the tears—you've got them, and the rest is anticlimax."

The strain, though, will be terrific. On the "big day," as he calls it, Jake appears in the darkest of somber suits. Court hangers-on call it his "bar mitzvah suit," and they believe it has some funereal dignity he wishes to impress on the jurors, or some lucky significance he has found in his crystal ball. Neither assumption is correct. On this day Jake will rise to such an emotional pitch that the perspiration will pour from his body. Only a dark suit will conceal the spreading stains until the verdict is in and he can change.

He won't relax when the case is over. As he wrenches off his sopping suit and slumps to the shower, Jake's body will be red. His skin will be stippled with "eighty million bumps." The shower won't remove them, and neither will a night's rest. They will not disappear for days.

They will be there when he drops down to Cookie's Bar, on Kearny, to accept the plaudits of reporters, bailiffs, judges from other courts, and a small army of admiring lawyers. The drinks will flow and the case will be reargued academically. Half a score of less successful lawyers will tell Jake in detail where he made this small mistake or that. To him they will all be a blur of faces, a jumble of sound.

Perhaps he will get in his Ford convertible and roar over the Golden Gate Bridge to his country place in Marin, with the sea wind blowing through his rumpled hair. Perhaps he will go to his office on Montgomery Street and fire off barrages of dictation: memos, abstracts, briefs, letters. Or he may drop everything and hole up in the cozy redwood library of his home and read until his eyes burn—one book after another, chain fashion, until it would seem he had crammed all the world's great literature into an indigestible lump in his aching head.

At such times Jake is apt to ponder his origins and struggles and to wonder whether the prize has been worth the game. He is not, as many suppose, indigenous to San Francisco. On October 15, 1900, Jake was born, a Southern Democrat and blooded Confederate rebel, on a plantation on the shores of the Potomac River, not far from Washington, D.C. He was the eldest of five brothers and one sister, and he had his eye fixed on the law even as a child. He used to accompany his fierce, goateed grandfather to the village of Rockville, to watch the periodic sitting of court. There he noted the rich, frock-coated lawyers with their high hats and fancy speech, and the respect they were accorded. He read tiers of books on jurisprudence, knowing in his heart that his mother wanted him to be a doctor. When he was seventeen, she died.

His father, a southern gentleman of aristocratic temper, objected to Jake's constant bookworming. He was a man of action and the first vested authority with whom Jake tangled. There were no appeals from his decisions, which perhaps was good training for Jake: very few of Ehrlich's cases reach the appeals courts today. Some of the arguments in which Jake was then involved were the bitterest of a career that has never been simple or tranquil.

At the age of seventeen, Jake left home with the Third Maryland Militia for the Mexican border. There they became a cavalry outfit in General Pershing's expeditions against Pancho Villa. Although sporadically in the guardhouse for contempt of regulations, Jake eventually became a sergeant.

When the campaign ended, he returned to Maryland and threw himself into day and night law studies at Georgetown University. Years later, when Ray Abbaticchio became special agent in charge of the FBI office in San Francisco, Jake recalled those faraway times. Introducing Abbaticchio around town, Jake said with deference: "Meet a Georgetown boy who made good." The G-man, with equal respect, patted Jake's arm. "But here's the Georgetown boy who made money."

Two semesters were all Jake got before World War I. He enlisted again and went to France as a lieutenant of infantry in the 163rd Division. There, in the trenches, he saw shots fired in anger, and he studied the personalities behind the triggers.

Home again, there was one final outburst with his father. "If I didn't feed you," roared the senior Ehrlich, "you wouldn't eat! If I——" Jake didn't wait to hear the rest. He shrugged—a gesture he would later perfect—and left. He made his way to San Francisco on freight trains, working as a harvest hand along the way. His first ride across the city was hitched on a vanload of furniture. The year was 1920. He studied law nights and worked days in a railroad office. He fought professionally as a lightweight. He washed dishes and he served subpoenas. The legend had its roots down.

Today Ehrlich maintains a luxurious suite in San Francisco's exclusive Stanford Court Apartments. He owns a $150,-000 country place across the Golden Gate with a patio-living room roof that rolls back to let in the sun. He has been married for thirty-five years to Marjorie Mercer Ehrlich, a quiet, pretty woman of Quaker extraction. Their son, Jake, Jr., who studied law but decided not to follow in his father's footsteps, now works for an office administering the business affairs of movie stars, and sometimes sits in on consultations at 333 Montgomery Street, Jake's office address. Their daughter Dora Jane is married to Guy Cherney, a professional singer.

Two grandsons, Joseph and David Cherney, and Jake's granddaughter Cynthia—his friends call her Cinderella Ehrlich—are his steady day-off partners. This self-appointed task of baby-sitting is a freshening change from the distractions of the week. It is like the starched collars, white cuffs and the pocket handkerchief which identify him everywhere.

Jake explains them wryly: "Soon after I was admitted to the bar I discovered that I was not going to be engaged by Standard Oil, Bank of America or the California Packing Corporation. I had to take whatever cases came to me. Some of my clients were not the wholesome type. They came to the bar of justice seedy and tarnished, in body and spirit. Fresh clean linen on their lawyer helped to suggest another effect—that of decency and cleanliness—if not godliness. We show a side of us that has had a bath."

In his post-trial reveries, sometimes, Jake wonders—as any mortal must—how it might have been. One brother is a successful lawyer in Washington, D.C., another a prosperous automobile dealer in Georgetown. A third has the largest advertising agency in Washington, D.C., and the fourth is in business in San Francisco. None of them is as famous as Jake. None of them can look out at great, warm, swashbuckling San Francisco and say: "That city is a part of me, and I am a part of that city." Jake can.

EARLY DAYS

ONCE upon a time, the San Francisco Chamber of Commerce maintained a Hospitality Committee to greet out-of-towners arriving at the city's two thousand hotels, classify them by business pursuits, and dispense luncheons and cards to the appropriate clubs. But in January, 1920, the committee, by some oversight, missed one J. Ehrlich, not quite twenty years of age, recently of Rockville, Maryland.

Sun-tanned after crossing the country by freight train, he arrived in the Oakland yards across the bay, where transcontinental train lines terminate. Clutching his one piece of luggage, a straw suitcase carefully padded with burlap (containing a Bible, some laundered personal linen and a Confederate battle flag), he dropped from the freight car at a practiced trot, ducked as two railroad dicks approached, passed in and out of a steam cloud from a locomotive, and boarded a ferry which, for five cents, would carry him the final ten miles of his journey.

When he got off the ferry he beckoned a Negro porter and gave him ten cents to carry the straw suitcase to the bus loading for the Palace Hotel. He didn't register there, however. He took residence in a waterfront hotel where a room could be had for twenty-five cents a night.

There he acquired some boisterous new neighbors, a hearty

lot of teamsters, longshoremen and sailors temporarily "on the beach." You spoke like a cavalryman if you were a little guy and wished them to hear you, as Jake did. On the fifteenth of that January they had occasion to become mournfully drunk, for on the sixteenth National Prohibition—which would provide many a legal fee in the years to come—became the law of the land.

Seeking employment, Jake suddenly found himself on the seat of a two-horse Wells-Fargo dray, collecting and delivering trunks for a weekly wage that was slightly better than none at all.

Frequently his deliveries took him out Kearny Street near the Hall of Justice, where Chinatown crowded down from Grant Avenue to border Portsmouth Square. Once this had been the Town Plaza, but now it fronted the chattering Filipino colony. Houses of prostitution stood open-doored there, and Jake delivered a number of trunks to them, shouldering them up dim hallways to mirrored, cloyingly-incensed rooms. Then he would tie his horses and step into the courts to watch the attorneys perform. There seemed to be room for a good little man among them.

Then and there Ehrlich decided to build a wardrobe and improve his personal appearance. In fact, it was the tailors of San Francisco who put Jake in the prize ring. A reasonably good suit of the kind he wanted, seamless along the trouser legs and back of the coat (and therefore less inclined to ridge or wrinkle with extended use), cost $25, approximately a full week's wage in the trunk-hauling business. A growing man, to make his own way in a community, must have additional income if he would pay his board bill, stand a round of drinks, eat an occasional meal out, and take in billiard tournaments, baseball games and the bouts at National Hall.

Repeatedly, at the fights with his gargantuan waterfront

friends, Jake would threaten to get out of his seat and wipe up
the ring with the boxers.

This vastly amused his friends and led to some betting.
The winner of one semi-windup bout looked particularly inept
to Ehrlich. "I'd kill that bum!" he howled. A week later he
was given his chance.

He came into the ring rusty but determined. The gloves
felt like snow mittens as he glanced over at the veteran they
had thrown him in with. Ring lights glittered off scar tissue
around the man's eyes and cheekbones. When the bell gonged
he came in, hammering.

For three rounds Jake felt as if all the trunks in the Wells-
Fargo lofts were bouncing off his head, and he couldn't seem
to get his left hand out of storage. Suddenly, though, the left
arrived and his tormentor collapsed. Jake collected $25 and
the promise of more "work" when he wanted it.

2

A day or so later he noticed an ad for part-time clerical
help at the U. S. Marine Hospital. He arranged to work eve-
nings as needed. At this time he also moved off the waterfront into a slightly less modest hotel. The difference in price,
he found, could be made up by taking supper at the hospital
in the officers' mess, to which, incidentally, he had not been
invited. There he was quick to praise the food and conse-
quently soon met the chief dietician, Marjorie Mercer. Jake
took one look at her and was on his feet bowing, holding her
hand and assuring her that her meals were the world's best.

Miss Mercer, with classic features and a lovely complexion,
was as dainty in her white uniform as a lace doily. She looked
at Jake from sparkling brown eyes and demurely withdrew
her hand. "Thank you, Mr. Ehrlich," she said quietly.

Was Miss Mercer a native San Franciscan perhaps?

No, she said, Wisconsin.

"I am working at the hospital only temporarily, you know," Jake heard himself assuring her. "I am preparing for the law."

"I wish you success, Mr. Ehrlich," she said, and turned back to the kitchen.

Every evening thereafter, Jake found some dish or other on which to compliment the chief dietician.

Miss Mercer could not determine what she thought of this brash young man. Raised, as she had been, as a Quaker on a Wisconsin farm, she had never seen anyone quite like him. He wore a different ensemble each evening, he greeted her with elaborate gallantries and, when he could hold her in conversation, he talked like a southern colonel, quoting with gestures from the Bible and Jefferson Davis' Farewell to the Senate.

One evening over coffee he looked up at Miss Mercer and announced that he had decided to "go into railroading"—he was now associated with the Western Pacific. Jake had indeed taken a position as secretary to the vice-president in charge of traffic after assuring the official that he "knew railroads intimately." He had clinched the job by announcing that he had "just recently" enrolled in San Francisco Law School "to better my lot." Thereupon he did enroll immediately.

During the next few weeks, Jake took Miss Mercer to dine at some of the little Italian restaurants in North Beach and the less expensive tourist places on Fisherman's Wharf. Of a Sunday they would ride the trolley out to Golden Gate Park, with a dietetically sound luncheon packed by her, and there at last they talked seriously. Probably it was the first time anyone had heard the innermost thoughts of Jacob W. Ehrlich, later developed for scores of juries. Basically, Jake's philosophy has never changed.

Shooting his cuffs and chopping the air with his right hand, Jake told Marjorie: "I've been around, I have done battle with the world, and I have never seen a rose without a thorn, or a tree without ugly branches. Nothing is perfect. You will never see a perfect life. The majority of unfortunates dragged before the bar of justice are simply unlucky—sick in mind to begin with. That is why I am going to be a defense lawyer."

He knew the Bible better than she, despite her Quaker upbringing, but he had his own ideas about religion. "I worship the Almighty in my own way," he told her one day as they sat at the beach. "I believe there is a guiding strength in nature—call it God or whatever—but the word religion means nothing to me. If a religious feeling means a kindly feeling and wanting to help someone, then I am a very devout man."

3

The Democratic National Convention of 1920 was due to open at the Civic Auditorium on June 28. Jake had to be there. California at that time had almost as many registered Democrats in residence as Fiji Islanders. The party needed him. With $3.70 in his pockets, Jake proposed to Marjorie and they took the Sausalito Ferry over to Marin County on June 30, 1920—two days after the convention opened—to be married.

They stood up before Justice of the Peace Herbert de la Montanya in San Rafael. Because it was a weekend and their marriage license could not be recorded properly, the judge wrote on the back of his business card that Mr. and Mrs. Jacob W. Ehrlich were duly married by him that day. He handed the card to Marjorie, who put it in her purse for later filing.

Jake laughed. "You know, Judge," he said, "some day

you'll have to have a riveting punch here so you can fasten the license on a collar around the bridegroom's neck where everyone can see it." Judge de la Montanya looked at the young man, but he didn't smile.

It was a chance remark from a nervous groom which might never have lingered in anyone's memory. However, there was occasion to recall it twenty-five years later, when the Ehrlich name had become legal magic around San Francisco. In 1945 a prominent stock broker was arrested for drunken driving, his third such offense; his obstreperous antics sent several arresting officers to the San Rafael hospital. When he sobered up and realized his predicament, he went to Ehrlich.

Ehrlich noted that Judge de la Montanya was scheduled to hear the case. He hadn't seen the old justice since that wedding day a quarter of a century before, but he thought of the card that Marjorie had put in her purse.

Judge de la Montanya was visibly impressed when the big-name attorney came personally to his little court and asked politely for a continuance of the drunken driving matter. Until June 30? Certainly. He did not seem to recognize Ehrlich.

On the trial date, his twenty-fifth wedding anniversary, Jake asked Marjorie to accompany him to court. They arrived early and met the judge in chambers.

"Judge," said Jake, "I want you to meet my wife."

"How do you do, Mrs. Ehrlich?" said the justice.

"You notice, don't you, that she still is my wife after all these years—and with no wedding license riveted to my neck?" Ehrlich asked.

The judge frowned, puzzled. "Uh—what was that?"

"Judge," said Jake, "haven't you ever seen my wife before? Haven't I ever been in your chambers before now?"

"Oh, no," said the judge. "I would have remembered if *you* had been here, Mr. Ehrlich."

"Sweetheart," Jake said to Marjorie, "show the judge that card."

Judge de la Montanya read his own slanting script. "The young man of the rivets!" he said. A smile played over his face. "Just think of that!" he said. "*I* married Jake Ehrlich! Twenty-five years ago and it's June 30 to the day! And now you say there is a son and daughter? This is, indeed, a day of celebration!"

Thus it was that one distraught stock broker in 1945 got off with a fine of $100.

On that first June 30, twenty-five years earlier, Jake was immediately concerned with the Democratic Convention. He hurried Marjorie to the flat they had rented on Fifth Avenue and caught a trolley to the auditorium.

Now his southern accent came in handy. The convention was being gaveled by a good Rebel chairman, Senator Joseph T. Robinson of Arkansas, and a few slurred words from Jake were credentials enough for the hall. He went directly to the Maryland delegation. Senator Ritchie welcomed the young campaigner and, as gentlemen will, they stepped downstairs to raise a glass.

Marjorie, though it was her honeymoon, understood when Jake scarcely came home during the next week. He was making scores of friends, thanks to the Maryland delegation, and rarely left the convention except to change clothes.

Down in the auditorium basement, Ritchie introduced Ehrlich to a number of personages. There was a gavel-voiced man from New York with a brown derby hat, Alfred Emanuel Smith, who in turn presented Charles F. Murphy, the big chief of Tammany Hall since 1902, and a tall, handsome New Yorker with dandified manners named Roosevelt. From time to time messengers arrived with liquid stocks released from federal warehouses.

On July 6, in the afternoon, a messenger fought through the crowd and tugged at Roosevelt's sleeve.

"Frank! You've got to come! They're nominating you for vice-president."

Roosevelt stormed, "Can't you see I am having a drink with a gentleman?" Jake turned to a companion. "A great guy!" he said in admiration.

In time Roosevelt did go up to accept the nomination, but as he set his glass down he shook young Ehrlich's hand and said: "Jake, my friend, whenever you come to the capital I want you to stop with me and say hello." Jake allowed that he would.

During the next year and ten months Ehrlich worked night and day. He continued in the railroad while studying law. Charles Levey, a sports-minded Scotsman who was president of Western Pacific, had taken a liking to the boy in the vice-president's office. He would stop Jake in the corridor to inquire how the studies progressed and, invariably, ask: "An' how is the famous left hook?"

"Fine, sir," Jake would tell him. "Last night in Oakland I killed them."

"First round?"

"Third."

"And the pur-rse?"

"That killed *me*—only $7.50."

The relationship got Jake a trip or two up and down the coast and gave him entree to other offices, particularly the general counsel's, for whom he was a willing messenger to the courts or offices of established attorneys.

On occasion, these men would pay him a dollar to serve legal papers. Along the way he met policemen, big affable Irishmen like Bill Houlihan and Mike Desmond, who had a cheery word for the bright young man with the good manners and the spotless appearance. Jake was beginning to establish an identity.

On May 29, 1921, a son was born to Marjorie. They named the baby Jacob W. Ehrlich, Jr. That night Jake stood alone on Nob Hill, close by the iron railing of the Pacific Union Club, and looked down at the twinkling city. Inside the rich and proud old club he was unknown, to be sure, but he was coming along. He was head of a family now. In another year he would be a lawyer. The ferries crossing to Oakland in their moving islands of electricity were clocking off his life. From now on it was Jake Ehrlich and San Francisco.

In the spring of 1922 he decided he was ready to attempt the bar. Other young men were nervous as they faced the three-day ordeal—two days of writing, one of oral exams. They saw Ehrlich pause to swing a playful left hook at a big policeman, and they decided he was cocky. He wasn't; he was just a little more used to the ropes. He went in to face the examiners exactly as he would have walked into National Hall with his little satchel to demonstrate what he knew about boxing.

On March 7, 1922, he was admitted to the practice of law in the state of California.

4

That same month, the name of J. W. Ehrlich first appears as Attorney of Record in a simple default divorce case. No further details about the case exist. No one recalls who the unfortunate spouse was who found himself (or herself) so incompatible as to require the youthful counsel. Jake could only remember that the client straggled in and won an uncontested decree when the husband (or was it the wife?) failed to appear. Years later he suspected the respondent mate had never been notified, and a neat little case of bigamy may have been compounded.

San Francisco was a transient city then, its five hundred thousand inhabitants for the most part restlessly on the move. There were many default divorces and the fees were inconsequential. Scores of fresh young lawyers were leaving state bar examinations, clutching their certificates to practice. They marched meaningfully, if unheralded, to scores of cubbyhole offices about the city, there to wait impatiently for cases, even default divorces.

This was the early Ehrlich era. Jake, with lights and gas cut off for inability to pay the bills, would borrow a calculated twenty from a friendly pawn broker and blow it on one round of drinks in the speakeasy near the Hall of Justice because "it made the gang mention your name." He didn't own law books, but deemed it important "background" to attend a World Series in Washington, D.C., and the Dempsey-Tunney fight in Philadelphia. They were rollicking years of short means and long campaigning, all deliberately designed to establish his unique identity while he waited for "that one big case."

At first he accepted all cases, and he didn't quote a fee. Those early clients came from the sordid places of society, he would later tell law classes. "It is down there that all good trial lawyers learn it if they are honest enough to admit it."

At this time, Ehrlich initiated two of his idiosyncrasies: never to carry a conventional lawyer's briefcase and never to carry his own pencil. During his secretarial days at the railroad, he had toted so many bulging bags of documents for the bosses that he came to feel like a redcap when he had to pick one up; he swore he would never pack one of his own. Anyhow he couldn't afford one, and so he began a lifelong practice of putting his trial material in accordian-board folders which grew as the case progressed and were filed intact at the end. In later years, clients and friends bestowed all sorts of fancy briefcases upon him but he has never carried one. Some of his best lawsuits might fill packing cases, but they all would be distributed through volumes of heavy paper accordians.

As for the pencil, he said one would mar the drape of his coat. Besides, he could always borrow a sharp one from the bailiff and it gave the officer an interest in him.

His first office was the smallest and gloomiest cubicle on the fifth floor of the rococo old de Young Building, a two-minute sprint from the Hall of Justice, on the strategic corner where Kearny Street bends west from Market.

New young lawyers hustled like insurance salesmen in those days. If they were interested in criminal law they gathered daily at the Hall, where the policemen brought in their culprits. If an officer was friendly with an attorney he would confide: "I've got a guy upstairs. He has money. I'll book him Wednesday." The lawyer, of course, would arrive at the proper time, would be introduced, and would share the resultant fee with his tipster cop. It was a bad system, and later it would be corrected. Suspects today are booked immediately "on suspicion" of the crime for which they were apprehended and the district attorney, after a study of the evidence, files the appropriate charge. In Ehrlich's day you hustled clients, or you sat and waited. Oddly enough, he waited.

A lawyer then might move along in San Francisco if he gave his allegiance to the McDonough Brothers, a powerful firm of bail bond brokers who used money and bail facilities to control operations of the police department. The day would come when they would be condemned as "the fountainhead of vice" in the city and would be smashed, but not before many a fortune had been made through them. If a young man found favor with them and joined their stable of lawyers he could keep very busy. If he didn't he got only the leftovers.

Ehrlich, though badly in need of fees, avoided the trap.

Inevitably, he knew, such machines fall before some wave of reform. He had many a drink under the same roof with old Pete and Tom McDonough, but he discouraged their interest in him. In time they came to regard him as a disapproving element and a potential enemy, a viewpoint that one day would result in San Francisco's most sensational Grand Jury investigation and some of Ehrlich's first great courtroom battles.

As a young lawyer, Jake was a student of many things, principally of success. He observed, for instance, that John Francis Neylan, the tall, oratorical firebrand who was William Randolph Hearst's attorney, did not cultivate the McDonoughs or cool his heels in the corridors of the Hall. And that, Jake decided, was to be his own style.

Dutifully he remained in his bare little office from 8:00 A.M. to 5:00 P.M. every day. One day, he hoped, this practice would bring him the pick of the criminal cases, as well as more dignified and profitable civil suits.

He cultivated Senator Tom West and his next-door tenants in the de Young Building, Lawyers Hilton and Christensen, former judges and successful practitioners who often had small legal chores for him to do. He made a deal with Senator West: when Jake had a client coming in, he would rush to the Senator's office and borrow eight or ten legal volumes. The client would arrive to find Ehrlich "busy as hell on a number of cases."

One memorable day Christensen had a minor matter on the calendar of Superior Judge Frank H. Dunne, a jurist feared for his cantankerous courtroom temper. Christensen had to be elsewhere at the hour and asked Jake to run over and get a continuance for him. When the case was called, Ehrlich jumped up and made his request. The judge looked up slowly, frowning, surveying the dapper young man distastefully. "Where is Mr. Christensen?" he demanded.

"Why, if Your Honor please," Jake said, "he was detained on another matter and asked me to appear for him."

"I am amazed at Mr. Christensen's imprudence," said Judge Dunne, "sending a mere beardless youth!"

Courtroom hangers-on guffawed. Jake flushed.

"Your Honor," he drawled, "if Mr. Christensen had known Your Honor attached such importance to whiskers, I am sure he would have sent over a billygoat!"

The old judge turned livid, angrily denied the request for continuance, and fined Ehrlich twenty dollars for contempt of court. Jake, of course, was stony broke. Before he could explain his predicament and apologize, he found twenty-dollar bills surreptitiously fluttering to him from all sides. He had done what a hundred established lawyers had never dared to do. This was to be the first Jake Ehrlich story to make its chuckling way around San Francisco.

Six months after Jake entered practice, his second child, Dora Jane, was born. She was a dark, laughing imp, temperamentally very much like Jake; the one in the family who, he said, "would make a great lawyer." Through the years, Dora Jane often sat in courtrooms to watch her father work. She became a fearless critic of his arguments and technique.

For a while, with one more mouth to feed, Jake had to take an after-hours job in a tire factory for $3.50 a night. However, he stopped his prize ring appearances as not in keeping with the dignity of a barrister.

Slowly the default divorce cases gave way to a parade of small bootleggers. Once Jake got ten months behind on the rent for his home. Mrs. Cruickshank, his landlady, obtained an eviction notice and came to serve it in person. Jake invited her in, explained that he had a $300 fee coming, and they sat talking like old friends. Mrs. Cruickshank, a widow with a young son of her own, laughed as she got up to go. "Keep

food on the table for these babies," she said. "Don't worry,
and pay me as you can."

Thirty years later her young son was a police inspector,
under suspension for a departmental infraction. He wanted
Ehrlich, but didn't believe he could raise that kind of fee.
Could he handle the fee with term payments? "No," said
Ehrlich. "Because for you there will *be* no fee." Then he told
the inspector of his mother's kindness to a struggling lawyer.

Ehrlich was appearing in court more and more frequently,
and he was being noticed. People hadn't seen a young lawyer
quite like him. One grizzled sergeant, years afterward, recalled his first experience with the embryo "Master."

"I went out on a burglary call," he related, "and I caught
this young guy kneeling at the safe with his hands inside it
taking the money. There were burglary tools on the floor beside him. Well, I collared him and jugged him.

"When I got to court here's Ehrlich standing with his hands
on the yegg's shoulder, and I hardly recognize my culprit.
He's all dressed up in Jake's fancy clothes—looks like a million. Then Ehrlich gets up before the jury and you'd think
my suspect was lawfully at that petey to count the money for
its legal owners. Ehrlich gives 'em this (handkerchief to his
eyes) and he doesn't say 'Ladies and Gentlemen'—he says
'Fathers and Mothers of the jury.'

" 'It's nearin' Christmas time,' he says, 'an' we should be
sending this boy home to his own dear mother and father.'
And you know, by the time he gets through, I'm not so sure
I *didn't* make a mistake. He just walks him out of there clean
as a whistle!"

As Jake's reputation grew, there were the inevitable seekers
of free legal advice. There was one pest in particular. For him
Jake painted a broad stripe across the top of his desk. When
the pest came in again Jake snapped: "Just lay the green

stuff on the line and we'll take up your case." The trouble
was that Ehrlich didn't know paints. What appeared to him to
be calcimine—and easily rubbed off—turned out to be enamel,
and it stayed on that desk top for years. From it came the
story of the little lawyer who took any case if you could "lay
it on the line."

5

Important friendships began to develop in the middle twenties. One day an attorney stopped him on Market Street and
introduced him to a chipper little man with pince-nez glasses.

"Lou Lurie," he said. "Lou, I want you to meet Jake
Ehrlich, an up-and-coming kid lawyer."

Lurie, already a fabulous dealer in seven-figure real-estate
transactions, invited Jake to luncheon at Jack's. There he
found himself chuckling at the young man's observations on
people and laws. He invited Jake back time and again, and a
friendship was begun that would last over three decades and
would bring Ehrlich to the attention of internationally famous
people.

Through another contact, Clarence Darrow hired Ehrlich
to do a research job in San Francisco, but when Jake met
Darrow he was disappointed. Clarence Darrow simply wasn't
Jake's style. They never saw eye to eye, even in the thirties
when Darrow, en route to Hawaii and his last big case, the
Massie trial, invited Ehrlich to join him in the defense. Jake
shook his head. He had worked hard to establish his inde-
pendent identity. His own big break, he was sure, would come
right there in California.

One of his younger friends was Rodney Pantages, whose
father owned a chain of sixty theatres. They often did the
town together and met occasionally at Rodney's apartment

over the Pantages Theatre, where they would play the piano and sing, and where Jake would play the violin for the first time since he had left home.

Young Pantages steered a little theatre work to Ehrlich and, finally, one day when Jake was going to Los Angeles, gave him a note to old Alexander Pantages: "This will introduce Jake Ehrlich. You will recall meeting him. He does our work here. Go out of your way to make his stay pleasant." The old man looked at the note, grunted, and proceeded to entertain Ehrlich personally—he taught him how to make vegetable soup.

Jake became the theatre magnate's "pet"; they had a lot in common. Pantages had come up the hard way after landing in San Francisco as an immigrant from Greece. He had washed dishes on the old Barbary Coast, gone on to the Klondike during the big gold rush there and, with $24 borrowed from a miner, set up his first stage show in a honky-tonk. Later he had moved to Seattle and then to Los Angeles, where he opened his first theatre in 1910. When Jake met him, he was worth an estimated $25,000,000 and was one of the most powerful theatre men in the country. He was one of the first really important men to tell friends: "That Jakey Ehrlich is a great little lawyer."

The single biggest source of legal fees in those years was Prohibition; the coves north and south of San Francisco splashed with rum runners landing their contraband and, frequently, getting caught. They gladly paid a lawyer $1,000 for a successful court appearance, $3,000 if there were two or more defendants in the case. Furthermore, they paid cash from huge rolls of bills, and when they liked the lawyer they would add another hundred or two. From one fee, Jake was able at last to pay cash for the first automobile he ever owned: a sporty 1926 Buick sedan.

He also bought the law books he needed, got some furniture for his office and put a rug on the floor. One day as he sat studying, a young lawyer acquaintance dropped in from upstairs. It was Roy Sharff, a brilliant legal student with bright blue eyes and sober ways but, unfortunately, no clients.

They chatted a while, and finally Ehrlich suggested: "Why don't you move in with me? We'll take the next office, open the door and be a firm." Sharff joined him that day. In years to come he would be the bulwark behind Jake in every major case he would try. The quiet book lawyer and the dramatic showman made a perfect team. The addition of Sharff also gave Jake more time to get out and mix. He began to emerge as a community figure.

The $5,000,000 Fox Theatre, heralded as the "World's Finest," opened with a world premiere featuring a galaxy of Hollywood stars headed by Will Rogers, a street parade and fifty thousand movie fans howling at the doors. By now Jake was well enough known as a character to be prominently displayed with the stars, and later went to lunch with Lurie, where he shared small talk with Louis B. Mayer, the movie tycoon, George Jessel, who would become a lifelong friend, and Will Rogers, who was "almost the only other Democrat in California."

In May, 1929, Rodney Pantages told Jake a good new comedy team was coming to the Pantages stage, and he wasn't sure the press agents could put them over in California. Ehrlich brashly said he could and began a round of calls, to the newspapers, to the mayor's office and, most important, to the city's used-car lots. The comedy team was Amos 'n' Andy. Years later, Andy—Charles Correll—would write gratefully about that San Francisco introduction.

"We were very nervous, naturally, about whether we would be received on the coast because we didn't know whether our show was listened to, or whether people cared about us as performers, or just what to think. We arrived in Oakland

and went to San Francisco on the ferry. Naturally there were newspapermen on the ferry—normal publicity for any attraction playing the theatre—but these newspapermen told us that Jake Ehrlich had arranged a reception for us in San Francisco.

"Upon our arrival we found about ten thousand people at the Ferry Building, including the mayor, chief of police, other city officers and a welcome such as we had never had before or since. Jake also had lined up a parade of broken-down cars rigged out as fresh-air taxicabs with two men portraying the role of Amos 'n' Andy in each car.

"We were paraded up to the steps of the City Hall and given the key to the city. Of all the cities we have ever played, the one that stands out in our memory is San Francisco. Ehrlich was practically our host for the two weeks we were there and gave so generously of his time we never had a dull moment.

"What a fellow! It was the beginning of a wonderful and lasting friendship, and I think I have been honored in having had Jake for my friend."

That was the beginning of Jake as a part-time impresario, never too busy to arrange a welcome for a coming star, set up a championship prize fight, or organize a tremendous milk fund for school children.

It was inevitable that he would also try politics. In that Coolidge-Hoover era there probably weren't thirty thousand Democrats in California, but Ehrlich was one of them. He became executive secretary of the State Central Committee, parading from San Francisco to San Diego as banquet speaker and toastmaster, making thousands of new contacts. It was Ehrlich who introduced the first resolution in California calling for the nomination of Al Smith, his 1920 convention acquaintance, for the presidency.

In 1930 the state convention at Fresno nominated Jake as

its candidate for State Attorney General, knowing he could
never beat old U. S. Webb, one of California's most venerable
public officials. Ehrlich stumped the state and tried his best;
he ran third in a field of three, with a surprising 52,442 votes
to Webb's 541,810. Webb was so impressed with the young
Democratic lawyer that he promptly offered Ehrlich a position on his staff. Jake politely declined.

It was Marjorie, rather than the electorate, who ended his
active political career. "You can be a good trial lawyer," she
told him one night, "but you can't be both lawyer and politi-
cian."

Of course, he could never quit politics entirely. The day
was coming soon when Jake would start a series of wagers,
as an equal, with the eminent John Francis Neylan. They bet
a ten-dollar hat on the outcome of the Hoover-Roosevelt race.
After FDR's fourth victorious campaign, Neylan wrote:
"Dear Jake: Enclosed find my check for ten dollars. To avoid
any unnecessary details in the future, I have asked my secretary to send you a check on the day after election each four
years as long as FDR is alive. I think this will simplify
matters."

Now Jake had recognition and respectability—he was
elected president of the San Francisco Aerie of Eagles—but
the Ehrlich legend was not to become too dignified to be rec-
ognizable. One day Jake accepted a client charged with rape
and went with him and a bail bondsman to the Hall of Justice.
As they walked in, an inspector said to the weeping girl victim: "Which of these men assaulted you?" She studied them
and pointed to Jake. The inspector opened his mouth to correct her, but Ehrlich shushed him. When they went into
court the girl was asked to repeat her identification. Again
she pointed to Ehrlich, and the case was dismissed. He had
won for his client in the simplest possible manner: had proved
it was a mistaken identity. Within twenty-four hours the story

was around town and friends snickered and pointed a finger whenever he appeared.

It was the type of story people wanted with their trial lawyers, and with Jake there always seemed a companion piece. He defended an armed robber for a promised fee of $5,000. The man paid $2,500 down, agreeing to obtain the rest when he was released. Jake got him acquitted and he went his way. One dark night when the attorney was walking home, a figure emerged from the shadows.

"Stick 'em up!"

Ehrlich recognized the voice of his recent client.

"Why you son-of-a-bitch!" he exploded. "You're not taking my money to pay my own fee!"

The robber peered closer—and apologized. "I didn't know it was you, Mr. Ehrlich."

The story was all over town by morning.

One day an old policeman friend stopped Jake. His son Johnny was graduating from law school, and he wished sincerely the boy could learn the ropes in Ehrlich's office. "Sure, Bill," said Jake. "Send him in. I'd be glad to have Johnny."

The old man hung his head. "It's his mother, Jakey," he said. "She don't like the kind of people you represent. She's afraid for our lad's good name."

"Bill," said Jake, "send the boy in. I represent churches and book publishers and fine people up on the Hill just as often as I represent the ones your missus hears about. Send me the boy and I promise he will be just as clean on the day he leaves me as he was the day he came. Tell his mother that Johnny has been raised in his religion, that her training has been good, and tell her no man is going to spoil that." The boy became one of his star pupils and later a civic leader in another California city.

"Jake," the policeman said, "was as good as his word. With him a man's word is sacred as scripture. I remember once we had him out to address our churchmen's group. He said he was going to give us the shortest sermon on record. Some of them sneered, 'Wise guy!' Then Jake spoke: 'Too many men kneel to Christ—not enough follow him.' He wasn't of our faith, but in that moment we were of his."

So it was, practicing a little of this law and a little of that, climbing in the community, but still waiting for his big chance, that Ehrlich picked up the papers one day and saw that his old friend Alexander Pantages was in serious trouble. He had just been convicted on the charges of a seventeen-year-old co-ed in the office of his theatre. As the telephone rang, Ehrlich knew that here at last was the big, nationally sensational case he had been expecting. Pantages himself was calling desperately for Jake.

Part Two: **THE CASE-BOOK**

Prewar Stuff

I

ALEXANDER PANTAGES

A Question of Rape

Every newspaper reader in America was familiar with the asserted sin of Alexander Pantages in 1931. It was the sex story of the season out of Southern California. In his first trial, which flamed through 1929, Millionaire Pantages, despite a high-power battery of defense lawyers headed by Jerry Giesler, had been convicted of criminal assault on co-ed Eunice Pringle.

The defense had appealed all the way to the State Supreme Court and finally won a new trial, which was set for July, 1931. By then only Giesler remained of the first defense staff. Pantages insisted that his smart young friend Ehrlich be brought down from San Francisco to help.

Jake's assignment was to be a delicate one. He was to prove that Eunice Pringle, the alleged rape victim and star witness for the prosecution, had actually lost her virtue long before she wiggled her way into Pantages' arms. It was a big order at that late date, for the first set of defense lawyers had scanned the ground thoroughly and without success. Furthermore, Jake was not used to disputing the morals of pretty young ladies.

Eunice Pringle, dark and attractive, was a co-ed at the University of Southern California. She was, as the tabloid writers had noticed, "mature for seventeen—the sweetest seventeen since Clara Bow." More than anything else, Eunice wanted to be a professional dancer, but her early auditions did not turn out well.

Still determined, she frequented theatres and talent-buying offices, and one summer day found herself in the lobby of the downtown Los Angeles Pantages. Precisely what occurred then was the subject of two long and lurid trials.

Both principals agreed that Eunice made her way into Pantages' company on the mezzanine. Neither the girl nor Pantages had a witness to testify what happened next. At any rate, Eunice soon ran screaming and trailing torn silk garments to the sunny streets, where she fell sobbing into the arms of a blue-shirted policeman, crying that she had been criminally attacked. "By M-Mister Pantages!" she shrieked.

Ehrlich had studied reports of the first trial in the newspapers, knowing there undoubtedly were many passages the editors had blushingly deleted. As he could see, it was a tough case for the defense. For one thing, Pantages was a rich theatrical man, and in those days show people, particularly the movie crowd in Southern California, were popularly supposed to have orgies for breakfast and seductions for lunch.

As he headed for Los Angeles, he read and reread the trial transcript and appeal briefs, searching for the line he might follow if he were chief counsel for the defense. It was Giesler's case all the way, but Ehrlich tried to prepare himself as if it were his own. He was coming in, he realized, where some of the country's biggest trial men had failed. And, for all his study, he couldn't find one point they had overlooked.

Reaching Los Angeles, still with no plan, he began to consider the benefits, if any, of an attack directed at District Attorney Buron Fitts personally. To that end he conferred with Giesler and put together a detailed psychological analysis of the veteran prosecutor, establishing how he might react in any given situation. It was revealing, interesting and eventually helpful, but it was not a valid overall defense plan.

The Pringle girl's story had not wavered in a detail. She still said Pantages had inveigled her to accompany him to his luxurious private office on a promise of a tryout for his stage shows. On the way up the stairs, she asserted, he had pushed her into a tiny janitors' supply room and violated her. In court she had feathered her dark lashes, blushed and wept, and the jury seemed convinced of her virtue. The defense lawyers had sought to question it in the first trial, but Prosecutor Fitts had blocked them. With the judge concurring, Fitts argued that it was not whether she was pure that mattered, but whether she was raped.

Pantages claimed that Eunice Pringle was a stage-struck young girl managed by a wily individual who was also a writer, actor and playwright, and who had written a dancing sketch he called "A Prince in Hollywood."

The girl and her manager, said Pantages, were trying to force him to book her on his vaudeville circuit. He proved that, with other young hopefuls, Eunice had obtained a regular audition with him and had not registered. After this, he claimed, she and her manager plotted to obtain a private showing, lurked in the lobby until she could corner him, and pleaded for a second chance. Pantages said he was only trying to be kind when he took her upstairs. He swore it was Eunice's hands, not his, that went groping among her unmentionables and tore and disarrayed them to produce the appearance of an attack.

Unfortunately Pantages was not as convincing a witness as the pretty, tearful girl. The best of lawyers could not change him overnight from what he was, a rich but rough old stone. For one thing he had to pick his words from a vocabulary accumulated around the world. When he spoke from the stand, churning inwardly with anger, self-pity, embarrassment and an understandable fear of being misunderstood, he growled. To the first jury he appeared a dark and scheming villain. Immediately after the guilty verdict was read, one woman juror rose from her seat and screamed: "Tell the world I voted to send him to prison!"

Jake boiled with anger and pity for his old soup-brewing friend. The new trial would have to be developed against a backdrop of the previous conviction. It would be a job for experts, and Ehrlich would never claim that he had more than a part in it.

Giesler, the big name in California law, was the direct legatee of Earl Rogers, lawyer father of Adela Rogers St. John and probably the most colorful pleader ever to walk a guilty murderer out of a California courtroom. As a young man, Harold Lee Giesler had migrated from Muscatine, Iowa, to the then sprawling little El Pueblo de Nuestra Señora la Reina de Los Angeles and, like the city, had lopped the unimportant handles off his name. As Jerry Giesler he became the famous attorney for famous movie names. When people insisted on misspelling his own name *Geisler* he ordered the telephone company to list it in the directory both ways.

As a youthful barrister he had admired the skilled, flamboyant Rogers and moved into his firm. Later, when Clarence Darrow was indicted for jury tampering in the Los Angeles *Times* bombing case, it was Rogers he engaged to defend him. Rogers, taking sick, left Giesler in charge. Darrow was annoyed, but Giesler went about his job competently and won an acquittal for the big Chicago lawyer. In one of his unpredictable moods, Darrow thereupon gave Giesler his best topcoat.

For Jake, then, joining Giesler in the second Pantages case was a sentimental linking with great trial men of the past: Rogers, Darrow, Giesler—and now Ehrlich.

He soon found that Giesler did not consider an acquittal

in the second trial impossible. The Supreme Court, in a forty-seven page opinion, had opened many of the avenues District Attorney Fitts had blocked in the original trial. For example, the high court ruled that the defense should be allowed to question the character and chastity of Eunice Pringle.

This ruling, incidentally, would change the entire trial procedure in California rape cases. Henceforth, ladies who screamed "Rape!" must previously have lived circumspectly. Giesler himself would use the new law to advantage in the sensational trials of Errol Flynn, the movie he-man accused of caprices with several pretty girls.

In the second Pantages trial the defense could also explore its theory that Eunice Pringle, with the connivance of her Russian manager, was "trying to frame" Pantages. In his opinion on the first trial, Chief Justice William Waste had noted: "The testimony of the prosecutrix was so improbable as to challenge one's credulity."

Using this observation by the court, Ehrlich and Giesler now proposed to develop utter incredulity in the second jury. Among other things, they planned to recreate Eunice Pringle's version of the rape itself, down to the next-to-last detail; perhaps to show the jury how ridiculous some of her charges were. One of the hilarious scenes of that second trial was to be "The Rape," with portly Jerry Giesler playing a clumsy and somewhat startled Pantages, and Ehrlich, looking like a suave floorwalker, trying to re-enact the tragic surrender of Eunice Pringle's virtue.

2

Jake went to work immediately on his primary mission, to establish what the relations were, if any, between Eunice and her manager, and show that she *couldn't* have been ruined in the theatre supply room, even *if* the actions she alleged did occur there. Certain discrepancies in her story indicated that this was a reasonable quest. Ehrlich set out to check at every place Eunice had lived in Southern California since reaching maturity. And for days he found the pickings slim. No one seemed to have noticed her. Finally he had only one more address, in Hollywood.

His taxi stopped in front of a court of small stucco bungalows, a typical Hollywood cottage court of the twenties, somewhat run down and life-weary, on a side street well away from the boulevards. Ehrlich found the manager's cottage and knocked. The woman who opened the door could have come directly from Central Casting and a charwoman part in an office building movie. She was wearing a drab, shapeless work dress, a ragged apron and shoes with holes cut for her bunions. Her hands were heavy veined and work bent.

Jake slid a toe inside the screen door. "I'm trying to locate a young couple," he said pleasantly. "Eunice and ———." (Jake named her manager.)

The woman nodded wearily to the last bungalow in the row. "They lived there. Gone now." She was not, Ehrlich saw, a gabby type, and she had little enough to be gabby about. The room behind her was furnished halfheartedly: no frills, no radio, only a few books, straight chairs along the wall, some faded paintings, a nondescript carpet, a round oaken table in the center of the room with a round, amber-glassed lamp dangling glass beads, and what might be a very old Bible on a clean white doily.

Ehrlich asked about the young couple. "Were they married, do you know?"

"Certainly!" she said.

"The reason I asked," he said, "the reason I'm here—you have heard of the Pantages case?"

"Yes."

She studied Ehrlich more carefully, eyeing the crisp pocket handkerchief, the broad flashing cuffs, the hard-creased suit. She sniffed. "I won't do anything to help that rich despoiler of women!"

Ehrlich was beginning to reappraise her. He smiled and pointed to the table. "That appears to be an old Bible you have. Do you know when it was published?"

Her gaze held steady. "I am not going to help Pantages."

Jake's smile broadened. "I can see you aren't, but remember the scripture: *'Let none of you imagine evil* (he emphasized *imagine*) *against your brother in your heart and love no false oath, for these are things I hate.'* "

"Are you religious, young man?" the woman asked.

Jake replied truthfully: "The Bible is an old friend."

She pushed the door open for him. "This one was printed in 1860," she said. "It belonged to my mother."

"It's a fine old copy," Ehrlich replied, opening it gently. "I have been fortunate enough," he observed, "to have read the old Scriptures in the original Hebrew and Aramaic. Some of the most beautiful verses are almost untranslatable into English."

He unbuttoned his coat and settled on one of the straight chairs, the old Bible in his lap. Then he began a learned discussion of the Book, from the first papyrus up through the Sacred Writings and to the remarkable translation by Martin Luther in 1534.

The old lady sat fascinated, head nodding. But when he laid the Bible back on its doily and turned directly to her, she said: "I am not going to help your rich, adulterous Mr. Pantages!"

"Rich?" demanded Jake. " *'Take heed and beware of covetousness, for a man's life consisteth not in the abundance of things he possesseth.'* I happen to know that Mr. Pantages was once as simple and hard working as you and I." He told her of the old man's early days and how he worked hard over half the globe before good fortune came to him. "It must have been the Lord's will," Jake observed. "You know, of course, that the Lord made many men wealthy in worldly goods—Abram, Lot, Job. *'And the Lord hath blessed my master, and he is become great and He hath given him flocks and herds and silver and gold.'* None of us prospers unless the Lord wills it."

She was working the apron between her fingers, listening. Jake looked out to the last bungalow. Suddenly his eyes clouded as if in anger. "The Lord punishes, too. And His edicts are strong against the adulterer. You knew, of course, that Eunice and —— were *not* married when they lived here? They weren't, and they still are not! *'For the land is full of adulterers and the land mourneth.'*

"Your Eunice Pringle sinned right here in your bungalow court, and did she cry out? Oh, no! She was here for carnal pleasure with this young man. *'Such is the way of an adulterous woman; she eateth and wipeth her mouth and saith, I have done no wickedness.'* Now she has gone with her soiled lips to accuse a fine old man who only tried to help her with her career!"

Jake was shaking his head in sorrow. He fixed the old lady with stern eyes. " *'Put not thine hand with the wicked to be an unrighteous witness!'* Oh, you know the warning! You know the scripture!"

Ehrlich told her that one response from an honest person might well free the old man from the unwarranted charge. One answer given at the right time in the trial might show the jury just who the adulterous ones were. He could envision the old lady just as she was now, sitting on the witness stand and solemnly stating the truth about Eunice Pringle.

"Of course," he told her, "the prosecutor would try to make unfair objections. He wouldn't want the jury to hear what you tell—the truth. Sometimes we lawyers call them persecutors." He smiled. "But you would want to tell the truth, wouldn't you? As God is your witness?"

"Yes!"

"Then you tell the jury that! Don't let the persecutors stop you. *'A faithful witness will not lie, but a false witness will utter lies.'* Remember that!"

She plucked at her rumpled skirt and complained that she didn't have the money to make a good appearance. Ehrlich was shocked. God's servants preening themselves to do His honest work! He instructed her to come to court just as she was—"your simple, honest, Christian self!" Slowly she nodded.

Jake told Giesler what he had found and what might be done with this strange witness, using just one simple question. Giesler knew a case wasn't won on a single question, no matter how dramatic. However, he gave Jake permission to try to work out a one-question shot from the old lady.

3

Ehrlich was concentrating on it when the trial opened on a steaming August day. The question, he had decided, must include everything and still not be involved, for it certainly wouldn't be allowed to stay in the record. Only in the jury's mind, he hoped. It must not sound contrived. He scribbled rough drafts on his pad while Giesler was selecting the jury and the first prosecution witnesses testified.

Jake kept one eye cocked on Giesler and the other on Buron Fitts, the celebrated district attorney. He was amused to observe that Fitts was reacting to each situation almost precisely as Jake had guessed he would.

As the trial proceeded, Jake had other duties. Among them

was the preparation of Pantages as a witness, trying to iron out the quirks a jury would dislike. Ehrlich also worked carefully with his surprise witness, cementing in the old lady's mind the kind of "unfair" stunt the "persecutors" would try. Almost before he realized it, the people's case was in. It was simple, direct and damning, an expansion of the evidence that had convicted Pantages the first time.

The jurors were apparently hostile from the moment the defense opened. They listened stolidly to attacks on Eunice Pringle's character. Of course they perked up when Giesler and Ehrlich put on their recreation of the alleged rape. It was a good show, with the immaculate Jake twined this way and that while Giesler puffed and demanded: "Was it this way? No? *This* way? No?" They even shared the courtroom guffaw when Ehrlich said: "I think a little more to the left will do it, Jerry." But the defense was racking up very few points.

Jake found himself losing weight and growing increasingly irritable. As the tension built, he started taking long walks at night, still trying to formulate that evasive, over-simple question he hoped Giesler would use.

One morning when he showered he found his body covered with a rash, "a million little bumps" that looked like measles. It was the first time it had happened to him, but after that the "eighty million bumps" always rose at the peak of every trial. He could only change linen, try to calm himself and plod on.

Then one dawn, as he sat alone at an all-night restaurant, the question suddenly unfolded on a napkin before him. He read it again and grinned. It was so simple his own Dora Jane would have asked it naturally. He hoped Giesler would try it.

The afternoon came, then, when Giesler turned, frowning, from one of his witnesses. Eunice Pringle was still intact. "All right, Jake," he said, "We'll try your hunch."

Ehrlich summoned his little old lady, noting that she had followed directions faithfully; she was dressed exactly as if

she had been lifted from her bungalow living room. She took
the oath and sat, hands in her lap, waiting. Giesler let her sit,
let the jury ponder, while he rummaged through his briefcase.
*What could this poor old woman say in defense of Alexander
Pantages?* Giesler lifted a sheaf of papers from his briefcase.
He leaned over to Jake and whispered: "Let's see what kind
of strategist you are." Giesler walked slowly to the witness
stand, paused before the old lady and gestured with his papers
to the star witness and her manager.

"Do you know Eunice Pringle and ――― ――― sitting there
together?"

That was the question. Simple, almost casual. Jake watched
his old lady hopefully.

"Yes," she replied, *"they lived together as man and wife in
my bungalow court."*

The courtroom gasped and Giesler frowned, presumably
surprised. There was a stir in the jury box, and an excited
muttering among the spectators. Prosecutor Fitts was on his
feet objecting, demanding that all the response beyond the
word "Yes" be stricken. Giesler glanced angrily at him and
quickly back to the old lady. "What's the matter?" she demanded. *"Am I not supposed to tell the truth here?"*

Her question fell like a sledgehammer. She was glaring
accusingly at the prosecutor, and at the judge who upheld
him. She shook her gray head at the jury. "The very idea!"
The jury appeared to have somewhat the same thought as
Fitts sternly insisted that the remark be stricken. Giesler
didn't argue. Instead, he excused the witness. The deed was
done.

Jake slumped back in his chair while the old woman came
down from the stand and went slowly out through the silent
crowd. Every eye followed her slow, plodding progress.
Buron Fitts, passing close behind the defense, muttered: "You
sneaky sons-of-bitches!"

Then Giesler was leaning over Jake. "Prepared like a master!" Jake smiled. It was high praise from the older lawyer, a real accolade. He liked the term, and it was well he did, for from that time on his colleagues called him "The Master."

Of course Giesler had to work like the Trojan he was for three more hectic weeks, and even then he couldn't be positive he had hammered an acquittal into the hearts of the jury. But he was pretty sure one old woman had disposed of Eunice Pringle's claim to chastity.

One other incident occurred that convinced Ehrlich this was his debut in the big time. Throughout the trial the bailiffs had to stretch ropes in the corridors to control the crowds. One day, returning from lunch, Jake tried to duck under a rope to get back into the courtroom. A deputy stopped him. "But I'm Jake Ehrlich," the lawyer said, "one of Mr. Giesler's associates."

"Go on," growled the deputy. "Get back in line like everyone else. Jake Ehrlich is a big attorney!"

Jake bowed from the waist as he produced his wallet and credentials.

The jury found Pantages not guilty.

Turning to his lawyers with tears in his eyes, the millionaire said: "I finally got a break." Ehrlich patted his shoulder. "Me too." And Giesler added: "I think we all did."

He and Ehrlich would be close friends and frequent associates. Years later, when Giesler was chairman of the State Racing Board, Jake had an offer to defend a bookie accused of bribing jockeys to throw races. The fee would be $25,000, but Ehrlich's presence on the defense would make Giesler's position more difficult. Jake turned down the case. "Our friendship had continued for more than twenty years," he said. "I wouldn't trade it for a million dollars, and certainly not for $25,000."

Of the thousands of autographed photos Ehrlich has collected during his practice, one was to find a place of honor on his office wall. It was a photo of Giesler and written on it was this: "To a very dear friend, a real pal and a fine lawyer, from his friend and erstwhile associate." Jake feels that the practice of law offers no higher endorsement.

II

Mrs. ALICE K. CAMPBELL

The Princess Who Wanted to Sing

Ever since its Barbary Coast days San Francisco has spawned rare and rollicking establishments for the diversion of adult males and females after nightfall. Probably the most extraordinary opened on New Year's Eve, 1933—Club Kamokila.

It was owned by a warm, gentle and beautiful lady, Princess Kamokila, otherwise Mrs. Alice Kamokila Campbell, the talented, utterly naïve daughter of James Campbell, sugar-pineapple-cattle king of the Hawaiian Islands, and Kuaihelana, a true Hawaiian princess.

As a child Alice had romped through King Kalakaua's Great White Palace, amid poets and artists, and as a young matron in San Francisco with $10,000,000 of her father's money she cut a fine figure as hostess, entertainer and patroness of the arts, particularly music. She herself liked to sing.

She opened the Kamokila night club, a fantastic replica of a Polynesian castle, in the basement of an old Methodist Sunday School hard by City Hall. There, as Prohibition bowed out, she offered American whiskey and Hawaiian drinks to socialite guests in a fern forest setting, with crimson draperies, gold pillars embossed with the royal Hawaiian coat-of-arms and an aura of night-blooming jasmine.

Mrs. Campbell established residence on the upper floors

with a staff of South Sea Island servants. She maintained a $30,000 fleet of automobiles, held musical teas and was obsessed with the idea of an upper-crust club "where husband and wife can meet on common ground." She said they could even bring the children.

Almost from opening night the Kamokila Club was beset with troubles, and soon the Princess was in Ehrlich's office. First it was a suit by ASCAP for using a song, "You're Gonna Lose Your Gal," without paying the customary royalties. That was comparatively minor. The police were not.

They said the noise made in the club disturbed the neighbors, and stationed uniformed men at the door. Jake got them removed.

"Why are the police bothering me?" the Princess asked. "I've already paid for protection."

Ehrlich shook his head disapprovingly and told her that protection was unnecessary, that Prohibition was over and her liquor license was in order. But soon the police were back with "an inside guard" to make sure that no drinks harder than wine were served and that there was no dancing. Again Jake got the uniformed men off the premises.

Without Ehrlich's knowledge, the Princess had written a check for $177 to a private guard hired by the club to protect the guests' jewelry. Of this, it developed much later, $27 was the guard's wage and $150 for distribution among assorted police sergeants, corporals and patrolmen.

That very night two officers burst into Club Kamokila on a surprise raid, frightening Mrs. Campbell's gold-plated patrons into the street and arresting her manager for serving hard liquor by the drink. It was the first such raid under California repeal laws, and somewhat confounding to Ehrlich. He had never seen policemen so obsessed with one gin mill.

Study of the new liquor regulations, furthermore, convinced him that the Princess was operating well within the law. A few days later the municipal court upheld his contention, noting that even the state authorities disagreed on the new statutes. "Until the law is plain," said the judge, "I will dismiss all such cases."

Ehrlich observed there weren't any other such cases, oddly enough, and that Club Kamokila was the single victim. Again he counseled the Princess to pay nothing but her honest bills and, if she must run a night club, to conduct it as an honest business operation. For three restful days nothing more occurred.

On the fourth day Princess Kamokila performed the most incredible act of her fabulously naïve career. She picked up her gold telephone and called Police Chief William J. Quinn.

"Is $150 the correct amount," she asked innocently, "to pay six police officers in my district?"

The Chief's startled roars carried to the offices of Mayor Angelo Rossi and to the newspapers. Everyone demanded a thorough investigation, and the Princess was still speaking. "A great many people," she said, "told me I would have to pay the police for protection. As soon as you pay, I was told, you will have the club open with flying colors."

Now she told about the $177 check she had given her club guard and the guard responded that he had never advised her to pay for protection and suggested that it might have been a young gentleman who sold her a fleet of Cadillacs and had a friend in the Mayor's office. The guard swore he had only told Princess Kamokila to give "gratuities" to the beat officers who worked so hard outside the place.

A rumor started that one police captain had initiated all the Kamokila troubles and that Ehrlich had had him transferred to "the fog belt." Jake flew into a rage.

All hell was breaking loose. Two grand jurors went to District Attorney Matt Brady and demanded an investigation. He replied that nothing criminal had been presented to him.

A headline appeared: U. S. OPENS PROBE INTO COPS' SALARIES. This was indeed news. Police salaries of that day were not subject to federal tax. Only income over and above the salary was taxable. And where would policemen be getting income over and above salary?

Mrs. Campbell kept lamenting: "All I wanted to know was how much." Ehrlich abruptly withdrew as counsel. "You've taken everyone's advice but mine!" he told her. The royal blood flared. "You're fired!" she said. She was back, however, a few days later, in tears. Somehow she had overlooked a dancing permit among all the applications she had made for licenses. The police were after her for that oversight.

The Grand Jury met and called her first. She sang a pathetic tale, but declined to furnish names or dates of payoffs though she did admit having written the $177 check. The young man from the Mayor's office denied he had instructed Mrs. Campbell to pay out money. He *had* advised her to "get rid of Jake Ehrlich." He didn't say why. An investigation of the Grand Jury itself was started.

One night the telephone jangled at the Kamokila and a harsh voice told the Princess to "drop the whole mess or you and your son will be bumped off." She demanded a gun permit, hired a small army of personal bodyguards and called Jake. He had been threatened too.

The police commission, disturbed at Mrs. Campbell's refusal to disclose everything before the Grand Jury, withheld action on her dance permit. Ehrlich fumed, but the commission ignored him.

Invited to a social function at the Palace one evening, he suddenly became aware that the commission was meeting in executive session at the same hour. He garbed himself in white tie and tails, called for one of the Princess' limousines with liveried Hawaiian chauffeur, and telephoned the newspapers to stand by.

Precisely at the stroke of eight, as the papers subsequently reported, "He rolled up in a black car half a block long, dressed like a ringmaster for a circus, attended by a South Seas giant and hula dancers." He strolled into the commission hearing and before the goggle-eyed chairman could rap him out of order announced:

"All other clubs have dancing, and we are going to have it too—beginning tonight. The police have made a circus of this little lady's attempt to start an honest business in San Francisco. They will have to break down the doors if they want to get in from now on." He turned and marched from the room.

Kamokila patrons danced that night (as usual) while Jake hovered angrily near a telephone at the Palace. No policeman broke down the doors.

But this was only a skirmish. Jake still couldn't find the enemy. He had a hunch, however. Six policemen were dismissed for declining to answer Grand Jury questions. A police captain sent word to the Princess to "get rid of Ehrlich," which was puzzling. Was it an indirect order from the omnipotent McDonoughs? Jake could only guess.

He learned that the police captain had said of the club: "It is a dive and one of the worst in San Francisco. She is not fooling anyone with that society bull. I am going to close it every night."

Jake filed a $200,000 slander suit, which goaded the police commission to take prompt action on the dance permit. They denied it forthwith.

Privately, this action suited Ehrlich, who believed that the Princess belonged anywhere but in the night club business. And for once she was reasonable. She was weary of singing and, it developed, in one of her spells of insolvency. She closed the doors. Ehrlich dropped his slander suit and hoped that was that.

But the payoff charges would not quiet down. The Princess was suddenly on page one with a block-buster.

"It is embarrassing, to say the least," she said, "to be the center of notoriety. When the community is not courageous, then it must expect vice and crime. When one has to pay for respectability it does not seem fair. San Francisco today is on trial. Let all good and patriotic citizens band together and clean up the city."

She proposed a committee of one hundred to raise $100,-000, hire a private investigator and get to the bottom of crime and graft.

"That should do it!" Jake said grimly to Roy Sharff.

He walked out into the night and strolled the streets alone. Usually he could feel the great hidden warmth of San Francisco. Suddenly it wasn't there.

A new Grand Jury was impaneled and demanded to hear Mrs. Campbell again. But she was weary of the publicity.

"The old jury did nothing," she said. "The new jury might just be trying to entrap me." At Jake's insistence, though, and under a threat of contempt if she refused, she did testify to the extent of reading her allegations from the previous transcript. The Grand Jury declined to bring in a true bill.

Shortly thereafter the Princess was married for the third time—to her voice coach—and went home to Hawaii on her honeymoon. On that Aloha day, as Jake watched her sail down the bay and out the Golden Gate, leaving behind a haunting refrain of police graft, he was heartsick. This singer had left an idea for a stern new tune in the city's mind—a song that would not easily die.

III

LIEUTENANT HENRY LUDOLPH

Matter of People vs. the Cop

ONE evening Ehrlich sat in a Mason Street tavern watching the proprietor polish glasses. "How's business, Manny?" he asked. The barman held up a glass and studied it. "Must be good," he grunted. "Everyone wants in. Been a string of strangers in town who want to open up. Want to know who you pay."

"Oh?" Jake slowly turned the ice in his Scotch. "Would you remember any of these guys if you saw 'em again?"

The barman thought a moment. "One I would. Great big man, like a lumberjack. Big hands and chin, but talks like a college professor."

Jake said good night and drifted along to the next bar. The big man had been there also, and at the next, always with the same questions: Whom do you pay? How much? And where can I get a girl for the night?

"She's rolling!" Jake muttered to himself.

The song inspired by Princess Kamokila had started.

Just that calmly did the cataclysmic Atherton investigation begin in November, 1935. A remark at a luncheon club by the Collector of Internal Revenue that "some San Francisco policemen now are paying income taxes" had provoked curiosity. Harvey Wing, an inquisitive *News* reporter, had heard of a captain with an income of $100,000 from prostitution. District Attorney Brady had made a quiet trip to the

Los Angeles detective agency Edwin N. Atherton had opened after resigning from the FBI. A few weeks later Jake Ehrlich got his tipoff.

Until then, probably, no one had believed that the omnipotent McDonough empire could be touched. For years Pete and Tom, the brother sphinxes of Kearny Street, had held tight reins over police with the telephone lines from their little bail bond office hard by the Hall of Justice. San Franciscans understood the situation in a general way and accepted it as they did the tides in the bay. They didn't know into how many dirty corners it extended.

The fifteen months Atherton took to write words for Princess Kamokila's original music became probably the most tormented in San Francisco's long and boisterous civic life.

The seventy-page report Atherton compiled spelled out details, down to the maiden name of the most anonymous prostitute hustling men in the Fillmore district. One million dollars a year, he disclosed, was being paid to cops to overlook vice, $400,000 of it from shady ladies in 135 long-established houses, twelve of which were within three blocks of the Hall, and none beyond reach of McDonough telephones or runners.

Illegal gambling, he disclosed, contributed another $15,000 monthly to those in power. Police captains and lieutenants had fortunes, and patrolmen were getting them. The "fountainhead of corruption" was the McDonough office, "with tentacles reaching throughout the city government."

"McDonough Brothers," said Atherton's report, "is willing to interest itself in almost any matter to defeat or circumscribe the law. It has officials and employees in key positions to take care of any contingency. No one can conduct prostitution or gambling in San Francisco without the direct or indirect approval of the McDonoughs."

Atherton got in touch with Ehrlich just before Christmas and came directly to the point. "I want dynamite," he said.

"How about that Kamokila Club?" Jake replied honestly that the Princess had brought him troubles, but no payoff checks. The investigator nodded and asked Ehrlich to forget his visit. Jake did, until some weeks later, when certain policemen and attorneys sidled up to ask for information and opinions. A civic buzz was growing into a growl.

On February 8, Atherton appealed to the public for help. "Crooked policemen are not going to give up lucrative practices without a bitter struggle," he warned. He asked for evidence of vice in any form. The announcement brought an avalanche.

Reformers cried for a new Grand Jury. Newspapers howled for police blood. Cops overnight were suspected thieves. Then it was that Jake told friends: "This is one Pete McDonough can't take care of."

The Sphinxes maintained an ominous silence. Atherton said they wouldn't quit without a fight. They didn't. They counterattacked.

A former U. S. Attorney conferred with Atherton at dinner and was promptly jailed, as "drunk." Officers on the beat found an Atherton investigator in the Tenderloin and booked him. It was twenty-four hours before they "noticed" his special credentials. Dozens of "suspicious characters" were marched to jail and released wearing black eyes and bruises. Police complained that "gumshoes" were snooping through safe deposit boxes and bank statements. Atherton announced that he was concentrating on captains and lieutenants and would have one hundred officers "on the carpet." Everyone complained that his telephone was tapped.

2

In April the Grand Jury got its first look at the evidence. It included miles of conversation recorded from the "whispering wires" of the McDonough offices. Atherton and the district attorney furnished this, with Grand Jury highlights, to the newspapers which printed every lurid word. The exhibits included a record of the intimate questioning of Dolly Fine, a comely blonde young woman of far-reaching reputation, later to be one of Jake's clients.

Q—What time do you usually go to bed at night?

A—Well, at different times. Any time from eleven to two or three.

Q—Any time business becomes slack?

A—I don't know what you mean.

Q—I mean when there are no patrons coming into the establishment?

A—I still don't know what you mean.

Q—I am going to ask you if you remember this conversation [picked off her own wires]: "Madeline, this is Dolly. What's doing?" And Madeline said: "I had a date. I could have used Lu tonight. Wanted something Chinese. I wish I could find somebody a little Chinese. Do you know of anybody I could get?" And you said: "No, but I'll try to find someone for you."

Miss Fine recalled no such chitchat.

Q—Isn't it a fact that for the last year you have been operating a house of prostitution in the city and county of San Francisco?

A—That question I refuse to answer, sir.

Q—The only ground upon which you can refuse to answer, Miss Fine, is upon the grounds of self-incrimination or that the answer will have a tendency to degrade your character.

A—That would degrade my character, that's certain.

Ehrlich was studying the testimony carefully. Nine policemen of varying ranks had refused to testify and had been suspended. His own office looked like the squadroom of Central Station, though most of his clients appeared simply to have placed bets with bookies, played the stock market or accepted cigars or whiskey as small favors. "Just keep calm," Ehrlich advised them. "Being a policeman is probably your worst offense right now."

3

Came then the Honest Dutchman.

Lieutenant Henry Ludolph, a big, balding, blond man from Harbor Station, was known to have smiled once shortly before the earthquake. He once had been a heavyweight fighter and, on the waterfront, where problems come in gross weights, he was a good man to have around. He could break an ordinary man in half with his hands. He was also probably the most frugal man ever to wear a policeman's uniform. He was worth perhaps $50,000, saved by great economy over many years, and he wished not to lose one cent of it—or the lieutenancy which paid him $250 a month. Suspicion made him furious, and when Ludolph was mad he had a habit of crunching his knuckles. He sounded at the moment like a boa constrictor full of skeletons.

"They're trying to scare me," he lamented. He dumped bank statements, receipts, canceled checks and deposit slips on Ehrlich's desk. "I save when other knuckleheads spend. All my life I save. I drink only when someone insists." Ehrlich could testify that Ludolph was a slow man with a buck.

He listened patiently, as Ludolph explained the origins of his wealth, back to July 4, 1908. On that date he had bet $250 on Battling Nelson against Joe Gans—the odds were 2½-1 on Gans—and Nelson won by a kayo in the seventeenth round.

Ehrlich respected Ludolph's sagacity. Jake had liked Nelson too, although he was himself only eight years old at the time.

"There's nothing down on the waterfront but fifty-cent bookmakers!" the lieutenant stormed, "and we raid them when we come on them. I never took a nickel of graft!"

A rumor soon arose, via Atherton, that Ludolph had had something to do with collecting $8,000 for the 1931 mayoralty campaign, which would have been a violation of police regulations. Jake didn't believe it and called Atherton to tell him so. The investigator said he would like to meet Jake's client. They met, for privacy's sake, in the Ehrlich apartment.

Afterward only Jake and Ludolph would agree on what occurred there. They said Atherton offered immunity if the lieutenant would "put the finger" on other officers. If not, he would be called to answer for the campaign funds.

Atherton, however, told the Grand Jury that Ludolph had asked for "a deal."

"Like trading an apple for an orchard," scoffed the investigator.

The three-man police commission heard Ludolph first. He swore angrily that his only sin had been to place a few horse race bets at a cigar store. This shouldn't have shocked the commissioners, one of whom (as Atherton would charge) had a monopoly on examining all prostitutes arrested in the city.

The dour lieutenant then went before the Grand Jury and bumped into an inquisition from Assistant District Attorney Leslie Gillen, the bulldog of Atherton's pack. Ludolph lost his temper. Pacing the corridor, Jake heard the voices rise until Ludolph bellowed: "Atherton tried that! He made me a proposition!" Gillen shouted back: "You're through!"

Ludolph burst through the door, almost taking the hinges with him. Gillen also was furious. "I am thoroughly disgusted with evasions and denials," he told reporters. "Ludolph promised the commission to answer questions fully in exchange for his job. He not only failed, but has gone out of his way to hinder my examination!"

During the next few days Ehrlich tried earnestly to persuade city editors to examine Ludolph's financial records, as he had. But there was too much "live" stuff from spicy witnesses like Dolly Fine. Any claim from Atherton blared from the front pages. Ehrlich saw little chance for a fair trial, so he made a move calculated to swing the blowtorch back on the oppressors.

He filed suit in Superior Court demanding that Atherton be dismissed immediately because he was not a San Francisco resident, as municipal employees must be. He further demanded that Atherton repay the $25,000 spent to date, which drew a chuckle from the public. Then Jake amended his suit to state that Atherton need return only $24,000, "inasmuch as he has been worth $1,000."

It got publicity, but Lieutenant Ludolph got indicted. He was charged with taking bribes totalling $175 from a bookie parlor run by the Beber Brothers. Four other officers, the first to be bagged in the big graft hunt, faced similar charges. Ludolph would be tried first.

4

The Honest Dutchman came to trial on December 2, 1936, in the court of Superior Judge Silvain Lazarus, a tiny, white-hair gentleman with a leprechaun humor. Gillen, the thorny young man who had wrung the indictments from the Grand Jury, would prosecute. He was a hunch-shouldered, serious lawyer who had been a newspaper reporter on the police beat. Meticulous, logical, a stickler for facts, he was disposed to sow objections through the trial like winter wheat.

"They talk in terms of million-dollar bribes and catching

big crooks," said Ehrlich, "and they bring in one honest Dutchman who admits he won $175 on some horse races."

Gillen retaliated with a press release of the latest wire tap from the McDonoughs', calculated to inflame any juror. *"They won't get to first base,"* it said. *"The jury won't be out five minutes, and that will blow up the whole thing."*

But the case didn't run off that smoothly. The six men and six women who went into the jury box looked tough. Gillen demanded that they be locked up forthwith "to save them from Ehrlich's publicity stunts." Judge Lazarus issued the order, which overnight produced an interesting state of affairs.

One newspaper reported that the jury's first dinner at the Fairmont Hotel cost the people of the city $39—de luxe eating in 1936. Next day the jurors refused to go to lunch and be "criticized by the papers." In time they changed their minds.

It was no secret that Louis Bucchiere, an immigrant vegetable peddler with connections in other merchandise, would be the prosecution's chief witness. Atherton had used him to trap a number of bookies. Around him Gillen had assembled a bank of honest citizens to introduce the facts which Bucchiere, when his turn came, would tie into the definite charge.

The first witness was a bank employee who testified that on or about the date of the alleged payoffs Bucchiere drew $100 from his account. Obviously, Bucchiere would testify that he took that money to the Bebers to pay Ludolph. Jake didn't cross-examine.

Then a procession of witnesses swore they had seen Ludolph at the cigar store on specific dates. Ehrlich let them go with never a word of cross-examination. They were reputable people; they *had* seen Ludolph.

Consternation began to show on the McDonough wire

taps: *"Ehrlich is terrible. He don't ask a question. It's murdering Ludolph."*

Meanwhile, Prosecutor Gillen was suffering. He sat only a few feet from the defense counsel, and Jake had discovered an interesting fact about him. In the parlance of baseball players, he had "rabbit ears"; he could be disconcerted by heckling from the side.

Gillen would pose a question sternly and Ehrlich, from behind cupped hands, would whisper: "You're a mean bastard, Gillen. You'd hang your grandmother!" Slowly the prosecutor began to boil. ("Gillen, your hair's falling out.") Once he tried four times to put a question. Each time he paused, lips pinched, to glare at Ehrlich. Finally, in a fury, he sat down and refused to go on. Judge Lazarus, who could hear none of the badgering, had to order him to stand up and proceed.

In spite of the heckling, Gillen built methodically to his key witness, Bucchiere. Ehrlich had been studying that gentleman on the basis of information from Ludolph's colleagues in the police department. Bucchiere had emigrated from Italy in 1922, got to San Francisco by 1929, jumped from vegetables to bootlegging and served ten months for impersonating a federal officer. Jake privately described him as "a snaky little rat of the furacious Mediterranean type." The proper fuse, he suspected, would blow Mr. Bucchiere sky high.

Bucchiere testified as anticipated. He was a friend of the Bebers. Ludolph had told them they couldn't operate a book unless they paid. He had personally watched Ludolph accept their money. As the banker had indicated, he, Bucchiere, had provided the payoff fund on one occasion. The Bebers, he stated, "wished to eliminate unfair competition with the assistance of police." At this statement Ehrlich's eyebrows went up but he said nothing until Gillen finished and Bucchiere sat back smirking at friends in the courtroom.

Then Ehrlich rose from the table with a blunt accusation: "Lieutenant Ludolph was indicted on the word of an ex-convict, and I will prove it is being sustained by Gillen and others." He fixed Bucchiere with a disgusted stare.

"You stated, and I quote, 'The Bebers wished to eliminate unfair competition with the assistance of police.' "

"Thatsa right."

Ehrlich drew back in astonishment. *"Thatsa right?"* he echoed. "Louie, you can't read or write, can you?"

The witness confessed he could not. " *'Eliminate competition with the assistance of police,'* " repeated Ehrlich. "Those aren't your words, Louie. They're Gillen's, aren't they? What you would say is the Bebers *'hoped to take the heat off.'* Now wouldn't you?"

"Thatsa right."

Ehrlich clenched his left fist and came at the squirming witness like a fighter. Bucchiere snapped broken, angry answers. Yes, he *had* run a book once. He *had* been arrested— "for somethin' else."

Ehrlich growled: "You're a liar, Louie! You impersonated an officer of the United States government!

"You were a bootlegger, too, in violation of the laws of this country, weren't you? You are an alien here right now, *aren't* you? You simply never bothered to take out citizenship papers in our great country—*did* you?"

Ehrlich put him through another round of questioning and, satisfied that he had destroyed his effectiveness, gave him back to Gillen. When the prosecution rested, Jake moved for a directed verdict of acquittal. It was denied. Next he moved to have all of Bucchiere's testimony stricken. Also denied. The jury, Jake hoped, would dispose of Bucchiere and his testimony both.

He turned back to that uncomfortable individual in presentation of his own defense witnesses. To the stand came

William Ferriter, an attorney who had represented Bucchiere in 1933. Prosecutor Gillen objected angrily that Ferriter's testimony would be "unprofessional." The judge overruled him, and Ferriter described his erstwhile client as "a thing that crawls."

"Would you believe Bucchiere under oath?" asked Ehrlich.

"No. He is a professional perjurer."

Now Jake turned to his own client and a theory he had often urged on law school students. "When a corpse has three bulletholes in his back and your client admits pulling the trigger three times when the other's back was turned—admit the obvious. There's nothing to stop you from challenging the state's contention of *why* your client shot." Or why, in this case, a police lieutenant was in a bookie parlor.

He called Ludolph to the stand and led him back through his frugal life. He started with the Gans-Nelson fight and, to get the jury's full attention, demonstrated it with left hooks and solid rights.

"Mr. Ludolph," he asked, "is it correct, as has been testified here, that you were on the premises of the bookmaking parlor on California Street?"

"Yes, it is." The big man was clasping his hands.

"Now is it also correct that you received some money while there?"

"Yes, it is."

"What was that money for?"

"Well, I had bet on a long-shot horse and it won a lot of money. I wasn't there when it won, so I came in to get my winnings."

"And as the winner you expected to be paid *not* because you were a police officer, and *not* so a bookie parlor could continue to operate, but because you were a legitimate winner on a horse that had won its race, like any other citizen here?"

"Yes."

Ehrlich didn't look at Gillen. He could imagine the prosecutor's expression, saying: "A likely story!" Nor did Jake fill in the other details of that likely story, such as the horse's name, the amount won, or how, indeed, Ludolph could possibly remember such details so faithfully. Let Gillen explore those things. Jake baited the hook and turned to other matters. When he finished, he had pictured Ludolph as a stodgy, introverted businessman who somehow got into a police uniform. "You may have the witness," he told Gillen.

Gillen leaped to the attack. "You have testified that six or seven bookmaking establishments are in the Harbor police district?"

Ludolph, brazenly honest, replied: "Bookmaking places are tolerated in San Francisco. This system of betting has been in existence for fifty years or more. Police can't cope with it."

Gillen frowned for the jury. "How many persons," he demanded, "have you arrested for gambling during your years in Harbor district?" Ludolph estimated "about one thousand." Gillen called his attention to 1933, when Ludolph had raided the Bebers' smoke shop, and asked why he hadn't gone into the backroom where race bets were taken. "I suppose I forgot," the officer said. "I got enough evidence in the front." Gillen was barking away: "There are a lot of foolish things about this trial—and your story."

Crunch went the knuckles. "You're a liar!"

Gillen asked Ludolph bluntly if the Beber raid wasn't just a stunt to convince people the police were onto the place. "It was not a phony!" Ludolph bellowed. "It was on the up and up!"

Now Gillen decided the witness was sufficiently nettled. He pounced on Ludolph's story of betting on a race horse, the story Ehrlich had left dangling. "If it is correct," he asked with slurring scorn, "that you won the money on a horse, *what was the name of that horse?*"

"It was a horse named Hidden Sight."

Gillen blinked. "And what race did this horse win?"

"It was the eighth race." There was nothing wrong with Ludolph's mental machinery. "I remember very well because it paid 16-1 odds and I was on the streetcar coming home, and just before we came to the Sunset Tunnel a fellow sat down next to me with a late paper and I saw the results on the front page. I remember it was printed in red ink as a sports bulletin on the lefthand side of the page. I remember, too, taking a pencil and paper and waiting till we got out of the tunnel to figure my winnings, since I bet $10 on the horse to win."

A blind man could have seen the jury mentally toting $10 on a 16-1 shot and coming up with $160 of the $175 the state claimed Ludolph had collected. It was clearly the lieutenant's story against Louis Bucchiere's now. Gillen was frowning. Probably he sincerely thought Ludolph was guilty. Certainly he hated to lose the opening trial of the five indicted officers.

He put everything he had into his argument. He drew skillfully on the Atherton disclosures, with which most people were becoming familiar. He argued that a Bucchiere might be everything that was said about him but that here under oath he had certainly told the truth. Told it to the best of his ability, under the badgering of a skilled criminal lawyer like Jake Ehrlich, who "calls himself The Master."

As Jake stepped lightly across the carpet to approach the jury, he felt the "eighty million bumps" of tension rising on him.

"Ladies and gentlemen of the jury," he declared vehemently, "this is not a trial. It is a travesty, an honored officer against a perjurer—a snaky little rat who would sell a man's soul for half a cent! The district attorney says the state had to dig deep to get its evidence. I ask you how deep did they have to dig into the muck, mud, mire and corruption to dig out a skunk like Louis Bucchiere?"

He dipped into the Atherton investigations and came up with illegal wire-tapping, scared rats squealing on others to win immunity, and a police force blackened by mere innuendo. He described how, in his opinion, it all came about from the case of the naïve Princess who wanted to sing on through to the Grand Jury indictments. He turned and pinned Gillen with an accusing finger. "Gillen here had to browbeat that Grand Jury for a solid hour, before he could persuade them to charge this honest lieutenant with a crime." All this, he reminded the jury, took place when Ludolph was a prisoner in the jury room, without legal counsel, and Atherton sat there calling everyone crooks.

Inevitably, Jake came back, sneering, to Bucchiere, "the key witness and the only witness."

"They have said only policemen and criminal lawyers condemn Bucchiere," Ehrlich cried. "Who else would know him? Clergymen? He is a liar, a skunk, a panderer, a perjurer, a convicted felon. He has no character at all! Yet he pits his word against that of an honorable police officer!"

His voice grew hoarse and finally, head down and clutching the rail, he cried out: "I don't defend Ludolph as a client, not as a policeman—but as an old and dear friend."

Tears actually were flowing down his cheeks. He sobbed and bit his lip. He asked the court, please, for a recess in which to regain control of himself. Judge Lazarus gently agreed, and Jake had voice enough to apologize to judge and jury for his emotions.

After the recess he resumed without a hitch. Spectators and jurors visibly were picked up and carried along by the dapper, earnest little man striding, chopping his arms, bowing, wiping his eyes and pouring a torrent of words. The subsequent wire taps from the McDonoughs' were ecstatic. *"We had a winner! Jake broke down. He actually cried! They hadda take him out of the courtroom. It was a masterpiece! The boys asked him if he had an onion in his handkerchief.*

"He talked about brotherly love, then he told how he was raised with Ludolph, how he helped him with his first examinations, and how he wasn't getting a cent for this. He'd known Ludolph for forty years and he wouldn't believe a thing anyone said against him. It was a masterpiece."

Perhaps it got overly emotional in spots. But time and again Jake returned to the solid themes—"that rat Bucchiere" and "the prosecution offered no proof at all." Finally, white from exhaustion, he tottered before the jurors with a voice that was little more than a croak. "I know before God," he cried, "that Henry Ludolph never committed a dishonest act or took a cent of dirty money in his life!"

The jury was out two hours and forty minutes. The verdict was "Not guilty." Gillen clambered to his feet. "I don't understand it," he mumbled. The jurors, when they were finally free to speak, said it was plain: "The prosecution offered no proof at all."

There was unrestrained celebration wherever policemen met that night, for the way was clear. Jake Ehrlich had got the first victim out of the web. Every one of the officers indicted in the Atherton probe was freed when his case came up.

Atherton produced his final detailed report in March and went his way.

George Sessions Perry noted in *The Saturday Evening Post:* "Atherton's purpose was not to clean up the town, which didn't want to be cleaned up, but merely to put the police department back in the hands of the people." Maybe it was and maybe it wasn't, but the Atherton investigation bound gay and roistering San Francisco in moral chains she would never quite shake.

"The old girl's not the same," Jake observed afterward. "My musical Princess didn't know what she had concocted, when she set out to realize her destiny. She sort of changed ours too."

IV

DOLLY FINE

San Francisco's Most Painstakingly Prodigal Daughter

LIKE the traditional garter snake killed by a small boy, San Francisco's vice would not die for some hours. The McDonoughs knew that, Atherton knew it, and so did Dolly Fine, called "the smartest madame in the racket." Before Atherton had even finished his report she was signing a five-year lease on a new seraglio and spending $20,000 on decorations.

To Jake Ehrlich, Dolly Fine was a good-looking young woman who dressed smartly, bought good books, read them and discussed them. He did not argue about prostitution with her. Nor did he visit her establishment. Under the McDonough setup she did not need a lawyer of his caliber; a fixer would do. If he ever pondered her choice of a profession, perhaps he recalled the words of Matthew Prior:

> That if weak women went astray
> Their stars were more at fault than they.

By 1937, however, he had come to understand that not all members of the "fallen sisterhood" were weak. Some, like Dolly Fine, could be very strong.

Ehrlich believed Dolly had misjudged the city's repentant temper and overplayed her hand before the Atherton Grand Jury, though she had made a fetching personal appearance.

She was no perfumed, mincy-hipped procuress, batting mascaraed eyelashes and slurring "C'mup 'n' see me." As women of sexful reputation often do, she appeared to be startlingly conservative.

Miss Fine said "if you please." She was a tall, fair woman of thirty-five, who had excellent taste in clothes and a figure to wear them on. She appeared before the Grand Jury in a tailored black gabardine suit with white gloves, a white blouse clipped at the throat with rhinestones, and soft, blonde-brown hair under a wide-brimmed sailor hat. She might have been any of the smartly styled ladies you saw that summer along Powell Street near the St. Francis. Feminine eyes on the Grand Jury widened with grudging admiration.

The working press, never so worldly wise as it pretends to be, was surprised to find that her clear blue eyes did not instinctively X-ray every male to determine what money he might have in his pocket. Dolly Fine, who was really Dorothy Harding, was shy. She blushed and bit her lip, covered her face, at times shed tears of mortification—and said virtually nothing.

Perhaps that was her first mistake. She tried to deceive San Franciscans, to pretend she was not what they believed her to be. Every man in the room blinked when she denied that she ran a house of prostitution. People frowned when she identified herself as "an apartment house manager." They were ready to forgive her when she acknowledged that she had been arrested a number of times, but not when she explained "for disorderly conduct."

Somehow they had expected more of Dolly Fine, more revelations like the tapped telephone conversation about "getting something Chinese." There was something unpenitently dishonest in her flat denials. They weren't quite in the spirit of San Francisco, which is usually honest with itself.

Of course San Franciscans had done nothing to punish her.

No one had expected them to. Atherton realized that. Two days after he made his final report he addressed a civic group in Oakland. "Has the investigation helped San Francisco at all?" they asked him. "No," he said sadly, "not so far. It is going to be a complete whitewash." He added that it might have gone better if San Francisco had had Oakland's district attorney, a husky young fellow named Earl Warren, who was later to be Chief Justice of the United States.

So the weeks went on and San Francisco's little vice serpent continued its death wriggles.

One April morning Ehrlich was strolling along Montgomery Street to pick up airplane tickets for Los Angeles. Ahead of him in the crowd loomed tall Dolly Fine, head erect, but seemingly preoccupied and lonely. Together they stepped into a cocktail lounge.

"What's the trouble, Dolly?" Jake asked. "The world got you down?"

"No," she said. "I've just finished reading a new book and I can't get it off my mind. It's *Gone With the Wind.*"

"A great story, ma'am!" said Jake. "Do I understand you are appalled at what the damyankees did to us suthernuhs?"

"No, Jake," Dolly said quite seriously. "It's that girl Scarlett. She intrigues me. How could any real woman be that beautiful, that determined and resourceful all at once?"

Jake studied the steady blue eyes. She was absolutely serious. "Dolly," he said, "sometimes you amaze me. I'll see you when I get back from Los Angeles." He didn't, though. While he was away Dolly Fine became the Scarlet One in San Francisco's own version of *Gone With the Wind.*

2

On Saturday, April 24, a socially prominent matron overheard her sixteen-year-old son making a telephone call.

"After the Prom," he was saying, "we're all going to Dolly
Fine's." The mother nearly swooned. She had read the story
of Dolly Fine during the months of the investigation and had
thought it all rather amusing. This was serious. She telephoned the police.

That night Inspector William Merrick trailed eight tuxedo-
clad youths as they left their exclusive private-school dance
and headed gaily for the shady apartment house on Bush
Street. Police closed in as the boys rang the doorbell, and
hustled them out of the building. There on the corner Inspector Merrick lectured them sternly and informed them that
he would tell their fathers. Then he returned to the apartment
and arrested four "scantily attired" women and a colored
maid. Dolly, he said, appeared "in a revealing red evening
gown."

One look at the police officers told her she was in trouble.
"Get Jake!" she ordered. Friends reached him by telephone
in Los Angeles and asked if he would represent her. Ehrlich
said he would, but that he would be busy in Los Angeles for
several weeks. "Get it continued," he instructed, and hung
up. Four hundred miles away, he could not hear the angry
cries of eight sets of parents or see the banner headlines in
San Francisco on "The Lady in Red."

Within an hour after her arrest, Dolly was released on
$1,000 bail provided by the McDonoughs. She was charged
with a misdemeanor only—keeping a disorderly house—
which usually involved a fine of $50 or less. Six months ear-
lier, she had been brought in twice on the same charge, and
before the same judge, Theresa Meikle.

Judge Meikle, an attractive and sensible young lady newly
elevated from the district attorney's office to the municipal
bench, had fined Dolly $25 on the first occasion and dropped
the charges the second time. Lawyers said of Judge Meikle,

"She knows life and, what's more important, she understands it."

But now she was staring down the big guns of righteousness. Byron Parker, a McDonough attorney, asked for a continuance of the case, granted automatically as a rule. Out of the crowded and ogling courtroom rose white-haired Police Chief William J. Quinn to protest and demand a speedy trial.

"We have been doing everything we can to drive such places as this out of San Francisco," he thundered. "We have raided the premises on Bush Street time and time again and tried to close them with no success." In less than seven years, he declared, there had been thirty arrests at Dolly Fine's.

That day Judge Meikle announced she would fine prostitutes from $200 for a first offense up to $1,000 for repeaters. She sent nine of them to the county jail for fifteen-day terms and gave two keepers of houses $2,000 fines, plus thirty days behind bars.

Next night the Grand Jury came to bat. In addition to the misdemeanor charge against Dolly Fine, it returned eight counts, one for each boy found in her place. And for the first time in San Francisco history it resorted to a state law—Section 702 of the Welfare and Institutions Code—which makes it a more serious offense (contributing to delinquency) to permit or encourage juveniles to enter brothels.

"We will be watching closely to see if police clean up the situation," the jury foreman warned. "If they don't, the jury will take further action."

Retorted Chief Quinn: "We have closed the place. It will stay closed."

During that wild week Dolly kept carefully out of sight, praying for the appearance of Jake Ehrlich. Police sirens shrilled through the nights with raids on neighboring apartments. District Attorney Brady was trumpeting: "Law-en-

forcement agencies must join in protecting youngsters from
the moral and hygienic dangers of prostitution."

At 10:00 A.M. Friday, April 30, Judge Meikle sternly
called the case of Dorothy Harding alias Dolly Fine. Everyone in the courtroom was looking for the exotic "Lady in
Red." Bailiffs had to chase one teenager after another from
the room before Nate Coghlan, an attorney, stepped to the
bar. "Your Honor," he said, "I was asked to represent this
defendant, but she does not appear to be here. Could this
matter go over a couple of hours?" Judge Meikle frowned,
and said she would call the case again.

She did so, at 2:00 P.M. Coghlan shook his head. "There
has been press discussion of increasing the bail in this case,"
he said. "The fear of that may have influenced my client to
disappear."

3

Disappear? Reporters sprinted for telephones. Judge Meikle
ordered a bench warrant for Dolly's immediate apprehension.
She told the bailiffs to take the four young women and colored
maid from the apartment into custody at once. A free-lance
streetwalker who happened to come up for trial at the moment
was given her choice of a $350 fine or thirty days in jail.

Thereupon began the longest—eighty-nine days—and
strongest manhunt for a woman ever pressed in the history of
San Francisco. The city was determined to get back the gal
it wanted run out of town.

Now a sensational discovery was made right in the gray
old Hall of Justice on Kearny Street. The Dolly Fine file was
found to be as bare as Mrs. Hubbard's pantry. Despite her
thirty-odd arrests, there was not one photograph or fingerprint of Dolly in it.

"They bring in so many prostitutes," complained a red-faced patrolman-clerk, "we'd have to move out in the street if we filed all the details." He could offer little more than a list of aliases and the limp red evening gown, which had been taken from Dolly as evidence.

This state of affairs did not silence the newspapers. The *Call-Bulletin* came up with "a slender, exotic, dark-haired dancer," who described how Dolly entertained night club employees at gay parties in a luxurious home at Sharp Park, a tiny seacoast town south of San Francisco.

"The house is beautiful," declared the dancer. "Everything in it is like a dream—silk and satin luxury everywhere. There was never anything wrong about the parties. We just spent the night having a swell time, drinking a little, and then came back in time to work the next day."

The *Call* put its most imaginative writers to work on the "sex castle" at Sharp Park. They reported "luxurious interiors built from the profits of vice," a boudoir with a central fireplace, Dolly's personal bed overlooking the Pacific, costly drapes, ultramodern furniture, two shelves of books—*Young Desire, His Hour, Trapped by Love, Poor Little Fool*—and a "big, lifelike, lonesome china doll on a chaise lounge."

"In her role as keeper of a bordello," wrote the *Call*, "Dolly, clad in a symbolic scarlet ensemble, directed the sordid activities of profit-sharing prostitutes, ruled over dimly lit, gaudily appointed rooms, played hostess to all sorts and conditions of men. In her daytime role as mistress of a home, she lounged in a costly negligee before a crackling fire, read typically lurid literature, and listened to the ceaseless rumble of the surf nearby."

Naturally, hundreds of San Franciscans took to their cars, bumping fenders and locking bumpers, and rushed down the narrow coast highway. All they found was a group of bored deputies watching a drab stucco house which needed a coat of paint.

The *Chronicle* printed an interview Dolly had given before she departed. "For years," she said, "I got along in this town, trying to run a decent house. I paid attention to details, kept my girls healthy. There is nothing more pitiful in life than a prostitute who has risen from the streets, tasted luxuries and liked them, and finds herself once again in the gutter." The *Chronicle* said Dolly had given herself four alternatives: commit suicide, "sing" to the law, plead innocent before a jury, or run away. "Whichever route I take" (it quoted her as saying), "I'm going first class."

Every day produced new rumors. Dolly was heading for France with a mystery husband and a $50,000 "nest egg." She was in Chicago (a rumor confirmed at one point by the Chicago chief of detectives).The State Department was asked to watch passports.

The *Call* produced a box score of Dolly's many arrests and the courts' disposition of them—"a paltry $145 in fines, slightly more than ONE HALF OF ONE MONTH'S RENT for her brothel-apartment."

The *Examiner* was the first to predict that Dolly would be back. "She has a $20,000 investment here," it noted. "Any competent lawyer can beat this. The prosecution would be no more successful than it has been in the graft and vice prosecutions of the past two years. She would never have run if able to confer with a certain criminal attorney who was out of town at the time. He is back and has been approached to defend her."

Jake was back, studying the box score and feeling like a man asked to defend a jug of gasoline in the middle of a brush fire. He spoke bravely: "I could stand on the steps of the Hall of Justice with a load of buckshot in my hand and hit so many houses of prostitution the district attorney and police would be busy for a year. Why are they picking on Dolly Fine?"

"No, I *don't* know where she is," he repeated into the telephone a hundred times. "I haven't talked to her since I left town. The heat's on now, but it will cool off." He said the same thing to Dolly's brother, Larry Brady. He also told the brother about a little-known law under which forfeited bail could be restored if the fugitive came back voluntarily within ninety days. Ninety days for Dolly Fine would be July 28.

As any firefighter knows, you start backfires when the glow is reddest. Ehrlich dropped into the district attorney's office. Would they consider reduced charges—say, a relaxing of those eight charges and a guilty plea? Indignantly they said no. Ehrlich suggested that some of their prospective witnesses might prove color blind in court when they tried to identify the "Lady in Red." The prosecutors told him to go peddle his papers. Jake shrugged and laid in some "props," a supply of dark glasses and one wine-colored veil that would screen a woman from head to toe.

4

On July 27, the eighty-ninth day, Jake sat in his office staring out across the bay toward Oakland. Larry Brady had stopped in that morning and the clock was ticking. The call came from Oakland, a man's voice. Meet him, he said, in front of the Oakland Auditorium. "You know the place?"

"I always kayoed my man in the third round there," said Jake. He found Dolly sitting in an inexpensive sedan at Lake Merritt, watching the kids fish for smelt. "Did you ever figure out Scarlett O'Hara?" he asked, handing Dolly the trailing veil and dark glasses. "No," she said. "That girl beats me." She was very nervous.

The veiled and muffled figure he guided up the steps of the Hall of Justice—Dolly Fine—looked and talked like a mourner arriving for the last rites of a loved one. "Make the public know I had nothing to do with letting those kids in," she pleaded. "Everyone knows my house was the finest in town."

Past tense, thought Jake. He got her bail money restored, got her case on the jury calendar in municipal court, and put up the $2,000 doubled bail Judge Meikle had set.

Dolly had another narrow escape. She appeared at a night club with her brother. Jake was there with Ted Lewis and Jan Garber, the orchestra leaders, and Jerry Lester, the comedian.

At the next table a patron questioned the price of his champagne. A knife flashed and, the papers reported next morning, "It was a half hour of seething uproar and one of the wildest scenes ever to turn a night club into a shambles." Just before the police arrived to cause Dolly more grief, she, Ehrlich and party departed on the double.

Jake once had defended a woman accused of offering to get a girl for a policeman. He had won by showing that the prosecution hadn't proved what the girl was to be gotten for. Now he went before Superior Judge Isadore M. Golden and moved, unsuccessfully, that the eight charges against Dolly be dropped. There was no evidence in the indictments, he argued, that the boys were now delinquent. Therefore, how could Dolly have contributed to their delinquency?

A few days later he got Judge Golden's ear and made a short speech. "These boys (who were taken in the raid) are as dear to their parents as mine is to me. (Jake, Jr. was then fifteen.) I wouldn't want to subject my son to such an ordeal (as appearing against Dolly Fine in a courtroom) and feel I should not do it to the sons of others." He moved to have the whole matter resubmitted to the Grand Jury. The motion was denied.

On September 7 Dolly appeared before a municipal judge on the original misdemeanor charge of keeping a brothel. Cloaked in the wine-colored veil, she entered the courtroom to watch the selection of a jury. Ehrlich was noticeably sedate. This case, though it involved only a misdemeanor, was vital to Dolly's fortunes. Acquitted here, she might escape trial on the felony charges. Convicted here, she almost certainly would be found guilty of entertaining the schoolboys.

The big question was: Who filled that red dress lying on the table before the clerk? Ehrlich, from the outset, suggested it was another woman, whom he would put into the gown. Prosecutor Ben Lerer promised the dress would fit only Dolly. And so they selected a jury of seven men and five women.

To the stand came Inspector Merrick, the stern officer who had rescued the laddies and claimed to have seen Dolly in the revealing red gown. The four other young women were in evening gowns too, he said. "Oh?" said Ehrlich. "And what is your idea of an evening gown, Inspector Merrick?"

The Inspector frowned. "Well—er—an evening gown is when a lady's dressed in scanty attire, I guess," he said. Ehrlich's eyes twinkled at the ladies on the jury.

The next witness testified he had collected utility bills from Dolly Fine at the Bush Street address. He glanced blandly at the veiled and muffled defendant, and admitted he couldn't be sure this was Dolly. And so it went, with the constant suggestion that another woman had been proprietress of the brothel that night, and finally the arguments by counsel.

"There are 580 bagnios in this town," Jake declared. "Why do they pick on Dolly Fine? I'll tell you why. The prosecution has picked up a hot potato and is afraid to drop it."

Nevertheless, the jury took only forty minutes to find Dolly Fine guilty of the misdemeanor. Judge Alden Ames fined her

$300, suspending a six months' jail sentence "if she changes her occupation immediately."

5

Now "San Francisco's most painstakingly prodigal daughter," *if* found guilty on the delinquency charges, faced incarceration for as much as sixteen years. Once more Jake argued for dismissal, declaring that Dolly had just been punished for keeping the house, and the new trial would place her in double jeopardy. The motion was denied.

Still in the background, keeping steady pressure on the law, were the socially prominent parents of the boys. Jake knew them all.

Ehrlich believed he knew teenage boys, too. If he did, then Dolly Fine didn't have to lean from any window and beckon them. Dolly was being spanked; he could understand that perfectly. But she was being spanked because the city was contrite over all the bad morals in which it had indulged itself these several years past, and Jake did not believe that represented justice for his client.

On the day before the trial Ehrlich cornered District Attorney Brady in Judge Golden's chambers. Jake had a batch of subpoenas in his hand. They were made out in the names of the parents. His meaning was obvious as he slapped them against his leg. He came directly to the point: "That State Welfare Code indicts my client for permitting or encouraging these boys to enter into dissolute lives. Now, if this matter must come to trial, the parents should come and testify that their sons' lives have become dissolute, as a direct result of that evening. If they haven't, then Dolly Fine didn't lead them anywhere, and you know it."

The district attorney snorted. "I don't even want to talk about it, Jake," he said.

Early the next morning a crew of process servers from Jake's office hurried to the exclusive neighborhood in which the boys and their parents lived. Precisely at seven o'clock, just three hours before court convened, they rang the doorbells of five homes. Maids who answered the door were brushed aside. Some of the startled parents were served before they could rise from bed, and found themselves under written order to appear at 10:00 A.M. in "the matter of Dolly Fine." It was 7:01 A.M.

At 7:05 Ehrlich's office phone began to ring. He let it sputter a few moments before he lifted the receiver and said, "Hello, Matt."

"Jake!" said the district attorney. "Do you think you could be in chambers a little before court? I think we ought to talk this over some more."

"I haven't anything to talk about," Jake said. "I've done my talking." He hung up.

Three minutes later Judge Golden called. "Jake," he said, "I hear you went through with your idea. Matt Brady wants to discuss it again. Would you come in, please?"

"I'll come in, Judge," Jake said, "but I haven't anything to discuss, except with those parents."

By the time he strolled through the corridors to Judge Golden's chambers he could feel the air of pandemonium. Brady explained nervously that he couldn't let Dolly Fine off after the months of hullabaloo. On the other hand, he recognized that he probably couldn't win a public trial without the parents.

Ehrlich shrugged. But he listened while the judge and district attorney discussed possible terms of sentence. One year on each count? (They looked at Jake, serenely staring out the window.) Nine months? Sixty days? A $2,500 fine? Would Dolly have that sort of money with her?

Jake let them mull it over for half an hour. Finally he

suggested "she might have $250 if there was any assurance she would be out of jail in thirty days." He turned and left the conference.

The body of the court was packed when Judge Golden trudged to his big chair and the bailiff rapped down the clamor. The people of San Francisco had waited months for this—through Grand Jury, Atherton investigation, lower courts, newspaper buildup. They wanted to see brazen Dolly Fine turned over the city's official knee and tapped with a hairbrush.

Ehrlich, suave, took the floor. "If Your Honor please," he said quietly, "if this case goes to trial, we'll have to have all those parents and boys in here. Miss Fine sincerely wishes to spare them all from this humiliation and I, as the father of a boy the same age, certainly would hate to have that happen. Therefore, if Your Honor please, Miss Fine will plead guilty to one count of the indictment." He stole a quick glance at Matt Brady, who rose and said quietly: "If the Court please, the people will drop the seven other counts of the indictment with the feeling that justice has been accomplished."

"She copped a plea!" protested someone in the audience. Before the buzzing could grow to a growl, Judge Golden spoke: "There is a definite question as to the outcome of this matter. The district attorney would have to prove Miss Fine actually had a part in the admission of these boys to the brothel, if the case went to trial. She might walk out of court a free woman." He glanced at his notes and pronounced sentence: a fine of $500 and sixty days in the county jail.

On November 22, less than thirty days later, Dolly Fine was given a pardon and left San Francisco forever.

Where did she go? If Jake knew, he never told. He returned to his office to work on a case for the Encyclopaedia Britannica. "She's probably curled up somewhere with a book," he suggested. "A good book like *Gone With the Wind*."

V

"LEO THE LION"

Fisticuffs for the King of Beefs

At about the time Dolly Fine was hanging up the gloves (and red gown) Attorney Ehrlich was summoned to a singular pugilistic display in Oakland. It was billed as a boxing contest between two nationally ranked heavyweights, Eddie Simms of Cleveland, Ohio, and Phainting Phil Brubaker of California, and it played to a packed auditorium because for ten astonishing days tomtoms had thundered from Los Angeles to San Francisco that it was to be the world's champion fake.

Big guns of the fight crowd were trained at the moment on Oakland promoter Leo Leavitt, a brash young man who called himself "Leo the Lion." Just before the bout a rival tried to hire away the main event and before it went into the record books, Ehrlich was involved in the longest, strangest and most violent combination of fists and forensics of his entire career.

"From the opening bell," he observed, "it was the worst mismatch, in or outside the ring, since Henry Cabot Lodge took on the League of Nations."

His client Leavitt, a gay and personable young man with flashing white teeth and a wavy black mane, had struck promotional gold in Oakland, a city sometimes described as the Brooklyn of San Francisco. The Lion started with a temporary permit to promote occasional fights and served notice on all competing fight clubs that they would have to hustle. His first card, Slapsie Maxie Rosenbloom against an unknown heavyweight, netted $6,500. From then on the Fight Trust was gunning for his scalp.

Established Oakland promoters were simply starved out. Leavitt tied up pugs all over the United States. Even Suey Welch, tops at fight merchandising, was cold-shouldered when he tried to hire bouts for his Los Angeles Olympic. Inevitably someone raised the cry that Leavitt was owning and managing boxers. Boxing Commission regulations said a man could not be both manager and promoter.

In response to all this the Lion roared happily and opened a fistic substation at Stockton, eighty miles away, to develop both fighters and fans.

Sportswriters of the San Francisco press, which is never happy to go to Oakland for its stories, wailed that Leavitt's monopoly had knocked the bottom out of their city's boxing barrel. They had a worthy opponent in Oakland, gadfly Art Cohn, sports editor of the *Tribune,* who later would write for the movies. A protégé of Damon Runyon, Cohn was Leo Leavitt's pal, and when Leavitt wasn't galling the San Francisco press, Cohn was. His favorite target was Tom Laird, hard-fisted sports editor of the *News,* whom Cohn referred to as "T. L-a-r-d."

Another gladiator in the fistic melee was Edwin W. Geary, a tall young Oakland lawyer on the boxing commission. Geary abhorred any monopoly, and the Lion unquestionably had obtained one. Furthermore, Geary had heard charges that Leavitt was disobeying commission law. He issued warnings.

Leavitt ignored them. He brazenly took Small Montana, a champion flyweight, on a barnstorming tour of the Orient. On their return, the fighter sued him for $25,000 in earnings. Leavitt blandly announced that he would promote a world's title match in Oakland featuring Small Montana; this made the Filipino boxer flash all his gold teeth in a happy smile. Rival matchmakers gnashed theirs.

But first Leavitt staged that heavyweight show between Brubaker and Simms. Local pride in Brubaker started a box office stampede. It didn't matter that Simms had kayoed Brubaker in seventy seconds a year before.

Then came the whispering campaign: "Simms is gonna dive to build up Brubaker. Leavitt's Brubaker's manager." The Los Angeles *Examiner* warned: "The fight is going to be one of those things." Fred (Windy) Winsor, usually well-informed fight pilot, declared authoritatively that Simms was to "dive for 20 per cent of the gate and a $750 blowback." Never had a box office thrived so lustily on such an odor of gorgonzola.

On the morning of the fight, Commission Inspector Donn Shields sent promoter Leavitt a registered letter: "I am locking the door before the horse is stolen. I have warned the boxers. The referee will be given instructions that if anything appears wrong both boxers will be thrown out, the bout called 'No Contest,' purses held up and officials of your club will be called at the next meeting of the commission."

And that is precisely what happened. After eighty seconds of the seventh round, with the fans in full hullabaloo and neither fighter putting on a show, Honest Billy Burke, the referee, stopped it. Ehrlich was at ringside with Slip Madigan, the old Notre Dame football player.

Fistically, it was California's biggest mess. "Hatched in Los Angeles and nourished in San Francisco," wrote Alan Ward, the Oakland fight expert, "a well-defined plot to discredit pugilism in Oakland is responsible for the boxing scandal now rocking the city." Art Cohn argued: "It couldn't have been a barney; it was too dull." He hunted down Simms before Eddie decamped for Cleveland. Simms swore that three fight men—Suey Welch, Windy Winsor and San Francisco promoter Evans—had telephoned him promises if he should "stink out boxing in Oakland." But he said he hadn't been trying to throw the fight. "Why," wailed Simms, "should I throw a fight to a bum like Brubaker?"

Leavitt, when cornered, was almost contrite. "The fight was a terrible thing to watch," he admitted. "But if rumors hadn't been spread, it would have gone down as a miserable exhibition, not as a fake. If it had been held in San Francisco, it would have been considered great."

Commissioner Geary cleared his official throat. "We have evidence that Leavitt is in actual fact Brubaker's manager." The Lion, he declared, should be deprived of his license as a promoter and barred from any further activities relating to prizefighting in California. Leavitt ran for Jake.

2

No other attorney, perhaps, had a better grasp of the fight game. Jake not only had fought as a lightweight in that same Oakland auditorium, but was also attorney of record for several world's champions: Maxie Rosenbloom, Barney Ross, and Jackie Fields. He was even, on occasion, an amateur matchmaker. One thing he understood: that boxing law very often is more lore than law. Politically appointed commission members do not conduct business as a court of law. They are ultrasensitive to rumblings in the press. However, they could easily destroy Leo Leavitt's career and his business.

"Serious charges have been made publicly against my client," Ehrlich announced. "We will demand a showdown, with Mr. Geary put on the stand to prove these charges or retract them." The public suddenly sat up to watch. "We are interested to learn if Mr. Geary is qualified to know the difference between a bad fight and a fake fight," Jake continued.

The commission hearing was held in an office suite near the Palace Hotel. Broken-knuckled fists rubbed startled eyes when Jake strode in and immediately demanded that Commissioner Geary be disqualified. The regular chairman shook his head. "I was fortunate enough to be 500 miles away when this thing occurred. Mr. Geary was at ringside." He handed the gavel to his colleague.

Before Geary could clear his throat, Ehrlich charged, "Raise your right hand and be sworn!" The commissioner reacted automatically. He raised his hand. In that moment he lost his power to rule on the issue; he had allowed himself to be sworn as a witness. "Geary took charge at 10:31," wrote Art Cohn. "At 10:32 Attorney Ehrlich took charge of Geary."

The attorney's approach was a feint, an academic discourse in his best jury-pleading style covering the fight game from its origins. He paced the room as he spoke, bobbing and weaving, shadowboxing, slugging, sweeping along with him the managers, trainers, promoters, seconds, writers, hangers-on, and commissioners. He traced the introduction of boxing to the early Olympic Games and described the metal-studded *cesti* used as gloves by the Romans.

"No Contests," he argued, "were not necessarily crimes." Even in historical days (citing Shakespeare's *Tempest*) there were fights that left *"a very ancient and fishlike smell."* As a matter of fact, he pointed out, switching suddenly from erudition to fight lore, Gene Tunney and Jim Braddock both participated in "No Contest" affairs before they became champions. "And you will recall the sad occasion when over-eager arbiters called the Carnera-Schaaf match a 'No Contest.' Schaaf died from his injuries that night."

Jake brandished a folio of enlarged photographs which showed Brubaker's bruised and swollen hands. He flipped them to Geary. "Do not persist, then, to retain at heart one sole idea—that the thing is right which your mouth utters, and naught else beside. That, my learned brothers, was uttered by Sophocles." They blinked.

He turned in time to Geary's witnesses. Under his questioning they proved to have lamentable memories, and of course Simms himself was far away. When Referee Burke protested Jake's contention that Brubaker had hit Simms so hard he had taken all the fight out of him, Jake showed Burke the photographs of Brubaker's fists. "What was he hitting: the ring posts?"

At noon the entire assembly adjourned to a nearby restaurant owned by Commission Inspector Shields, for a luncheon at which the defendant Leavitt was host. It was a jolly repast, with the Lion borrowing a dollar from Shields to pay the bill. "As a restaurateur, Shields is a second Oscar of the Waldorf," Cohn reported. "But of course he still is one of the worst inspectors in boxing history." The luncheon broke up laughing, but the moment the gavel sounded again, Ehrlich resumed his attack on Commissioner Geary.

"Do you have one bit of evidence to support your statement that Leavitt is acting illegally as a manager?"

There had been hearsay, the commissioner said.

Then Jake threw a haymaker: Geary was not legally a commissioner; his term had expired six months before and he had not been officially reappointed. "Isn't it true, Mr. Geary," he asked, "that you have a strong animosity against Mr. Leavitt and always voted against him in his commission dealings?"

Geary shook his head. He could not recall, however, when he had voted *for* Leavitt.

"Do you have any evidence that Mr. Leavitt was in any way responsible for this fiasco?" Ehrlich thundered.

The commissioner shook his head. He admitted, reluctantly,

that Oakland boxing had thrived under the Lion's promotion.

As Cohn reported: "It was a moral victory for Geary. He wasn't convicted."

No one was. Simms, long gone from the state, was suspended for six months. Brubaker was reinstated and paid. And the newspapers clamored for Governor Merriam to appoint Jake Ehrlich to the boxing commission. Ehrlich ducked. "That," he growled, "would be very bad matchmaking."

3

Once more the Fight Trust watched helplessly while "Leo the Lion" roared. Ed Geary was replaced on the commission by Jerry Giesler, the famous Los Angeles attorney. Oakland again pulled big fight crowds. Then Uncle Sam demanded $1,885.35 in unpaid amusement taxes on one of Leavitt's matches. Small Montana renewed his suit against the Lion for $25,000. Another promoter entered the Oakland field and cut gallery prices to fifty cents. (He didn't prosper, but neither did Leavitt.) The Northern California Managers Association declared a boycott on the Lion's shows, claiming he was actually manager of Little Dado, a money-making Filipino.

The final blow came when the commission granted a promotional permit to Charles Marsalli, a twenty-nine-year-old Hollywood musician with a fat bankroll. The commission gave him one set of Wednesday nights and the rest to the other new promoter. There simply weren't any Wednesday nights left for Leavitt.

Young Charlie Marsalli boasted that he had swung Little Dado away from Leavitt with a $1,500 guarantee, and had matched him against Tony Olivera. Leavitt wouldn't have the remotest connection with the fight unless he paid his way

through the gate—which is what Leavitt thereupon did. Acting very much like a manager, he counseled Dado not to fight
unless he collected his $1,500 in advance. This constituted a
double violation of boxing laws, for a main eventer may not
be paid *before* he fights.

Dado refused to fight. Marsalli pleaded with him. Inspector
Shields ordered him to get in the ring. He wouldn't budge.
They summoned Ehrlich from the audience. After listening to
all hands, he suggested that the money be deposited in a
nearby hotel vault. With three thousand fans screaming for
action, this finally was done. By then, Olivera, the challenger,
had cooled off and gone home. Shields climbed wearily into
the ring, announced there would be no fight, and ducked. The
good burghers of Oakland thought all hell had exploded.

"Leavitt perpetrated this to ruin me!" wailed Marsalli.

"I was only coaching Dado as a friend," retorted the Lion.

"What were you doing *advising* another man's fighter?"
demanded Inspector Shields. "And what about demanding
the purse in advance?"

Once more Ehrlich's client was in hot water.

At the moment, Jake was handling the sensational divorce
case of Municipal Judge Frank Dunn. He paused in stride
to file bankruptcy proceedings for Leavitt, thereby reducing
the pressure of Small Montana's continuing demand for
$25,000.

Several days later, Jake came back to the commission hearing room. The official personnel had changed. Jules Covey,
a Hollywood lawyer, was in the chairman's seat for Jerry
Giesler.

Ehrlich studied the grim faces of the four commissioners
and decided to attack. They wanted Leavitt punished for acting as a manager? He put Leavitt on the stand. "Is it true,
Mr. Leavitt, that you are the actual and legal manager of
Little Dado, the fighter?"

"Yes," said the Lion, glancing guiltily at the commissioners and the press row. They did a slow double take. Jake thereupon read a letter from Charles Dreyfus, deputy of the State Labor Commissioner.

"My client, who admitted today he is Dado's unlicensed manager," said Ehrlich, "will continue in that capacity. The State Labor Commission in this letter grants him the right to be such an agent by fulfilling the single requirement of securing an employment agency license, and that is just what Mr. Leavitt will do in the morning."

Jake advanced on the commissioners. "And if you threaten other promoters with penalties if they negotiate with Mr. Leavitt, I will take the commission into the courts. We'll see whether it has more power than the Labor Commission."

Cohn dashed out to telephone his paper. "The commission," he dictated, "was supposed to bar Leavitt from boxing. Now the commission is fighting for its life."

He returned in time to pick up Ehrlich's continuing statement: "Bar Leavitt and the State Athletic Commission will lose jurisdiction over all fight managers, because they will be licensed by the Labor Commission. Bar Leavitt as Dado's agent because he refuses to take out a manager's license, and I will prove that no boxing manager in the state of California needs a manager's license. Yes, gentlemen, we will abolish all licensed managers, and with them the commission too!"

Chairman Covey said he didn't think the Labor Commission had jurisdiction over the Athletic Commission. "But," he added hurriedly, "I don't know——"

While they puzzled, Ehrlich affably offered suggestions for settling the matter, principally by paying Dado his $1,500.

Emmons Bryne of the *Post-Enquirer,* who had never before seen "The Master" perform, wrote: "After observing him in action, we can readily understand why he is regarded as the most brilliant of the younger legal lights. He pleaded, he thundered, he cajoled and he promised—and he got Little Dado a contract which calls for 30 per cent of the gate. . . . Dado is a very fortunate Filipino to have a man like Ehrlich representing him."

Byrne was right. The commission readily approved a Dado-Olivera rematch and Dado was paid $900 immediately.

Ehrlich returned to his other fight, the Dunn divorce. Leavitt openly managed Dado at the rematch. Charlie Marsalli gave up fight promotion and opened a restaurant.

Leavitt left Oakland after a bit and moved to Hawaii, where he became the Mr. Big of territorial boxing.

Ehrlich would continue to represent fistic figures, among them Middleweight Champion Bobo Olson, as well as his gentler clientele. He would also continue to fancy himself as a matchmaker. Several years later he blissfully agreed to help arrange a world's heavyweight title fight at Los Angeles' Wrigley Stadium. It brought together the thunderous Joe Louis and an old trial horse named Jack Roper.

Both boys were duly licensed by the California Boxing Commission, as were their managers, trainers and seconds. Neither got his fee in advance. Leo Leavitt wasn't closer than three miles from ringside and it was, without doubt, one of the worst mismatches in the history of boxing.

VI

JEAN COLLINS

Murder is an Act of Love?

"Do you believe it sound practice," a fledgling attorney asked Ehrlich, "for a lawyer to be seen in these honkytonks?" He had caught Jake in an amiable mood and drifted with him into a tavern in San Francisco's Tenderloin for a holiday drink. Rain was driving last-minute shoppers to shelter. Many chose the neon doorways where jukeboxes caroled. It was a few nights before Christmas, 1940.

Ehrlich considered the young man's question. "In my practice," he said gruffly, "it once was vital. You come out of the hallowed halls of law school and defend any client you can get—until you make your name. Today I defend a street sweeper and tomorrow I take a Nob Hill divorce. Big Larry there owns this joint. I defended him once." Jake smiled indulgently. "In the practice of criminal law you may win on the law you know or the kind of life you know. I keep in touch."

He returned to his observation of the bar patrons. He had been watching one oversized young man in a pinstriped suit with padded shoulders, a flashy zircon ring, feline eyes and long black hair. The man turned from whispering to an alkali blonde, caught Ehrlich looking at him and drawled: "Good evening, *Mis*-ter Mouthpiece." Others heard it and turned to stare. They recognized the snowy handkerchief, carefully

starched and folded, rising in four sharp crests from the breast
pocket of a dapper brown suit. They noticed Jake's cuff
adornments, miniature dice in tiny gold cages (a gift from
Paul Small, one-time producer of the Ed Wynn Show).

Ignoring their stares, Jake waited until the young man
swaggered off to the restroom, then beckoned Big Larry.
"Who's that punk?"

"Tony Barcelona," said the bar owner. "Got a string of
tarts hustlin' for him. He's dynamite."

"He's a very careless young man," Jake observed. "His
coat collar bunches in back."

Ehrlich might not have noticed the girl hesitating in the
doorway except that she didn't appear to belong there. She
had dignity. She also had warm brown eyes, a smooth olive
skin and fluffy chestnut hair. Her transparent raincoat revealed the rounded figure of a young woman of perhaps
twenty-five.

To Jake's amazement she stopped behind Tony and slipped
an arm about his waist. He lunged to his feet at her touch,
towering above her. His right hand cuffed and cut her across
the mouth. She crumpled against the jukebox.

Ehrlich came off his stool jabbing. "You son-of-a-bitch!
Why in hell don't you pick on men?"

Tony sneered. "Okay, Mister Mouthpiece, how about
you?"

Big Larry and the second bartender closed in. "Take a
duck," they grunted. Jake chuckled as the young lawyer
squeezed by him in the doorway.

2

December slid into January. On the evening of the ninth,
Jake and Mrs. Ehrlich attended Bob Crosby's opening at the

Golden Gate. They were home early at their Stanford Court apartment when the telephone rang.

"Mr. Ehrlich!" a woman wailed. "I just shot a man!"

"Well now," he replied calmly, "how did that happen?" He reached for a pencil. "And who is this?" He was deliberately conversational.

It was a girl named Jean Collins, and she was on the thirteenth floor of a downtown hotel. Jake knew the place; not a good address.

"He was going to throw me out the window!"

"Was going to throw you *through* the window," Ehrlich suggested. In a defense, that would connote greater violence.

They had fought, she said. She had grabbed his gun and shot him. It was Tony Barcelona.

"He threatened to kill you?" Ehrlich repeated.

"He—he's dead!" she sobbed.

"It will be all right now," Jake said gently. "You call Sutter 2020 and ask for Homicide. They'll send someone to help you. Don't make any statement until I talk to you."

Her name meant nothing to him. Jean Collins could be any of Tony's stable. Anyone who killed Tony Barcelona was, in all probability, justified.

Ehrlich went directly to the Hall of Justice where, he found, trouble awaited him.

"Holy hell's busted loose on you, Mr. Ehrlich," the elevator operator warned. "The newspaper boys are gobblin' it up. She's a prostitute—Tony's woman for eight years—and she ain't stopped talkin' since the inspectors got her."

The big Irish cop who unlocked the gate at the fifth floor added some more. "Boy, is she singing! Shot him four times. Inspectors Norton and Corrasa are on it, and you know them!"

Ehrlich knew them, both "square cops." Down the corridor to the right, in the women's section, he saw the camera flashes. Policemen at the booking desk came wide awake when they recognized him. Then the reporters spotted him.

He eased through them, ducking a camera, patting an arm, nodding. Suddenly his face nearly changed expression. This Jean Collins had fluffy chestnut hair, a clear olive skin and dark brown eyes. She was the girl in the bar.

"Mr. Ehrlich!" she cried. "I didn't mean to! I didn't mean to murder him!" Jake winced.

He spoke gently. "It's hard to picture a little lady like you in here. I guess it's just one of those things that maybe we can do something about.

"Come on, boys," he said to the reporters. "Jean has nothing to hide. Give them the whole story, Jean." Leaning close, as if to hear her reply, he snapped: "Say one more word and I'll kick your brains out. I'll see you tomorrow."

On the way out he checked Tony Barcelona's record: assault, burglary, suspicion of armed robbery. A bad man, but it is illegal to kill even bad men.

Ehrlich smoked a lot of cigarettes the next morning, one after the other in his long gold holder, as he discussed the case with Roy Sharff. The newspapers were spread before them. One said that Jean Collins had been arrested for keeping a brothel at Kearny and Broadway, just three blocks from the Hall of Justice. Another recalled the time she had handed a card for a red-light house to a stranger who turned out to be Police Chief William J. Quinn. The photos showed her clutching a long-curled French doll in the jail. "Sentimental wench," Jake observed.

He bridled at a story that said he had called her "a pretty classy dish."

"I never said that in my life!" he snapped. It violated three of his rules: 1) Never talk the language of your clients; 2) educate the client to look up to you; 3) never put yourself on an equal basis with a client like this.

He read a newspaper paragraph aloud: "Inspector Norton brought the gun and asked her in official language: 'I will now show you a .32 caliber revolver, number 42848, hammerless type, and ask you is this the gun you shot Tony Barcelona with?' "

"Hammerless type," mocked the lawyer. "What the hell does he think she is—Annie Oakley?"

A final line caught his eye. "As she was being taken through the hotel lobby, Jean turned to the manager and apologized: 'I'm sorry this had to happen here.' "

Jake rubbed his long straight nose. "I wonder if I'm going to be sorry, too."

Self-defense, of course, is a defense for murder in most cases. There was no doubt in his mind that Jean Collins had fought for her life. But there was no chance in the world that she could be tried by a jury of her peers. Jury panels simply aren't drawn from the shifting tenderloins of a city, and responsible citizens have no understanding of the semi-society in which prostitutes live. Respectable householders believe that a woman who can invite a strange man in from the streets can just as easily take a life.

Could Jake convince jurors, some of them women, that Jean Collins might never have lost the basic instinct of all women? That her love for Tony Barcelona, a brutal lout, could be as consuming as the love of a housewife juror for her respectable spouse?

"I've got to make it pathetic," he told Sharff, and his eye fell again on the newspapers. Juries read all the tawdry details.

That gave Ehrlich something to start with. The moment his name went over the press wires as counsel for the defense, long-distance calls began to come from papers in Chicago, New York, and even London. "What's this Collins thing?" they asked.

Jake replied: "It's a justifiable homicide, the kind we defend out here in San Francisco as if they were big important people. No, she can't pay a big fee and a girl in that profession can have no friends. There may be no fee at all." From their responses he guessed the unknown girl from San Francisco's streets would become the object of some Grade A sob-sistering.

3

The facts of Jean Collins' life came sparingly. Born in 1916 and abandoned by her mother when she was three, she had run away from an orphanage at fifteen. She was nearly mature then and had to fight off the boys. But she had stayed "good." At seventeen, in Sacramento, she had met Tony, big, handsome and cocksure, a dark Prince Charming who took her to night clubs and on moonlight drives along the river. He had promised to protect her. She had surrendered to him. Jake did not ask the next obvious question: How did Tony turn her to prostitution? The answer is always involved, never articulate, and usually implausible.

At any rate, Tony "owned" her and took her earnings. In 1939 he had needed a lot of money. There had been quarrels and sometimes he left her. He always returned to beat her, make love to her and demand more money. Once she tried to break away from him. She took a job as cigarette girl. He simply got other girls. She hated him and she needed him —a feeling more than one mistreated wife has had about a worthless husband.

"Jake," a reporter asked, "how much money do you suppose Jean Collins produced for Tony in eight years?"

"Who the hell are you?" the lawyer snapped. "The financial editor?" He could guess she had earned $80,000 for

Tony Barcelona, but he didn't propose to picture her as a big commercial enterprise. His defense must be predicated on the issue of her slavery and self-defense.

Surprisingly, Jean did have friends. They wrote anonymously, saying they might deplore what she had become, but they would try to help.

There was a curious flow of mail to her cell. One woman wrote that she was "a mother who can't help cheering you in your time of need." An office clerk wrote from Pennsylvania, offering to marry her. There were many more letters, which Jean read listlessly and jammed into her pockets. Ehrlich studied them carefully. They spoke for a segment of the public.

A *Call-Bulletin* writer suggested a series on Jean Collins' life. "How she became the slave of this man?" Jake suggested. He helped supply details, and the story ran on Page One for three days. So great was the interest that the editors asked readers to write their verdicts on the case. It was the only time in his career Ehrlich would get this service. "It's like reading the jury's mind!" he exclaimed to Sharff.

Jake had decided to have a lifesize dummy made of Tony to contrast his six feet two inches and 218 pounds with Jean's slight five feet four. He searched through stores. Finally he had to construct the thing himself, out of mannequin parts, the legs and arms extended by cardboard mailing tubes.

It would be highly objectionable as evidence, and he doubted whether he would be allowed to drag it into court, but as he explained to Sharff: "Suppose it's the last of the ninth inning, three men on and two out, the score tied and we've got two strikes on the batter. A spitball is illegal as hell, but any pitcher will throw it and hope the umpire doesn't catch him."

The "umpire" in this case would be Judge Robert Mc-

Williams, "a judge you don't fool with," and McWilliams would be trying his first murder case.

As January passed and the trial date approached, Jean Collins retreated deeper into herself. Jake had few interviews with her, and these were far from satisfactory. He was afraid she was beginning to crack, as every murderer he has defended has done. "Every person who commits a killing," he has noted, "gets to a point where it stalks him. At some point these poor people will disintegrate. That is why I am opposed to the death penalty. They're dead anyway. Meanwhile, it's hell on the trial lawyer." Jake consulted the jail matron, who decided to transfer Jean to a hospital. Once more there was an outburst of public pity for her. People were praying for Jean Collins in the churches.

She was brought to court briefly to hear the date set for trial. The room was packed. Jean stood, pale and haggard, clutching Ehrlich's hand as the judge spoke. Suddenly her legs went out from under her and she sagged. Jake caught her as she fell. Flashbulbs erupted. The photos stole space across the nation but they did not gladden the lawyer. His client had to appear as a woman—not a wreck—and she was getting nearer the breaking point.

4

On the day the trial opened, February 17, 1941, Jake brought relays of fresh shirts and cuffs to his office and dressed in a cheerful gray suit. The hospital had told him Jean was calmer. He studied her carefully as he threaded his way from the jammed corridors down the center aisle of the courtroom. She had a blue ribbon in her hair and was wearing a demure blue skirt and sweater. Her smile was wooden. She twisted a handkerchief between her fingers.

Ehrlich set his cardboard briefcase on the counsel table and nodded politely to the prosecutor, Joseph Garry. The white-haired man was a highly respected civic leader, head of the San Francisco Commandery of Knights Templar. He was impeccably fair. Once, he had stood up to Judge Twain Michelsen, a crusader against narcotics, and demanded that a drug trafficker be freed because the evidence was not sufficient to convict him fairly. But Garry's first job was to protect the people of the state of California. In his hands was Jean's damning confession.

Quickly they agreed on a jury, seven men and five women. Undoubtedly all of them had read the newspapers. Jake asked them to consider his own deep conviction: that in this extremely serious matter the prostitution label on Jean Collins must be considered no more relevant than a blemish on her skin. Although a prostitute, he argued, she was no more inclined than any woman on the jury to take a human life. She had had a relationship with this violent, brutal man, Tony Barcelona. It had been, in her poor mind, the same relationship as that of man and wife. She had killed to defend her life.

The jury followed his words impassively.

The first witnesses, Inspector Corrasa and Norton, should have come and gone without a hitch, with routine accounts of the scene, identification of the gun, and the arrest of the girl. But suddenly Ehrlich felt Jean Collins' shoulders shudder spasmodically. She was clutching his left hand under the table. Her own hand was dripping. The left leg of his gray trousers was dark with her perspiration. Without attracting attention to it, he waved the officers off the stand. The living death of Jean Collins had begun.

The courtroom mechanics proceeded. Garry began to read the confession, unmindful of the girl's low sobbing: "Tony said he was moving out. . . . He came over to the bed and grabbed me by the hair and said: 'There are a few more things I want to settle with you.' I said: 'Tony, every man has his day and there will be a bright day for me, too. . . .' "

Jake had his arm about the sobbing girl's shoulders. Garry droned on: "*I* said: 'Tony, you are the type of man that dies with his shoes on.' He picked up a shoe and hit me." Several jurors frowned at that.

In that moment Jake felt one of his hallways of light begin to open. He rose quickly, walked to the judge's chambers and returned with a glass of water. The girl gulped it gratefully.

The prosecutor continued reading: "Tony said: 'Your days are numbered. Do you know what I'm going to do to you? I'm going to make you a cripple. I'll throw acid in your face and disfigure it and give you a tin cup so you can go and beg dimes and nickels. . . .' I said: 'That's all right, Tony. I am not too proud for that. You have threatened me for the last time. I am not taking it, Tony, any more. Tony,' I said, 'you are as crooked as a corkscrew. Your own mother said you were no good!' "

Jake glanced over his shoulder at the spectators. Somewhere out there were Tony's mother and sister. Two more variables who might create pandemonium for the defense lawyer.

"Tony said: 'I'll throw you out that window!' (Jake mentally winced.) I looked down. 'It's not so far,' I said. 'Only thirteen stories.' He grabbed me . . . I opened the drawer . . . got the gun there. He looked at me and said: 'Don't shoot!' I just shot him in the right arm. Then I shot him twice in the back and then once more in the head. When he fell . . . I walked over to the telephone and asked for the police and told them to give me the murder detail. 'I just murdered a man,' I told them. 'I will be waiting here.' "

The only thing she didn't tell them, Jake fumed inwardly, is that she'd just as soon be in the gas chamber. His collar

and cuffs were wilted. His gray suit was rumpled. He was trying to hold Jean in her chair. He all but missed Garry's quiet
announcement that the prosecution rested. The court, for-
tunately, adjourned for the day.

Ehrlich did not read the papers that night. He did not take
the long-distance calls. He slept fitfully and for only three
hours. Long before sunrise he was up pacing the apartment,
and then his office. The frown lines over the bridge of his nose
were deep. He shaved and changed to a dark suit—the "bar
mitzvah suit." He pinned on the lucky gold cuff links his wife
Marjorie had given him in the early days of their marriage
when he was struggling for a practice.

5

This was the big day. Jake goaded himself to get into character, to feel for Jean Collins as a person, as she must be
feeling for herself. It had to be sincere.

He was poker-faced as he edged through the corridors to
the courtroom.

He called three policemen to the stand, none coached, to
describe Tony Barcelona's reputation. They said he was
vicious, a dangerous, violent man. One added impetuously:
"A dirty son-of-a-bitch!" Jake's eyes widened on the jury.
This was better.

He paused, then said quietly: "Miss Collins, please take the
stand."

It was a gamble. She had not been readied for this. But in
her mental state she should tell a story that would be straight,
honest and stark with sincerity. It was the moment of which
he had spoken often, when a lawyer should know his client
as well as a merchant knows his wares.

"You walk into a shop," he had said by way of illustration,

"point to a piece of meat and ask: 'How much is that?' The
butcher says casually: 'Oh, about a pound and a half—ninety-
seven cents' worth!' He puts it on the scales and that's what it
is." There comes a moment with a lawyer, Jake said, when
long experience tells him the correct weight of a witness.

He expected Jean to cry a little when he took her back
through her relations with Tony, hammering on the slavery
angle. She cried a little. In the dead cold tones of a grieving
woman, she testified to her doglike devotion. "I gave everything, everything, to Tony."

Jake spoke over his shoulder, to no one in particular: "Will
someone please get her some water?" The only pitcher in the
courtroom, as he knew, stood squarely in front of Joe Garry.
Without a moment's hesitation, the prosecutor jumped up and
walked, carefully balancing the glass, toward Ehrlich. No
one, thought Jake, can offer a glass of water carelessly to another person. He stepped aside. Garry had to hand it to Jean.
She drank and thanked him with her eyes. The jury saw it,
and they saw Garry's courtly bow. They did not see his lips
twist as he passed the defense lawyer.

Jake launched into Tony's brutalities. Jean's sobs came
faster. The jurors leaned forward to catch it all.

Suddenly Joe Garry was on his feet. Jake frowned. Garry
was not protesting or objecting. He was more subtle. He stated
kindly: "Mr. Ehrlich, in order to relieve the witness, I will
stipulate that this man Barcelona was a violent man."

Jake grimaced, but he turned his back to the jury to do it.
He began to shuffle papers. He needed to collect his thoughts.

"If Your Honor please," he said, "at this time I would like
to introduce, for the purpose of comparison, a life-size effigy
of Tony." Without waiting for the court's ruling, he pulled
open a doorway to a side corridor near the jury box. For
an incongruous instant the dummy hung over him like a
Frankenstein monster, a rough creature six feet two, plus

Ehrlich's extensions for exaggeration, a foot taller than his own five foot seven.

"Miss Collins," he called, "please pick up that book from the table." She rose obediently and came around the table near him. The judge was hammering for order. For one electrifying moment she paused, incredibly frail in the shadow of the dummy's wavering arms, fifteen feet from the gaping jury. They couldn't miss the graphic comparison.

"You will not make a hippodrome of this court!" thundered Judge McWilliams and Jake backed down with simulated haste. He had seen what he wanted on the jurors' faces. He could appear to be chastened and save the court's dignity. Eyes downcast but spirits exulting, he trudged back to the counsel table.

"In that case," he said quickly, "I am through with the witness." He gestured to the prosecutor. "You may cross-examine."

Judge McWilliams ordered a recess to let the girl compose herself. As the jury filed out, Jake turned to the audience, located Tony's mother and beckoned her to come inside the railing. She spoke no English, but her daughter, apparently speaking for them both, touched Jean's cold hand. "We feel bad about Tony," she said. "But we realize."

That was one loophole Jake had wanted to plug.

The judge and jury returned. Jean got up unsteadily to resume the stand. Jake thought: *Garry's nuts if he whips her any more. She'll blow sky-high.* He felt the "eighty million bumps" beginning to burn over his skin.

"When you—did this," Joe Garry asked hesitantly, "you were in fear of your life?"

"Yes!" She almost leaped from the chair.

The prosecutor frowned. Then he stepped back, shrugging. That was all. He waved to Ehrlich. The lawyer was up instantly to help Jean from the stand. Now to wrap it up. He shuffled papers, thinking it over.

As he rose for his summation, he was mentally gathering the threads. He would play it extemporaneously, feel the mood of the jury, sensing the moment to stop. No woman sitting there, he now believed, would punish Jean Collins.

Ehrlich balanced on his toes before them, eyes closed, chin upraised, thinking himself back into her woes. "Jean Collins," he declared, "is not guilty of a crime." He nodded as if in agreement with himself. "She is no more guilty than a person who stamps on a poisonous spider."

As if it were shocking to him too, he retraced the career of Tony Barcelona. He spoke of panderers, "loathsome rats gnawing on the weakness of the weakest members of society." He described the life they forced girls to lead.

He held up straining hands, as if clutching the girl's body like a sack and threatening to dash it to the ground. "I ask the ladies of the jury to consider what you would have done in this girl's place? What would any reasonable woman have done if placed in the same position by a man six feet two inches and weighing 218 pounds?

"I *demand* of you that you either send this girl to the gas chamber or release her entirely."

He regarded the jurors coldly. "If you do the first, you hereby pin a medal on all the dirty curs like Barcelona. He had it coming to him! It had to happen! There was no good in him! San Francisco is better off for the death of Tony!"

He paused, the gesturing hands still. The jurors expected the obvious now, the sentimental, traditional story of the woman taken in sin and released by the words of Jesus. Their minds already were reaching out for it. The heads were bowed and two of the women jurors were weeping. Ehrlich shook his head sadly, looked at Jean Collins and sat down.

For a long moment the courtroom was still. Then as Jake,

bowed and sweat-soaked, sat with his chin on his chest, eyes closed, and one hand grasping Jean Collins', a spontaneous ovation broke out from the spectators. Judge McWilliams rapped sternly, threatening to clear the courtroom, and Jake glanced sidewise at the prosecutor, Garry. ("He was a human before that moment," Jake would say of him, "and he would be a human after it.")

Garry rose. He said: "This is not a murder, and by no stretch of the imagination should it be called a murder. It could only be called involuntary manslaughter. I am not asking you to compromise your verdict. You must find her guilty or not guilty, according to the evidence." He cleared his throat. "Tony has been pictured—and I have stipulated—a panderer, a debaucher of young girls and an assailant of defenseless women. He that soweth the flesh shall reap the flesh."

Joe Garry, thought Jake, *is a very righteous man.* The prosecutor glanced at the stern-visaged judge and frowned. "If by this trial we have driven that lesson home to one person, it was well worth the time and expense. I feel sure you ladies and gentlemen will have no trouble reaching a fair verdict." He sat down.

The jury went out at 3:05 P.M. Jean's hand in Jake's was cold and dry. She breathed but she had paid the extreme penalty. He, too, felt gone inside. The hands of the clock dropped down one click at a time—3:10—3:15—3:17—and a buzzer sounded. It was 3:18. Only thirteen minutes had elapsed. The jury was coming back. Judge McWilliams came from his chambers and warned the spectators against further demonstrations.

The five women and seven men filed self-consciously to their seats. The foreman handed his paper to the clerk. The judge glanced at it and read: "Not guilty."

There *was* a demonstration. It shook the walls. Even bailiffs and newspapermen were clapping Jake on the shoulders. Judge McWilliams rose from the bench and strode to his chambers.

Photographers crowded around the table, shouting, congratulating, snapping pictures. Jean Collins, bewildered, stood mechanically. A cameraman asked her to smile. Her eyes were dull. "I won't ever smile again," she said.

That was all of it. Jake walked slowly out of the courtroom, down the alley, down Montgomery Street and up to his office for a change of clothes. Jean Collins went her way. . . .

Ten months later, Christmas again, he got a card. "I love you," it said, "because you were good to me." A mechanical greeting from a mechanical heart. He got another Christmas card from her in 1942 and a third in 1943. On January 18, 1944, almost three years from the date of her acquittal, Jean Collins was committed to a state hospital as insane.

It was no surprise to Jake. He had felt her mind slip through his fingers that day she clung to his hand.

VII

FRITZ WIEDEMANN

Nazi Spies and a Woman to See Hitler

W HEN the girl at the office switchboard announced a Mrs. Alice Crockett, the name did not register on Ehrlich's mind. Then she tossed in the name of Captain Fritz Wiedemann and Jake sat up sharply.

The Nazi Consul General in San Francisco was a dynamo of good fellowship, particularly in social circles. In other circles, specifically Jake's, he blew fuses. Mrs. Crockett, the switchboard girl said, wanted to sue Wiedemann at once.

"A fine idea," Ehrlich observed. "But what does Mrs. Crockett expect to sue Fritz about?"

"She says about seeing Hitler for him."

"Adolf Hitler of Nazi Germany?"

"That's what she says."

The legal brief Ehrlich had been studying fluttered from his fingers. "Ask Mrs. Crockett to come in and tell us about it."

In the whole wide world there was no one Ehrlich would rather sue at that moment. He had tried earnestly to tip people off to Wiedemann, the "laughing boy of the Third Reich." Clapping a make-believe monocle to his eye, jutting out his chin and guffawing, Jake would give a fair imitation of "Fritz, the jolly front man." But Wiedemann, with his chuckle, his London tweeds and Mercedes-Benz, had set out to make people like him from the moment he arrived in San Francisco and he was succeeding.

He was a huge, athletic man who looked ten years less than his stated forty-eight. He had beetling brows and a dark pugnacious face much like that of the ex-heavyweight champion, Max Schmeling.

"There is nothing forbidding in his frank, natural manner," reported *Life* in September, 1939. "He has a disarming way of laughing uproariously when his English lapses or someone asks him an embarrassing question . . . a forceful man of strong character, but incapable of subtle intrigue and not worth much copy, was the conclusion at the bar of the San Francisco Press Club."

Jake fumed. Incapable of intrigue? Hadn't Fritz once been Hitler's private secretary? Hadn't he flown to London before the Munich appeasement pact to help set up Prime Minister Chamberlain for the coup? Princess Stephanie Hohenlohe, the redheaded glamor girl of intrigue, had helped him on that job and had since come on to San Francisco to join him. (She currently was in custody of the Immigration Service.)

Wiedemann's disarming chuckle sounded often as the panzers blasted through Denmark, Norway and France. It was irritating to Ehrlich but it seemed to charm others. They bowed to the Consul General's Continental air and thrilled to his tales of sports: tennis, dueling, boar hunting, fine car racing (he never mentioned gas chambers, Fifth Columns or concentration camps). He was a wonderful storyteller, they declared, a most agreeable companion.

The Wiedemann boosters were an odd hodge-podge, starting with the "international set," both pro- and anti-British. There also were the isolationists, those who believed that Hitler would destroy communism, the racial purists, the antiSemites and others.

"This man doesn't act like a Nazi at all," people said.

Wiedemann worked hard not to. He never spoke Hitler's name in public. He insisted he was at San Francisco merely to stimulate German-American trade. "Politics," he said, "is the business of the Embassy in Washington." If pressed about the German-American Bund's disturbing activities, he would swear it was an American organization over which he had no control.

Until his family came from Europe, Wiedemann disported himself at the smarter night clubs (and in other nocturnal sports, if rumor could be believed). Usually he lunched at Schroeder's, a German restaurant on Front Street, but he also got around to many places where important men broke bread—Solari's, Jack's, the Palace—and of course the Chamber of Commerce "to stimulate trade." Sometimes the Martinis prompted embarrassing questions and his uproarious laughter echoed all the way to Twin Peaks.

But he was winning his way. He rented a twelve-room home in fashionable Hillsborough and somehow got his name proposed for membership at the exclusive Burlingame Country Club. He brought his family on, and his followers got a look at one son, Eduard, fourteen, and a daughter, Anna Marie, nineteen. Wiedemann said little of a second son, Klaus, seventeen, who was serving with the motorized Hitler Youth.

Of course there were minor annoyances, too, which got Fritz' hearty, angry laugh into the public prints. He took an old mansion on Pacific Heights for his consulate, and the labor unions decorated it with picket lines. Two American sailors scaled the walls and tore down the swastika flag. Eddie Cantor told some anti-Nazi jokes at the Golden Gate International Exposition on Treasure Island and, as newspaper columnist Herb Caen reported it: "Fritz got into his fancy car and roared over there. 'An inzult to my guntry!' he shouted. Nobody paid any attention."

Jake Ehrlich did, for there was more to it than anti-Nazi

jokes. Eddie Cantor was Jake's friend and a prime mover in the worldwide campaign to rescue German Jews from Hitler's clutches. At one luncheon in San Francisco, he raised $75,-000 in forty-five minutes, thanks to Ehrlich, Louis Lurie, the Reillys, the Sullivans and a gang of their friends. Not all the United States was neutral about the Third Reich.

Some people suspected that Fritz had not, as he pretended, "fallen from grace" in Nazi Germany but had picked San Francisco as an excellent place to organize isolationist propaganda and resistance to President Roosevelt's foreign policies.

One noon, walking through Solari's bar, Jake came face to face with Wiedemann. He glanced at the big man and started to pass. The German accosted him.

"You do not like me. I'm a pretty good fellow," he said. To prove it, he let loose his bellowing laugh.

Jake stared coldly. "If burning innocent women and children in furnaces makes a pretty good fellow, then I guess you're a pretty good fellow."

Wiedemann lowered his head belligerently. "This is an inzult!" he muttered.

"If it's an insult," Jake snapped, "why don't you put up your hands?"

The German threw back his head and roared with laughter. Ehrlich walked away.

2

In due time, Jake thumbed through a dossier on Wiedemann, F., first lieutenant in the 17th Bavarian Infantry in World War I. As regimental aide-de-camp in charge of communications, Wiedemann had Adolf Schicklgruber as a dispatch runner. He had recommended the little corporal for the Iron Cross. He also had been one of the Brownshirts in the

Beer Hall Putsch. After the blood purge of 1934, he had become Hitler's personal adjutant and a member of the Nazi Supreme Council. He had often shared Hitler's luncheon table.

Speaking before the American Chamber of Commerce in Berlin before he sailed for San Francisco, Wiedemann had declared: "My first task is to serve my Fuehrer and my people faithfully."

"When he said that," Ehrlich noted, "he didn't laugh."

As for Wiedemann's Hungarian friend, Princess Stephanie Hohenlohe, she had once been considered a close friend of Hitler but had also known Chamberlain and had represented the British publisher, Lord Rothermere. She had come to San Francisco in December, 1939, as Wiedemann's house guest, and Ehrlich had begun to see her at social affairs. There were rumors that the FBI had trailed her and Fritz to Yosemite, but had withdrawn, blushing, when they found activities not strictly within their scope.

Ehrlich suspected that there was some sort of parallel between Stephanie's work for Wiedemann and that of Mrs. Crockett who now wished to sue.

Mrs. Crockett was thirty-seven, a native of Switzerland, and an international getabout. As Alice Gulden, a striking blonde, she had been a Hollywood bit player and for ten years had been the wife of Major Gilman Crockett, a peacetime Army officer.

The record showed that in 1936 she had divorced the major and that she got $150 a month alimony, but later settled for $1,000 in cash and some insurance policies. Reputedly, she was still "a looker, with a terrific figure."

The lady who arrived in Jake's office fitted that description, except that now she was a brunette. She was well-mannered and intelligent, and she soon demonstrated that she was a woman who came to the point.

Fritz Wiedemann and she had had an arrangement, she said, and he had reneged. He was head of all Nazi espionage and propaganda in the United States. Fearing that rivals at home might undermine him, he had hired her to see Hitler and determine his true status. For this service he had agreed to pay her $500 a month and expenses. She had gone abroad, interviewed the top men in Nazi Germany and reported back that Hitler had told her personally: "Fritz Wiedemann is the best man for the job we have to do in the United States."

Ehrlich was finding it difficult to maintain a wooden face. He paced the room. Finally he settled behind his high leather chair, leaned on his elbows and simply stared at the charming creature with the amazing story.

She had reported back to Fritz, she said. He had refused to pay. She figured he owed her six months' salary, $3,000, plus $5,000 for legitimate out-of-pocket expenses, a total of $8,000.

Leaning on the chair back, Jake studied Mrs. Crockett as she blurted out tales of Wiedemann's machinations: trips to Mexico to deliver secret documents, employment of men in American munitions plants, storage of ammunition in New Jersey, hiring of U. S. government employees to report information about the Panama Canal. This, Jake decided, was an angry woman telling all.

She had a sheaf of documents in her purse which she turned over to him. He read some and his own anger flared. Before he agreed to take the case, though, he weighed his own position.

He had never sued anyone with the stature of Consul General for a powerful nation. And some of this stuff that looked potent on first reading might not stand up in court. He informed Mrs. Crockett it would be a tough, perhaps an impossible, case to win. Yet perhaps, if the cards fell right, he could bring in Fritz Wiedemann on a civil suit and cut his throat at the same time. The suit would be for breach of contract.

But first Ehrlich called a press conference and explained: "This little lady felt she must sue Captain Wiedemann quickly because she has information that he is about to leave the country." The reporters stared. Wiedemann leaving? Why? Jake looked stern. "My duty as an American citizen forces me to disclose certain facts which my client here will detail."

Alice Crockett quietly retold the fantastic spy story. Wiedemann, she said, had engaged her originally to help him improve his English. "He expressed admiration for me," she said modestly and named some places in which he had done so—in his Hillsborough home when the family was out, in various private rendezvous up and down the coast, and sometimes in the vicinity of the Mexican border. As his trust in her grew, she said, he had explained his jitters about the homeland and finally—because she spoke German fluently and was "such an attractive woman"—he had asked her to go see Hitler for him.

Upon her arrival in Germany, Mrs. Crockett related, she went to a cheap rooming house. She had a letter of introduction from Wiedemann to Propaganda Minister Goebbels. She presented it and was transferred immediately to the swank Central Hotel on Friedrichstrasse, with all chits picked up by the Nazi government. "I then went to a small affair at the Kaiserhof, where I met Hitler and Hermann Goering."

The reporters looked incredulously at Ehrlich. "The whole world should know this story," he declared. "I'd like to rent the Civic Auditorium and charge a dollar admission, the money to go to British War Relief."

San Franciscans at first sniffed at the tale as preposterous— "an Ehrlich stunt in very bad taste." But soon many felt that there might be something in it. "This feeling was strengthened," said an editorial, "by recent rumors in London diplo-

matic circles that Wiedemann was about to be recalled because Hitler was angered at his persistence in associating with
Princess Hohenlohe, now at Palo Alto awaiting outcome of
deportation proceedings."

Wiedemann denied everything. "I met Mrs. Crockett when
she came to the consulate to inquire about two missing aunts,"
he said. "She was impressed with Nazi doctrines and wanted
to get into German movies, so I gave her a letter to Heinz
Paul, a German motion picture executive."

After several red-faced lapses he finally admitted that Mrs.
Crockett might have visited his Hillsborough home.

On February 20, 1941, as headlines announced that 600
U-BOATS MASS FOR RAID ON BRITAIN, Ehrlich filed
his suit. City editors read it through hastily and printed it in
its entirety. The allegations were strong:

I. . . . Fritz Wiedemann . . . was and is the head of the
espionage service of the government of Germany in the United
States . . . charged with the dissemination of all Nazi and
German propaganda in the United States;

II. During the year 1939, the defendant Fritz Wiedemann
had serious misunderstandings with the official government of
Germany . . . and the Nazi party . . . the misunderstandings
. . . concerned the ability of Fritz Wiedemann to properly
fulfill . . . his duties as head of the propaganda division . . .
head of the espionage division of the government of Germany
in the United States;

III. In order to ascertain whether he was in the good graces
of the government of Germany . . . on or about the first day
in May, 1939, he engaged the services of the plaintiff to travel
to Berlin and confer with the authorities . . . and did then and
there agree to pay to this plaintiff for her services the sum of
$500 per month and all expenses . . . that pursuant to said
agreement, and at the special instance and request of Fritz

Wiedemann, this plaintiff did travel . . . to the city of Berlin, Germany . . . did visit and talk with Adolf Hitler, Joseph Goebbels, Hermann Goering and other high officials . . . and she did then and there determine and was informed by the said officials that Fritz Wiedemann was properly carrying out his duties as Consul General . . . as head of the propaganda division in the City and County of San Francisco . . . and as head of the espionage service of the government of Germany in the United States.

"This is blackmail!" thundered Wiedemann. "Several months ago, Mrs. Crockett wrote and asked me for $500 to buy a little shop. I didn't send it and this is the answer. I did send her $120 when she said she was ill and $20 on her birthday. I sent it as a friend."

Wiedemann's attorney, Otto A. Hoecker, a capable and respectable member of the San Francisco bar, enlarged on Fritz's protests, citing the inconsistency of Mrs. Crockett's asking Wiedemann for a $500 "loan" while claiming she had money due her for services rendered.

Ehrlich continued to press. He got a Superior Court order for Wiedemann to give a deposition. Fritz ducked into the consulate's immunity. So Ehrlich hired a young man who had been successful at serving papers on untouchable people and caught Wiedemann at a full-dress affair. Wiedemann accepted the summons but he did not appear.

"I am going to keep Fritz running until his legs hurt," Ehrlich announced. The court-appointed notary continued the session for ten days, at which time Attorney Hoecker filed his argument. "The proceedings taken herein," he stated, "are void . . . jurisdiction over foreign consuls is vested in the courts of the United States, exclusive of the courts of the several states." He noted that President Roosevelt had not demanded Wiedemann's removal as consul.

"No," Ehrlich said. "But my friend in the White House doesn't know Fritzy like I do. Give him time."

Ehrlich threatened to give details of a certain trip Mrs. Crockett had taken with Wiedemann. Wiedemann protested righteously: "I have never been to Mexico since I have been here. The FBI knows everything I do." (Nat J. L. Pieper, special FBI agent in San Francisco, replied: "We are *not* checking up on Captain Wiedemann. He has diplomatic immunity, which is rigidly respected.")

Jake announced that he had documents which would place Wiedemann in a certain caravansary near the border.

3

Suddenly, though not unexpectedly, Ehrlich found himself under heavy pressure to drop the suit or at least modify it. Some felt this was a job for the United States government rather than a San Francisco trial lawyer. Others among Jake's friends feared his attack on Wiedemann would prove injurious to Jews. Jake stormed. "I believe Wiedemann is doing a terrible thing in my country! He is a very bad man."

Wiedemann suddenly was blackballed from membership in the Burlingame Country Club. Society editors noted that an increasing number of cocktail parties to which the Consul General had been invited had been "postponed indefinitely."

When the Wiedemann case came up in Superior Court, Hoecker, appearing without his client, argued that the court lacked jurisdiction. The judge upheld him. "Okay," said Ehrlich, "I'll file in Federal Court and make the complaint tougher. Americans have a right to know the position Captain Wiedemann occupies in our country."

The suit filed in Federal Court on March 5 presented more accusations:

That Wiedemann had received . . . from the German government and carried out espionage directions, employing Princess Stephanie Hohenlohe as a sort of superespionage paymistress.

That Wiedemann supervised espionage activities in . . . the Panama Canal Zone . . . to determine how the canal could be rendered useless. . . .

That he . . . informed Mrs. Crockett . . . officials of the U. S. government were in his employ. . . .

That Wiedemann made many trips to Mexico from San Francisco, one of them with the plaintiff in the first week of April, 1939, at which time Wiedemann assertedly delivered secret documents and gave instructions to other members of the espionage service.

That Wiedemann informed Mrs. Crockett . . . it was the plan of the German government to promote strife and class hatreds in the United States, to employ ruffians to stir racial hate, and . . . encourage strikes for the purpose of destroying unity and undermining the strength of the United States. In this regard . . . Wiedemann had in his employ many superintendents, foremen and workers in manufacturing plants . . . in particular . . . steel and munitions industries.

That Wiedemann informed . . . plaintiff . . . he directed work of the German-American Bund and was active in secretly storing large quantities of ammunition in eastern New Jersey to be used by the Bund in fighting against the government of the United States.

That Wiedemann directed propaganda activities from the consulate and . . . named to Mrs. Crockett his subordinates: Dr. Friedhelm Draeger, East Coast; Dr. Mathias Schmitz, New York; Hermann Schwinn, West Coast, and others . . .

Dr. Draeger, German Consul General in New York, got out of bed at midnight to disclaim his role. Princess Hohenlohe added her denial from the federal detention facility. In San Francisco, Attorney Hoecker protested: "We have called this thing a shakedown from the start."

Jake was in full swing. There were telephone calls, local, long distance, and even international. There were telegrams, letters, and postcards signed *The Bund*. Some threatened Ehrlich's life. Official voices were among the callers. The FBI checked in. Jake was pulled and hauled but he stood fast. "I have a duty to my client, and I'm going through with it," he said. "I was an American long before I was an attorney." He didn't believe the FBI was unhappy at the public hounding of Fritz Wiedemann, nor did he believe the Secretary of State objected.

4

Federal Judge A. F. St. Sure, who would hear the suit, was as American as "The Star-Spangled Banner," a thin, white-haired little man with silver-rimmed spectacles. He called the case on June 9, 1941, at a moment when the Nazis were holding sway over much of Europe and Africa. Wiedemann did not appear. Attorney Hoecker moved to quash the suit on the ground that America's peace treaty with Germany after World War I did not permit individuals to sue representatives of the German government.

The argument went on for two hours. Jake contended that a treaty or contract has no greater validity than the moral intent of parties to carry it out. This German government, he argued, had no intent of carrying out any treaty terms; so the old treaty would not apply, and Wiedemann could be sued.

Attorney Hoecker, well prepared, came back with a strange contention: that the oral contract between Mrs. Crockett and Wiedemann was illegal because it engaged her to perform services "against the public policy" of the United States. Since it was thereby illegal, he contended, there could not be any contractual violation.

Before Ehrlich could counter again, Judge St. Sure cut off all argument. He glanced down at the surprised lawyers, adjusted his spectacles, and picked up three typewritten pages which he began to read. "Assuming," he said, "under all the rules of pleading, the allegations contained in the complaint are true, it appears that the defendant is guilty of violating the Espionage Act of the United States. It further appears that the plaintiff aided and assisted the defendant in his unlawful acts and she likewise is guilty."

Judge St. Sure glared at Mrs. Crockett. "If the allegation in her complaint is true, the plaintiff entered into a contract against all public morals and decency." Gruffly he dismissed the suit without leave to amend, rose and strode to chambers.

Ehrlich and Hoecker looked at each other in amazement. "He ruled you were right," said Jake, "but he tore Wiedemann's head off!" The judge had implied that Wiedemann was guilty of everything charged, but added that because of the law he could not be punished.

Both lawyers noted Ehrlich phrases in the judge's statement. It was as if the United States government were saying: "This man Ehrlich is right, but we'll handle it our way."

The two lawyers shook hands and Jake turned to his client. "Well, my dear, we lost." She smiled. Like many a bit player who aspires to stardom, she could lose gracefully. Ehrlich strolled meditatively back to his office.

There was not so much as a giggle from the consulate mansion on Pacific Heights. Instead, there were reports that the staff was busy burning records. Just seven days later, on June 16, 1941, Undersecretary of State Sumner Welles picked up Jake Ehrlich's allegations in an ultimatum to the Hitler government:

It has come to the knowledge of this government that agencies of the German Reich in this country, including German consular establishments, have been engaged in activities wholly outside the scope of their legitimate duties.

These activities have been of an improper and unwarranted character. They render the continued presence in the United States of these agencies and consular establishments inimical to the welfare of the country.

I am directed . . . by the President . . . that all German consular offices . . . be closed . . . and officers . . . returned.

Fritz Wiedemann left San Francisco with his party on July 5. Three planes flew them east to join other Axis envoys sailing for Lisbon on the liner *West Point*. A German national was intercepted carrying secret dispatches from Wiedemann to Nazi agencies in Central America. Wiedemann, it was revealed, had been in on a plot to assassinate the British monarchs on their 1939 visit to the United States. He was, as Ehrlich contended, a very bad man.

In September, 1941, big Fritz became Consul General at Tientsin, China. When the Japanese bombed Pearl Harbor and put the United States into World War II, Wiedemann fled to Japan. Later he was captured, was a War Crimes Trial witness, and was himself tried in a denazification hearing. He was found guilty and fined two thousand deutschmarks. In 1952 Herb Caen reported: "Fritz now is riding high, wide and ugly in Cairo, Egypt, representing a German film outfit." In due course, the cold consulate on Pacific Heights became a more thoughtful place: Mortimer Adler's Institute of Philosophical Research.

Princess Hohenlohe spent time in a Texas alien camp and bobbed up after the war in Beverly Hills, where she denied having had any truck with Wiedemann. "I was pro-British," she protested. Mrs. Crockett was around San Francisco for a while, pestering the FBI "for a clean bill of health." Then she walked offstage.

There were other echoes. Earl Warren, then Attorney General of California, asserted: "Wiedemann was ready to head a Fifth Column in the United States." Senator Josh Lee of Oklahoma charged in Congress: "Wiedemann was the head man in Nazi undercover activities against the U. S. government."

Ehrlich simply glowed. "That's all I was trying to tell them!"

VIII

TAINTED LOTUS BLOSSOM

A Murder in Old Chinatown

ONE balmy night in October, as Chinatown lay dreaming in its many beds along the hillside, Louis Quan, efficient young manager of the American Finance Company, tossed and turned in his private quarters behind the insurance offices at 843 Clay Street. He got up at last, dressed, and walked the several blocks through silent streets to his home, a crowded apartment on Stockton Street, where his beautiful young wife, Choy Lin, awaited him.

Their murmurings in the bedroom had scarcely quieted when a low knock sounded at the door. Mr. Quan went to answer. In the dark hallway he heard whispered syllables and recognized the voice of Henry Yee, a suave young singer and man-about-Chinatown. An angry outburst of male Cantonese followed, and the walls trembled to the thunder of gunfire. There was a quick shuffling of feet, a grumble of protests through the old structure, some slamming of doors—and silence.

At 3:00 A.M. the police arrived, summoned by an anonymous call through the pagodaed Chinatown exchange. Inspector Harry Husted found Henry Yee dead in a pool of blood at the closed door of apartment 202. Three bullets had hit him, one in the heart. Pretty Mrs. Quan, fully dressed when she answered the inspector's knock, said she had heard some shots but that her husband usually handled such things. "Go see him. His office is on Clay Street."

Inspector Husted sprinted to the insurance and real estate office in the heart of Chinatown, and found Louis Quan patiently sorting policies while he waited. The gun, a .38 caliber pistol which he readily admitted having fired at Yee, lay on his desk. Quan smoothed his black hair, carefully squared his conservative businessman's hat, and walked out into the dawn with the officers.

At the homicide bureau he calmly dictated a statement to the police stenographer. "I went home," he stated, "and I was talking to my wife at night time. I heard a knock at the door. Then I opened it. I saw it was Henry Yee, and I thought he was going to do something to me. I then pulled the gun out. Then I tried to knock his head with the gun and the bullet came out then. It went through his head. Then I left. That's all. Now please, I get Jake Ah-lick."

The Grand Jury, meeting a few days later, was as interested in Quan's choice of lawyers as it was in his confession. Like most San Franciscans, the jurors had heard the current Jake Ehrlich story. It involved Ehrlich's appearance before a municipal judge to seek reduced bail for a client. "Your Honor," Jake was quoted as saying, "this bail is pretty high for a man who is innocent." "Innocent, Mr. Ehrlich?" retorted the judge. "Then what are *you* doing in the case?"

The grand jurors inquired if Quan, as reported, had immediately said: "Get Jake." Homicide inspectors assured them he had, and they promptly returned an indictment for murder. The district attorney assigned the case to his toughest prosecutor, John J. McMahon, whom trial lawyers called "Ropes," because he always pulled hard for a death penalty.

In his first talks with Quan, Ehrlich had recognized certain defense possibilities: self-defense, the eternal triangle, the unwritten law. Quan, a solemn, hard-working executive of thirty-three, was the fond father of four children. His wife Kathleen, nee Choy Lin, was thirty, rounded and full-bosomed. Henry Yee, who sang Chinese love songs over KSAN, had pursued her for several years, how successfully the husband, and Jake, could only imagine. Two months before, Yee had broadcast a serenade to Choy Lin by name, and it had been heard by everyone in Chinatown.

This was the "Case With No Witnesses." Despite their endless noisy chatter in the shops along Grant Avenue, the Chinese became taciturn as turtles in the face of Occidental justice. Choy Lin, the wife, demurely avoided intimate details of her relationship with Yee. Quan himself, after his first confession, became thoughtfully silent. Not a shadow crossed his bright moon face when Jake reminded him of the gas chamber waiting at San Quentin Prison.

It was not a good case for a trial lawyer. Chinatown murders rarely are. Jake was forced to go prospecting in the homicide bureau. He sauntered in, drew up a chair and began what appeared to be a conversation with himself.

"You know," Ehrlich drawled, addressing the busy desks generally, "it's a hell of a note to go around putting innocent men in jail. I'd hate to have such a job." No one answered him. He shrugged. "Of course if you didn't put men in jail I wouldn't have this case, which should be a walkaway." A few heads came up. "It's a funny thing, though, how Henry Yee got two bullets in his precious hide."

"Three," corrected an inspector.

That was better. "Two," argued Jake, flicking lint from his sleeve. "I don't believe three shots were fired."

"Three shots hit him," the inspector snapped. "Your man emptied his gun and reloaded. Or didn't he tell you that?"

"You found all the bulletholes, I suppose? Or did those dark halls scare you out?" Jake smiled. "I don't believe you even examined that apartment."

"We ransacked the joint!"

Ehrlich was listening. The police seemed to think more than one gunload had been fired, though Quan, not a man to lose count of such things, told Jake he had fired four shots. Three bullets had hit Yee. If that fourth bullet could be found, Jake might have a silent witness casting doubt on details of the prosecution's case. He got up, pretended to left hook the nearest inspector, and strolled out. Fishing hadn't been too bad.

2

Even in Chinatown an observant man can learn things if he is patient—and has contacts. Sergeant Jack Manion, grizzled veteran of the Chinatown detail, was no man to give away police secrets but neither was he one to offend people. Lawyer Ehrlich had been courteous to him through the years. Manion knew the Quan family, as he knew everyone in the Chinese colony. He recalled Louis Quan's father, a fine gentleman who had saved his money and returned to the homeland to be buried with his ancestors. Manion remembered Louis' arrival in Chinatown, a slender sixteen-year-old, neat and studious, with a head for figures. Louis had studied nights at University Extension. In no time at all he was manager of American Finance, a credit to himself and the community.

Others recalled Louis' wedding ten years before to Choy Lin, a big-eyed girl with full red lips and an intriguing figure. She was attractive in either Chinese silks or American frocks; and, when she walked, she had a provocative bounce that Henry Yee would notice. Sergeant Manion knew Quan had befriended Yee. Everyone knew about the love song Yee had sung to Mrs. Quan, by name, in August. It had gone over KSAN and KGEI, the short-wave station, to China.

Quan had complained to his tong. Then he had come to

Manion and demanded that Yee be driven from Chinatown. The sergeant had sent Officer John O'Connor to warn the singer to keep away from pretty Mrs. Quan.

After the third day of Ehrlich's prowlings the tong sent a delegation to his office. Three ancients in mandarin costume, with wispy chin whiskers and tiny black caps nodding on their heads, filed in with three young Chinese businessmen. The old gentlemen tucked their hands into voluminous silk sleeves and perched in a semicircle staring at the great lawyer.

Ehrlich, familiar with protocol, sat wooden-faced in his high-backed leather chair and waited. They stared at his huge white cuffs and the jade cuff links (a gift from the Cal-Neva Gambling Casino). From time to time, without change of expression, they uttered torrents of Cantonese. One of the young men explained that the ancients spoke no English. "What you think will happen to Mistuh Quan?"

Ehrlich pondered the question while his eyes ranged over the old men. "You," he said politely, "do not believe in the Mosaic Law of an eye for an eye. That is our law.

"It is a bad law," Jake continued, "for it makes us practice vengeance rather than compassion and justice. It will be difficult in the case of Mr. Quan. I have no witnesses to prove Mr. Quan's innocence, not even a scrap of paper." The Chinese gentlemen bowed and filed out.

3

A man seeking out secrets in Chinatown by night must not be squeamish. During the late watches, there are creakings in the old buildings, stealthy footsteps that might be cats or might be other men. There are tinkling ornaments, bamboo curtains that rattle, and the mutterings of oldsters dreaming on their hard beds. Foghorns groan from the bay. Ehrlich, though generally self-assured, fortified himself with hookers of Scotch before he shrugged into his topcoat and climbed the hill to the murder house.

No light broke the gloomy face of 1104 Stockton as Jake eased through the narrow front door. The stairway creaked as he groped to the second floor. He allowed himself a quick flicker from his pencil flashlight, stepped over the dark red stain and through the unlocked door of 202. He didn't care to use the room lights.

As the police had before him, Ehrlich searched through cabinets, drawers, suitcases and closets, finding nothing but the things of family life. He passed up Chinese paintings, paper lanterns and one large ivory statue of some grotesque divinity. Kneeling, he crawled slowly around the room, using quick flashes to examine the lower walls. At the doorway, exactly in the juncture of floor and baseboard, he found what he was looking for—one bullethole splintered into the cracked old wood. He could find no other.

Placing a pencil in the bullethole, he stood back to gauge the line of fire. Quan apparently had been truthful. He had fired not three bullets, which the police had from the body, but four. His wild fourth shot had hit the floor at an angle. Ehrlich would send a ballistics specialist in the morning to dig out the bullet and identify it. Now he made a final sweep of the room. The light glinted on the ivory statue, passed it, and suddenly came back.

The creamy statue wore a soft veil of dust, as did its walnut base; but the top was glossy clean. Human hands, it appeared, had lifted the head so many times that a protective film of oil had adhered to it. Jake stooped to the base. Something was hidden there: a fat bundle of letters. They were letters addressed in a man's hand to "Choy Lin." Jake jammed them into his pockets and tiptoed to the door. In the apartments around him early-rising residents were beginning to stir.

As Jake suspected, they were love letters from Henry Yee, but he didn't have time to examine them thoroughly before taking off for a series of Los Angeles court appearances.

4

During his absence Waxey Gordon, the New York mobster, arrived in San Francisco and was arrested as a $1,000 vagrant. Roy Sharff cleared him out of town, and he took the noon plane for Los Angeles.

Officers there, hearing he was coming, called Jake from court and drove him in a police limousine to the Burbank airport, where the ex-beer baron was to land. "I feel sorry for old Waxey," Ehrlich said on the way. "If he had a surefire chance to make a million dollars honestly, he still would figure a way to do it crooked." Jake steered the old gangster through another "thousand dollar vag" arraignment and saw him off to the next city where, presumably, another limousine full of cops would meet him with another high-priced attorney.

Ehrlich was in Southern California on Sunday December 7, and was sleeping late after a particularly hearty celebration at the Hollywood Knickerbocker, when the telephone jangled. "Jeezus!" shouted Bill Saroyan, "what do you think of it?"

Jake, who had had a full night of Author Saroyan, muttered: "Think of what?"

"The Japs! They're bombing Pearl Harbor!"

"Bill," croaked Jake, "you've simply got to stop drinking." He hung up the receiver.

Later he got the full appalling jolt. By nightfall all the Ehrlich brothers had checked in by telephone. Myron, the Washington attorney, was already in uniform. A Naval Reservist, he had been summoned with thousands of other men from Griffith Stadium, where they had been watching the Redskins play football.

Jake flew back to San Francisco on the first plane next morning. While Franklin Roosevelt was addressing Congress on "a date that will live in infamy," Jake was trying to enlist in the Marines. Alvin, his second brother, head of a Washington advertising agency, enlisted as a private in the Army; Jack and Samuel, the other brothers, were hammering on the doors of recruiting offices. Jake, just forty-one and a veteran of the Mexican campaign and World War I, was confounded when the Marine Corps advised him there would be a delay in his request for combat duty. He turned back to the Quan trial with a heavy heart.

5

It was the hardest trial he had ever faced. He had developed a fondness for Quan. The patient, trusting young man had done what any husband might do when a predator fouls his nest. But this trial would start on December 18, just eleven days after Pearl Harbor, and Jake was defending a man of Oriental birth.

San Franciscans still were in the first shock of war. Honolulu, where their own great fleet lay ruined, seemed only a gull's cry beyond the Golden Gate. There were reports that the conquering Japanese were steaming for California. The blacked-out city shivered. Hadn't Jap planes reconnoitered over San Jose and Santa Rosa? Wasn't an Oriental task force massing to march troops up Market Street?

Justice for a Chinese-American at that moment? People who wouldn't know a Jap from a Hottentot glared at the chattering citizens of Chinatown, where loyal residents hastily donned lapel buttons proclaiming: "I am Chinese." A China-

man protecting his home? Ehrlich felt he might as well have
Tojo himself for a client.

He slept poorly and was astir by six each morning, reading,
pondering, preparing. He made a careful study of the letters
from the Quan apartment. Here, in Henry Yee's own handwriting, was an intimate account of trysts with Choy Lin; the
cuckolding of honest Louis Quan. Here was startling intelligence! At this very moment, Mrs. Quan was carrying the
unborn child of Henry Yee! Jake took a deep breath.

In the first hours of the trial he appeared preoccupied,
sifting through the jury panel, studying faces, weighing responses. There was no time for clowning with cronies in the
corridors. Quan, the impassive defendant, was human. Somewhere along the way he would break under the strain, for he
had taken a human life.

Ehrlich watched intently as "Ropes" McMahon, the dark
little prosecutor, spread his noose. He had Quan "dead to
rights," McMahon claimed; he expected the jury to return a
death penalty.

Husted, the homicide inspector, was a stern and forceful
man who knew his business. He recreated the murder scene
and the finding of the body. He said Mrs. Quan was up and
dressed because she had been heating milk for one of her
babies when the shots were fired.

The medical testimony was blunt. Yee had been hit by
three shots at pointblank range; one in the head, two in the
chest. Good shooting, McMahon sneered, for a supposedly
meek businessman with a gun conveniently left by a father
these ten years gone in China.

Sergeant Manion was a potent prosecution witness. Prosecutor McMahon used him skillfully to indicate that Louis
Quan had been on the prowl for his rival.

Before he rested, McMahon adroitly prepared his noose,
topping his case off with Quan's almost casual statement:

". . . the bullet . . . went through his head. . . . Get Jake Ah-lick." Ehrlich looked up at Superior Judge Edward Preston Murphy and felt the "eighty million bumps" beginning to rise on his skin.

He called Choy Lin. She appeared almost drab as she minced to the stand. Watching her, Jake gave particular attention to her figure under the nondescript cloth coat. It held a secret that no one in that room knew but her—she thought. Ehrlich fed her tentative, leading questions. She shadow-boxed.

As he questioned, Ehrlich had been pacing restlessly. Now, fingering the lapels of his blue, pinstripe suit, he paused.

"Uh—Mrs. Quan——" he hesitated, then turned to counsel table and reached for a big paper envelope. "Mrs. Quan, I will now call your attention to some letters."

He heard her gasp as the packet spilled on the table. He picked it up and turned to her. "Mrs. Quan, I will now ask you some further questions and then, maybe, I shall want to ask you about these letters." She bit her lip.

He went back to his original interrogation. Slowly the reluctant answers came.

Q—When did Henry Yee first call on you and talk to you personally about yourself?

A—It was last year.

Q—Will you tell the court, tell Judge Murphy and the ladies and gentlemen of the jury what the circumstances were?

A—One time . . . while my husband was away from home one night . . . he came to make love to me. He touch me . . . and then I said: "You shouldn't do that" . . . and I slapped him on the face . . . and I said, "If you do it again I will tell my husband about it. . . ."

Q—Did you see him any other times?

A—While I was home . . . I caught him several times standing in our fire escape place and I said: "What are you

doing around here, standing over there?" He said: "I want to
find out when your husband gets home."

Q—Did he stop coming to see you after you told him
that?

A—No, he still came up.

Q—Did you see Henry Yee often?

She hesitated. He tapped the letters in his left hand, waiting
patiently.

A—Well, he came up to the house often.

Q—Did you tell your husband that Henry Yee was bothering you?

A—Yes, one time . . . I gave him a hint. I said to my
husband: "I don't think Henry is a good friend of yours." But
my husband didn't pay attention. He was kind of busy.

Q—Now at any time when your husband was not in town
did Mr. Yee call on you?

She frowned, crossed her legs and fumbled nervously at her
skirt. "Yes."

Q—What were the circumstances?

The packet of letters was tapping like a metronome.

A—Well . . . after I told him not to come up . . . he still
came up. And one time I was not feeling well. He said he will
fix me some tea. So . . . I was drinking the tea . . . and so he
made love to me . . . and finally, that night . . . I gave in.

Ehrlich stopped and faced the jury, his face expressionless.
The admission spoke for itself.

Q—Did your husband come home while he was there?

A—He got home and he found our apartment door was
locked and it took Henry a long time to open it . . . and my
husband was mad, and he told Henry not to come up to the
house or to his office any more.

Ehrlich slapped the letters angrily in his palm.

Q—Did he call on you again?

A—Then he came up again a few days later and he said

he could not sleep . . . I said, "Why couldn't you sleep?" And he said, "Because I miss you very much" . . . and he said, well, he is sick . . . and he said he had written out a song for me and he said he would sing it on the radio that night . . . and he told me to listen. And so that night on the radio he sang this song.

Ehrlich permitted the witness, utterly miserable, to step down temporarily and compose herself while he called Charles Jung, an interpreter, to read into the record the now-famous serenade. Jung gave a rapidfire translation.

 Always I am dreaming of you. . . . I hope you will pardon me for what I have said . . . I do not experience pain if I should die because of love . . . I am sick because of love. . . . Oh, take pity on me. I have no other love but you. . . . If you should keep me in suspense my date of death shall not be far away. Is it preordained that we should be separated? And what prevents me from pouring out my intense love for you? Oh my dear Choy Lin, why should romance be denied us? Where is the God of Love? I am like a lone goose. . . .

And so on.

Jung's droning was not as romantic as Yee's crooning of it over the rooftops to Choy Lin. Louis Quan, the husband, sat stolidly as if he had not heard, or had heard too many times. Jake glanced at him again. A nerve was twitching at Quan's mouth. The lawyer scowled and called Choy Lin back. What about that night Quan had "to break open the door" to catch her with Henry Yee?

A—They quarreled and said a few words and Henry pushed my husband out.

Q—*Pushed your husband out?*

A—Yes, he pushed him out the door and [Henry] said, "I will get even with you some day." *And then he threatened to kill my husband.*

Ehrlich spun around and slammed the letters on his table

as Mrs. Quan stepped down. He hunched his shoulders and stood with clenched fists glaring at "Ropes" McMahon, while the jury absorbed the full impact of the declaration. He might have stopped there. That should have been enough for any jury. But there still was more to this story—more to showing Louis Quan as the good American husband who had been betrayed and had killed to defend the sanctity of his home. Jake asked for a weekend recess.

6

On Monday the twenty-second, three days before Christmas, he called Louis Quan. Jake watched carefully as Quan walked to the stand. Ehrlich knew he must hurry. Quan had taken a life and he could sense now, as anyone in that room could, that the battle was almost over. With release goes the will to fight.

Quan related how in 1939 he had received a letter from Yee, then in Seattle, asking help to come to San Francisco. Jake prodded him on. "I gave him $5 to get a room. Then about a week later I got him a job at the New Shanghai because he wanted to work at the best café. He was getting $5 or $6 a day. He stayed about a week and came back and told me he didn't like the job and he wanted to be his own boss. He asked me to advance him money for a laundry business."

Quan searched his memory for details. He had let Yee live in the basement of his office building. Then in July Quan had gone to an insurance convention in Galveston. When he returned he learned that Henry Yee had been staying with his wife. His daughter Evelyn came to him and complained that she was hungry, that her mother was neglecting the children for Henry.

Quan's lip quivered, and tears appeared on his cheeks. "I

heard the broadcast—Henry Yee singing the Chinese love song to Choy Lin—my wife." Quan's shoulders were quivering. "I went to the Chinese tong, the Chinatown detail, to Sergeant Manion." He held up his hands and collapsed in a massive outburst of sobs.

Ehrlich grabbed the distraught man, half carrying him to a chair. When Jake faced the jury, his face was dark, almost furious. He shook his head and patted the quailing shoulders of the defendant. On them he rested his defense.

Prosecutor McMahon argued long and logically. Sternly, again, he demanded the death penalty for Louis Quan.

Ehrlich rose. He advanced to the jury rail and spoke solemnly of the mass murder now loosed on the world. Of America, the last haven of justice, even for one insignificant Chinese-American businessman. He built upon the wholesome structure of family life and its destruction in this case by the predatory love of a Chinatown rat, Henry Yee. His voice thundered through the afternoon.

It was one of Jake Ehrlich's great arguments, though not a line of it made the San Francisco papers. They were preoccupied with the Japanese. But for two solid hours the jury of men and women were snatched from the world of war and made to live the drama of a man named Louis Quan. Their heads were down when they got the case. They were out less than forty-five minutes. The verdict: "Justifiable homicide."

Louis Quan was a free man. Broken in mind and heart and spirit, but free. He composed himself temporarily. He ordered one of the greatest feasts Chinatown's Far East Café has ever prepared. To it he invited not only Ehrlich and his family, but the members of the jury, the judge, bailiffs and every person in the courtroom who had helped him through his great tribulation. Only the judge declined the invitation.

It was a gourmet's feast, rice wine, pressed duck, buns of a thousand layers, bird's-nest soup—every delicacy. Jake, as toastmaster, explained that this was Louis Quan's grateful toast to American justice.

Ehrlich went back to court to get Quan a divorce from the faithless Choy Lin before she gave birth to Henry Yee's child. Quan quietly resigned his managership of the insurance company and dropped out of Chinatown society. He was a very sad man.

And so, after it all was over, was Jake Ehrlich. The Marines turned him down for combat duty, offering instead a commission at a desk. He and Jake, Jr., not yet twenty-one, went together to register for the draft. Brother Myron became a Navy captain, and served as Inspector General of Navy Courts and Boards.

There is a final word in the case of Louis Quan. The wispy-whiskered ancients of the tong summoned him before them and tried him privately for taking a human life. Their hearing was not complicated by Mosaic Law. They fined him $600.

Part Three: **THE CASE-BOOK**

The Shooting Never Stopped

I

GENE KRUPA

Reefers for the King of Drums

IN THE early years of World War II, Young America was jumping to a form of syncopated bedlam known as boogie-woogie. The personality who, above all others, sent the kids was a handsome, boyish jazz drummer named Gene Krupa. When Krupa mounted his percussive paraphernalia and began to fire, all hell broke loose. In his first year as "King of Drums," Krupa pelted out $100,000.

Early in 1943, having shattered eardrums and attendance records at the Hollywood Palladium, Krupa moved his band to the Golden Gate Theatre in San Francisco. On the night of January 18, after drumming his subjects into a frenzy, he jumped down from his podium, bounced off into the wings, and into the arms of two federal narcotics agents. They had a tip that Krupa's zip did not originate in vitamin pills, and they proceeded to search his dressing room.

A wide-eyed witness to the scene was John Pateakos, a slender, curly-haired, sensitive lad of twenty, who had signed on a week before to tend the drums. Probably Krupa's most adoring devotee, he tried to anticipate the drummer's every wish. He chose this moment to slip out of the theatre and sprint for their suite at the St. Francis Hotel. One of the narcotics agents was close behind him.

He nabbed Pateakos coming from Krupa's room and in his pockets found marijuana in two envelopes. Pateakos was sufficiently scared to tell everything or anything, but no arrests were made that night. This may have been in deference to the theatre, which had billed one more day of Krupa. At any rate, the drummer had time next day to telephone long-distance distress signals north, south, east—and west to Montgomery Street.

After the show of the nineteenth, the spotlight took Krupa to the wings, and narcotics men took him to his dressing room where Attorney Ehrlich waited. Krupa, perspiring from his toils, was permitted to shower and change clothes under scrutiny. Then he was taken to the city prison and booked on a misdemeanor charge of contributing to the delinquency of a minor. Ehrlich provided $1,000 bail, and that should have been that.

It should have been, but it wasn't. Krupa was "the idol of thousands of young Americans," a national figure. The newspapers pounded out a chorus of their own on the theme of "Dope and Delinquency!"—and it was louder than any solo the thirty-four-year-old drummer had ever performed. Moreover, it was election year in San Francisco and the district attorney was up for office.

Jake took one look at the headlines and knew he was in for trouble. Only a felony charge would fit these headlines, and a felony would mean San Quentin Prison for a young entertainer at the zenith of his career. It could destroy a million dollar entertainment property. It could blight the character of a young man who, offstage, was a quiet, God-fearing lad. Krupa, son of a onetime Chicago alderman, had studied for the priesthood before he turned to music.

The Krupa case grew steadily more malignant. There was the judge Ehrlich would always give the coldest lizard eye in the future and the district attorney who got greedy. There was Ehrlich futilely pleading a basic tenet of American justice, and Krupa drumming solos in a jail cell. Behind the case was

one of the most vicious lies ever told—one not to be untold
for a long, long time. "I don't know anything about this,"
Krupa insisted that night at the city prison. His dark eyes
flashed angrily. "If the boy had marijuana," Krupa swore, "I
certainly don't know where he got it."

"There is absolutely no merit to this complaint," Ehrlich
declared, glumly watching the officers mug and fingerprint
the musician. Old Matt Brady, the district attorney, wasn't
present that night but Ed Leonard, one of his assistants, was.
If the preliminary evidence stood up, he announced, Krupa
would also be charged with the felony of having a minor
transport narcotics.

Krupa was worried. "The thing I'm bothered about," he
said, "is that it will get to my sister. She brought me up. When
you print something like this, the people think you're guilty."

The papers printed it, with the prominent use of the word
"dope," photos of the drummer, and the allegations of the
narcotics agents. They made much of the facial contortions
peculiar to Krupa's frenetic craft. By some mischance they
had Pateakos' age as seventeen, which hurt. He was just short
of twenty-one and Army induction.

Krupa told Ehrlich he had hired the boy when his regular
valet was drafted. Pateakos, originally from Massachusetts,
was a jazz-happy kid who had jumped to Hollywood to be
near the big bands, and particularly Krupa. He had got a job
at the Palladium and hung around rehearsals. When the band
went on one-nighters, he had helped carry instruments and get
the uniforms ready. Given the chance to come to San Francisco, he had jumped higher than usual.

2

Two days after the arrest the district attorney's office added
the felony count, charging that Krupa *used a minor* to trans-

port narcotics." Ehrlich frowned though he saw a slim ray of light. "This may be a break," he told Krupa. "I think they're making a mistake." Preliminary examination followed in juvenile court, before Judge Thomas M. Foley, a tall, graying, heavy-set jurist who had graduated from Georgetown shortly before Ehrlich left there. Jake would have taken his word on anything.

Federal Agent Giubbini was the principal witness. "We received information," he said, "that Krupa was in possession of a quantity of marijuana. We carried on an investigation and, on the eighteenth of January, went to the theatre and met the defendant as he came off stage. We asked him if we could talk to him privately. We identified ourselves and told him we were interested in marijuana—and searched the room.

"After about fifteen minutes, Mr. Krupa asked us if he might wash, as he was perspiring quite a bit, and he left the room. I followed. He was walking with John Pateakos. I separated them. I asked Mr. Krupa where he lived and where the keys to his room were. He stated he lived at the St. Francis Hotel and that the key was at the desk.

"I became suspicious and telephoned the St. Francis, identifying myself, and asked them to give the keys to Mr. Krupa's room to no one but Mr. Krupa. I then left Mr. Krupa with Agent Polcuch and went alone to the St. Francis. I went up the elevator. As I stepped off, John Pateakos was waiting there to step on. I stopped Pateakos and took him with me to the band manager's room. I searched Pateakos and took from his trousers pocket one envelope containing two marijuana cigarettes and one half of a smoked marijuana cigarette, and another envelope containing thirty-seven such cigarettes.

"I questioned Mr. Pateakos and the band manager, who was in the room, and a few minutes later Agent Polcuch came in with Mr. Krupa. I then took Mr. Krupa into his room, where I talked to him a few minutes. Then Agent Polcuch came in. We conducted a search of Mr. Krupa's room and I found, in the writing desk drawer, fragments of marijuana—approximately one-tenth of a regular marijuana cigarette—which was lying at the bottom of the drawer.

"We questioned Mr. Krupa for a while and after about twenty-five minutes we took Mr. Pateakos to our office, where we allowed him to sit down and think it over. He finally stated——"

Ehrlich, frowning through the chronology, suddenly interrupted: "Was this in the presence of the defendant?"

"No."

"Then I object to it."

Judge Foley sustained him and whatever Pateakos had to say was held in abeyance. A chemist was brought to the stand to identify the material in evidence as marijuana. He described the weed as a plant growing over much of the United States. Usually it is rolled and smoked, the chemist explained, and it has a narcotic effect. Its results are unpredictable, varying greatly with individuals. Ehrlich made a note of that, but declined to cross-examine.

Pateakos came to the stand noticeably ill at ease. He wet his lips nervously, as he swore to tell the truth, the whole truth and nothing but the truth. He refused to meet Krupa's eyes. The prosecutor took him up to the moment near the dressing room when Agent Giubbini had separated him from Krupa.

"Mr. Krupa," Pateakos said, "asked me to go to his room and get an envelope from his coat pocket. I said, 'Is it the camel hair?' He said, 'No.' So then I left."

Q—What did you do?

A—I went to the hotel to get this envelope from the coat pocket.

Q—How did you travel in going to the hotel?

A—I ran part of the way.

The desk clerk had informed him that only Krupa could have the room key, so Pateakos had talked a bellboy into unlocking the suite. He said he had got the envelope from Krupa's coat, then had bumped into the federal agent at the elevator. He identified the envelopes in evidence as the ones he got from Krupa's room.

Ehrlich whispered to Krupa: "That kid's not *testifying!* He's repeating manufactured evidence!"

Krupa nodded. "Can you kill him on cross-examination?"

Jake shook his head. "We *can't* cross-examine. This boy's hot about something. Probably they threatened to throw him in jail. Only a fool starts an argument when all the signs are up."

The prosecutor, noting that Jake was making no move to examine the witness, addressed the court. "Your Honor, there is a possibility that this boy is leaving the jurisdiction. He is subject to military draft. I would like to put counsel on notice that, if he wants to question him further, now is the time to do it. Otherwise he may have to depend on the transcript in the trial of this case."

Ehrlich shrugged and shook his head. "I have nothing to do with his leaving the jurisdiction. It will be a simple matter to clear Mr. Krupa before the jury."

Judge Foley held Krupa to answer to Superior Court on the felony count, but permitted him to continue free on bail. The musician headed east to reassure his sister and join his band.

A month later, Ehrlich spoke to Judge Foley about the delinquency charge. Because it was only a misdemeanor, Krupa could not be forced to come across the continent, nor could he be extradited. Jake thought he understood Judge Foley quite clearly: *Bring Krupa back voluntarily for the misdemeanor; we will fine him $500, and that will be that.* He

telephoned Krupa to come, announcing that he intended to
plead him guilty of the misdemeanor.

As Jake saw it, the publicity was doing the entertainer ir-
reparable damage, though there was no evidence that Krupa
used narcotics. By disposing of the case quickly and quietly,
Ehrlich hoped to keep it out of the election oratory.

But the case was not so easily settled. *Admitting* the delinquency? This was an unexpected dividend for the prosecution. They could concentrate now on the felony.

3

Pateakos was released from protective custody pending the
trial and went his way. Subsequently he let it be known that
he was filing a claim with the State Labor Commission for
pay while he was in jail and reimbursement of expenses he
had incurred as a result of the arrest. Ehrlich discussed this
claim one evening with Roy Sharff who suggested that he go
to Southern California and settle it, since a disturbance by
Pateakos would only fan the publicity. Ehrlich told him to go
ahead.

On May 18 Krupa flew in from Providence, Rhode Island,
and went with Ehrlich to the Hall of Justice. "Are you sure
I'll only get a fine?" the drummer asked. Jake patted his
shoulder. "I never break my word, Gene, and I deal with
men who won't break theirs." He admitted that Matt Brady,
the campaigning district attorney, might "try to lower the
boom."

The district attorney had been raising a stentorian voice
over narcotics and entertainers. Ehrlich's mail reflected public
feeling on the subject. Most of the postcards and letters protested that Brady was pushing Krupa around, but others criti-
cized Jake for taking the case.

Ehrlich couldn't understand why Brady, a San Francisco political institution, needed any such hullabaloo to win re-election. He had had the job since 1919—some twenty-four years. At sixty-eight, he seemed as solidly rooted as Fisherman's Wharf, what with his annual birthday party for kids and a staff that handled office detail while he got about at social gatherings with his charming Irish smile.

Jake stood beside Krupa while the musician pleaded guilty to the delinquency charge. Ehrlich had $500 for the fine in his pocket. He reached for it. He was unprepared for what followed—*"and ninety days in the county jail!"* Ehrlich stared. The next words should have been *"sentence suspended."* But Judge Foley had finished. In that moment Jake "died eighteen thousand deaths." Anger surged to his lips, but there wasn't a word he could say. Krupa, though stunned momentarily, was still a trouper.

"Look, champ," he said, "something went wrong. I'll make it—somehow."

But Jake was looking to the future. He had just pleaded his client guilty to an offense that, in essence, was *included* in the felony to be tried. Perhaps Musician Krupa couldn't see it, but usually there isn't much defense left after a man admits he's guilty.

The judge specified that Krupa could serve his ninety days in the jail there in town, which had an excellent view of Alcatraz, while awaiting the second trial. That day, carrying a set of practice drums, Krupa surrendered himself to the custody of the sheriff.

Brady had assigned his top prosecutor, Leslie Gillen, to the Krupa case. Gillen had been waiting for five years to face Jake again—ever since Ehrlich beat him in the Ludolph case and washed out the whole Atherton probe. He picked up the narcotics-kid theme eagerly. Three times, though, he had to ask for continuances.

It took Ehrlich some time to discover why. The district attorney was having trouble finding its star witness, John Pateakos. Through his own contacts, Jake knew the boy had gone to Chicago to see his mother and then had returned to Los Angeles, where Sharff had located him.

"They're so damned busy making speeches they haven't taken time to use their heads," Jake growled.

4

The court of Judge Foley was crowded to the railings on June 28, when the Krupa case was called. Bailiffs working like ushers packed Krupa fans, lawyers and reporters into seats around the room. Krupa came from the jail pressed and polished in a plaid suit.

Pateakos still could not be located. He had not answered his draft board's request to come in. The FBI was searching for him. The trial would have to go on without him.

Jake, standing wooden-faced, waited for the complaint to be read and moved immediately for dismissal. He began to cite law, and the prosecutor suddenly recognized his strategy. Ehrlich was claiming double jeopardy. In effect, he was saying: "You have put this young man in jail for an act, and now you want to put him in the penitentiary for the same act. Because it is the same act, it is an included offense and double jeopardy."

For the first time, Prosecutor Gillen and Krupa's public saw why The Master had not even brought Krupa to trial the first time. If he had planned to, the prosecution, in whose hands the choice lay, would simply have said: "Fine, but we'll try the felony first. It's the more serious offense." Jake had also foreseen that the prosecution would be greedy. They were delighted to have a cinch conviction, a guilty plea, for which they had spent nothing.

Judge Foley refused to dismiss the felony charge. He said it would not be proper for him to decide the double jeopardy issue. That was the jury's task. Ehrlich almost exploded. Now Gene Krupa *did* face the penitentiary. He had already pleaded guilty to the same offense.

Only Krupa was calm. He tried to reassure Ehrlich as they began to question jurors. Jake could only try to educate the jurors in the technical matter of double jeopardy. Finally he accepted nine men and three women.

Agent Giubbini was back to open the prosecution case. He added a few new details. "I asked him if he had ever used marijuana, and Mr. Krupa stated he had at one time. He said that was about ten years ago, when it was the fashion for everyone to use marijuana, but lately he had had nothing to do with it."

Gillen asked: "Is it common knowledge that marijuana is frequently used because of its definite propensity for distorting time by so-called hot musicians? Jazz musicians?"

Ehrlich was on his feet, storming. Krupa, he declared, was not charged with smoking marijuana. "The question is irrelevant, immaterial. It is grossly unjust." He demanded that it be stricken and the prosecutor admonished. Judge Foley permitted the question to be answered. The agent said that was the purpose for which marijuana was used by musicians.

Q—And that is so they can beat the drums or play a cornet or trombone without feeling the effect of doing it?

A—That is right.

Krupa leaped to protest, but Ehrlich shoved him back. He strode to the center of the court and demanded that the judge stop the whole line of questioning as creating prejudice in the minds of the jury. He was overruled. Gillen persisted for several minutes longer, then sat down smiling, and offered the witness to Ehrlich. Jake had one question:

"Now is it true, as you said a few minutes ago, that marijuana cigarettes have *no* effect on some people?"

"That is right."

Jake looked at the jury and brought their gaze around to Krupa, calm, clean-cut and smiling. He sat down.

There was a confused conference at the prosecution end of the table. They finally asked permission to read the testimony of the key witness, Pateakos, from the transcript. Judge Foley nodded.

Gillen, an earnest young man, stumbled over the jive slang. Then the prosecution rested.

Again Ehrlich asked for dismissal on the previously stated grounds of double jeopardy. This time, it appeared, the judge was listening. Gillen leaped to his feet. "This plea of twice in jeopardy is not made in good faith," he declared. The judge sustained him.

Krupa appeared anything but a depraved addict as Ehrlich escorted him to the witness stand. Jake addressed the drummer as he might a learned colleague.

Q—Mr. Krupa, are you addicted to the smoking of marijuana?

A—No, sir, I am not.

Q—You have smoked it?

A—Yes, I have.

Q—And what effect did it have on you?

A—I became violently ill every time I smoked it.

His face reflected the nausea he said he had felt. Ehrlich nodded to the jury, and asked Krupa if he ever had asked or ordered John Pateakos to bring him marijuana cigarettes. The musician said he had not.

In cross-examination, Gillen went doggedly back to his

theme that marijuana was a necessary prop for jazz musicians. Krupa indignantly shook his head.

"My own experience among bands—big-time bands— bands that have responsible work to do," he said, "is that if you have a half-hour radio program, and have to make a tune last just thirty seconds, say, and there is a difference of tempo —I am afraid the marijuana would be apt to hurt you rather than do you good. It may be all right, but I don't know it."

He smiled at the prosecutor. "You say marijuana is used by musicians, but if you will look you will see that those musicians who use it are playing in small bands and small dives. I think you will find that the musicians in the big-time bands, like my own band today—the leaders and members of these organizations—are pretty clean-living boys. I mean it is necessary. If you don't think so, I would like you to try it some time."

Wasn't it a fact, Krupa was asked, that he had the reputation of being able to attain a faster tempo and faster rhythm with his trap drums than any other trap drummer in the world?

Krupa glanced at Ehrlich. "I don't know," he said. "The question of speed is a question of technique. Now, when you say play faster that sounds silly to me. When you stop to consider that a good trap drummer is able to beat his drums faster because of his technique—better technique—naturally it is harder to keep up a steady, fast tempo. But a man's ability to beat his drums faster than someone else is because he has developed his technique to a higher point and it is easier for him to play fast than it is for someone to play slow. That is the reason why I say it sounds funny to me. But if I am able to play faster than someone else it is because I have studied it, and developed my technique."

Gillen scowled. "I don't think he has answered the question."

Ehrlich raised his eyebrows but the judge ordered: "Answer yes or no."

"Well, Your Honor," protested Krupa, "there is no such thing as fast rhythm. Rhythm cannot be fast or slow or anything else. That is the only way I can answer you. I am considered pretty fast, sir. If that is what you want me to say—yes."

Q—Isn't it a fact . . . that when an orchestra plays particularly hot, as they call it, that means fast?

A—No, it does not. Hot does not mean fast.

Ehrlich, swiveling in his chair, was enjoying Gillen's predicament. Lawyers, he thought, stumble into many pitfalls.

Q—But when an orchestra plays either hot or cold . . . it is a common expression that they have been, or must have, smoked marijuana beforehand?

A—No, sir.

Q—You never heard that?

A—I have heard it, but it is not a common expression.

Q—I mean it is a stock joke, is it not, that if the boys play good, fast, hot music, they must have smoked a few reefers?

A—Certainly a joke, but nothing else. Certainly not the truth.

Krupa was losing his patience. Ehrlich tried to gesture to him to calm down. Finally, though, the drummer snapped at Gillen: "You told me you were not a master of ceremonies. You told me you were a lawyer. Be one!"

Gillen returned to Krupa's admitted use of marijuana. He demanded to know the specific occasion and the witness' reasons.

"I was feeling low," Krupa said. "I was a little put out with the band for giving a poor performance. I felt lowdown and sick. I had lots of worries on my mind. Lots of troubles." He ignored Jake's warning scowl. "I was sort of grabbing at a straw, like a drowning man."

The musician said the cigarettes found in his hotel room had been given him by an unknown fan outside the stage door in Hollywood, just before the band came to San Francisco. This intrigued the prosecutor.

"Who?" he demanded. "Who was this mysterious donor?"

"He was not too mysterious," Krupa retorted. "You can't call them by name, but you see them around the country as you play, at dancehalls, sitting up front in theatres—and they hang around the stage door and arrange to sit up in front of the bandstand. You are bound to see many of them the country over. When you come out of the stage door there are often kids—men—all kinds of people who will say, for instance, 'Here is a song, will you play it?' Or 'Here is a lyric.' "

In his final argument, Ehrlich argued the double jeopardy theme again. On June 30, his twenty-third wedding anniversary, Jake watched the jury go out. Probably they felt quadruple jeopardy was little enough if it turned up one offender as vile as Gillen had painted Krupa. They took less than three hours to find him guilty.

Still the trouper, he asked Ehrlich: "What's next, champ?"

"Keep practicing your drums," Jake said. "We're not through yet." He served notice that he would appeal.

Two days later Judge Foley sentenced Krupa to a term of one to six years in San Quentin Prison. Execution of sentence, however, was to be withheld pending the Appellate Court's decision on Ehrlich's motion. The "King of Drums" was still in custody, with more than a month to serve of his term in the county jail. Actually, the Krupa case was just beginning.

II

MADGE BELLAMY

Rootety-Toot for Mr. Big

ON THE day Jake was called to help Krupa he was also summoned in a second criminal occurrence. Madge Bellamy, the movie actress, had taken three potshots at a prominent man and needed a lawyer at once.

Among womany Hollywood actresses of the bare-bosom twenties and thirties, Madge Bellamy had been a legend of dovelike virtue. It was not that she lacked curves, for she had lovely ones, displayed in such piquantly titled productions as *Silk Legs, Soft Living* and *Ankles Preferred.* Madge was a golden blonde Texas gal with wide brown eyes. "The most beautiful woman in America!" artists had said. And to all appearances as untouchable as Eve.

To discover, then, that she had leveled an angry gun at A. Stanwood Murphy, San Francisco's strong, silent socialite, was revelation indeed.

Ehrlich had come home to his apartment exhausted. That first day of the Krupa case would have flummoxed an owl. Everyone in the world had a telephone, he was convinced, and the operators were giving everyone his number. Marjorie Ehrlich recognized the symptoms when Jake slammed in.

"If that damned telephone rings again," he instructed, "tell them I have gone out to the Farallon Islands to consult with a gull. I won't talk to anyone."

Of course it rang, with the flash on Madge Bellamy. (Ehrlich prides himself on getting the very first call, from one source or another, on all big San Francisco cases.) He listened out of curiosity, for he knew both of the principals well. Then there were calls from certain gold-plated telephones in Beverly Hills, and one from Madge herself, from the women's quarters of the city jail.

Jake left immediately for the Hall of Justice.

It was a misty evening with Alcatraz booming a mournful foghorn voice from the bay. According to first reports, Madge had loitered outside the Pacific Union Club—that "temple of dignity"—a big, square stone building up on Nob Hill, which snubs even the Mark Hopkins and Fairmont on adjoining corners. It is surrounded by a wrought-iron fence atop heavy parapets of concrete, and lacks only a moat.

Among the least garrulous of its members was A. Stanwood Murphy, the lumber baron. Not even the registrar of births knew what the "A." in his name signified until that eventful year of 1943, when Murphy was fifty-four years of age, a husky, balding sportsman and financier and, as it developed, a connoisseur of lovely ladies.

Murphy was president of the Pacific Lumber Company, which owns more California redwood trees than the State Park Commission, and even has a town of its own, Scotia, on the north coast. Some eulogists claimed Murphy had worked his way up from logger to tycoon, but others, including Ehrlich, swore the man had inherited his vast holdings without so much as swinging a hatchet.

"He is the type," Ehrlich had remarked, "who would look down on me from a very great height if I weren't Jacob W. Ehrlich, Esquire, and somewhat of a showpiece myself."

As a lawyer he had noted Murphy's recent divorce. Then, on New Year's Eve, Murphy had married June Dibble-Almy, in Baltimore. She was a daughter of British General Lionel

Dibble, had once been a Paris model and had recently divorced a millionaire Arizona cowboy-rancher. Jake suspected that the gunplay by Madge Bellamy was somehow connected with Murphy's recent marriage.

Madge, he judged, would be reaching early afternoon, as age goes. She was eighteen in 1921 when she hit Broadway in *Pollyanna*. At nineteen she was a Thomas Ince star in *Lorna Doone, The Playgirl, Hail The Women, Summer Bachelors* and *The Iron Horse*, with George O'Brien, whose father once was police chief of San Francisco.

Ehrlich had chatted with her at Hollywood gatherings, asking for her mother since she had no husband or children to inquire about. In her heyday, he recalled, she had owned "The Cedars," a $200,000 mansion in Hollywood. Her father, Dr. Will Philpott, had been a University of Texas professor. When he died, she had had her mother moved to a ranch near Riverside. By 1943, nearing forty, she no longer was a sunpower star.

Wheeling his car through evening traffic, Ehrlich recalled Madge's one experience with matrimony. In 1928, when she was twenty-six, she had eloped to Tiajuana with Logan Metcalf, a San Francisco stock broker who met and fell in love with her on the set of *Mother Knows Best*. The marriage had lasted four days. Metcalf told the divorce court: "All I eat for breakfast is ham and eggs. She said my tastes were vulgar." Madge tossed her golden head and sought neither alimony nor settlement. "Mr. Metcalf didn't get his money's worth," she murmured. The legend of untarnished virtue seemed durable.

Some would wonder how that record now stood. On a drizzly day when the headlines shouted BIG DAY RAID OVER LONDON and ALLIES IN TRIPOLI why was Little Miss Angelface stalking the fortress Pacific Union with her .25 caliber popgun? There would be bigger headlines tomorrow, Jake knew. Krupa *and* Bellamy!

The first move obviously was to get Madge out on bail, which could run to $25,000. That was too high. It would make the affair too serious in the public eye. A lesser bail—say, $500—would imply that the authorities did not take her prank too seriously.

2

Jake parked and went to the jail elevator. "She's still a honey!" exclaimed the operator. That would help. She had, however, admitted firing three shots at Murphy. Two passersby had disarmed her, which meant witnesses. Ehrlich listened carefully to the operator's briefing. Madge had come peaceably, crying that she did it because he married the other gal.

The officer who controlled the barred gate at the jail floor advised Jake that Madge had been booked for assault with a deadly weapon, which carries a maximum penalty of ten years' imprisonment and a $5,000 fine. What was the feeling of the department about her? "Well," chuckled the big Irish officer, "it must of been a sight to see Mr. A. Stanwood Murphy doin' that commando crawl under parked cars!"

Jake didn't laugh. Murphy was too big in San Francisco to be treated with levity.

At the jail, the press was having a field day. Madge was smiling regally from a perch on a table, silken legs crossed under a lynx coat. In plaid skirt and a tight sweater, she was still extremely attractive. Jake bowed and took her hand. "What have you been up to, my dear?"

He noticed the crumpled paper tissues and the torn cigarette packages. Madge was nervous. "I told him," she was saying, "that if he ever married anyone else I would kill him and her too."

Jake chuckled aloud. "Why don't you stop misleading these people, Madge? With your ranch background—shooting rattlers and tarantulas down there in Texas—you could have hit this man if you'd wanted to." He added: "Why don't you tell them how he made love to you?"

The actress studied his face a moment and caught the dead earnestness in his eyes. Ehrlich was working for a position. She nodded slowly. "I didn't intend to shoot him, of course," she said pleasantly. "I only wanted to scare him. I am a very good shot."

Jake nodded encouragement and she continued. "I never believed it was possible for me to love anyone as I loved this man. He is everything to me: the heart of my hearts. It was crazy, probably, but I simply could not bear the thought of living without him."

Her brown eyes appealed to the reporters. "He is a proud man. I wanted him to suffer the same thing I have. I knew publicity would hurt him more than anything else. I wanted to hurt his pride, not his hide." Satisfied, Ehrlich slipped out to call a judge.

The one he finally located was Municipal Judge Clarence Morris, a stocky, handsome man, kindly in appearance and action. He was at dinner with his wife. "I know this little girl," Jake told him. "She's a beautiful little thing. But of course you remember Madge Bellamy." The judge came right over.

Ehrlich made no attempt to minimize the seriousness of the episode. "Miss Bellamy has made a mistake," he pointed out. "She knows what she has done, and why it was wrong. I'll vouch for her. Don't you think five hundred would be adequate under the circumstances?" Judge Morris pondered.

"My idea of complete marital happiness," Madge was saying, "is to marry and settle down on a farm. I've always wanted what any woman wants—a home and a man to love me."

"Miss Bellamy," the judge interrupted, "you realize that Mr. Ehrlich has given his word? You are not going to let him down?"

With wide innocent eyes, Madge protested that she would certainly not let anyone down. The $500 was posted quickly and Ehrlich drove her to her hotel. Because he was busy with the Krupa matter, he asked a nine-day continuance, and Madge went home to Hollywood.

3

She returned to San Francisco in ample time to be seen, admired and interviewed before the preliminary hearing. Jake and his wife took her to dinners at expensive places where attorneys, judges and his prominent friends could flit about her as if she still were a queen bee. He had noticed the fear in her big eyes and he pitied her.

She was giving the San Francisco newspapers titillating columns on A. Stanwood Murphy. "When I met Mr. Murphy," she said, "he looked like a crude, honest lumberjack. I thought he was the type of man who, when he said he loved you, meant marriage."

A. Stanwood Murphy's silence was complete.

"Stan was so playful and sweet," Madge told another reporter. "He used to call me 'my little Easter Egg' and 'Wifey' and 'Monkey.' One day we were out in a rowboat and Stan said: 'Oh, those cute little legs!' Then he'd take pictures of me."

Reporters sought Murphy's version of these trysts, but a maid said he and his bride had gone out of town. "They probably went to the country," she said. "What country?" snorted Jake.

Madge was only beginning her recollections. "I had some

beautiful moonlight walks with him at Scotia," she said. "The
redwoods were majestic. In the house, on the divan, he would
bounce me up and down as though I were a four-year-old. He
was so rugged and strong." Ehrlich began to pity Murphy too.

"We used to talk about his affairs," said Madge. "I've gone
over his whole set of books trying to figure when he could
retire and we could spend our entire time in the cottage. Then
he would tell me different reasons why we couldn't get married right then. There was always some reason."

The newspaper-reading world hung on her revelations.
Jake's telephone was busy day and night. He talked with jour-
nalists in South America, Spain, Hawaii, London and the
Scandinavian countries, and to reporters from Denver to
Boston.

4

Press and public were agog at the prospect of a bare-
knuckles match between Ehrlich and the austere and untouchable Murphy.

Madge, meanwhile, was delighting Page One. "I was at my
mother's ranch when he wired me to call him," she related.
"I did. He told me he was not going to marry me. A few days
ago I read he was married, so I got the gun and went up to
the Pacific Union Club. I waited."

The actress said she had spent the entire drizzly afternoon of January 19 near the club, reading *Harper's Bazaar*
and watching the members come and go. When people began
to drift into the Mark for dinner, she had walked around to
Sacramento Street and waited by the parapet fence. She had
seen Murphy stride from the back door, toward his car, had
thrust her little pistol through the wrought iron and let fly.

"Miss Bellamy said he ducked," the *News* reported. "Other
reports to police were that Mr. Murphy violated all tradi-

tions of the stately old club by dropping to hands and knees and crawling around its parking area with the agility of a lumberjack at the cry of 'Timber!' However he managed it, Mr. Murphy got back into the club without having been contacted by any of the bullets."

Out in the sprawling city were the people who would eventually be Bellamy case jurors. Ehrlich trusted they were reading avidly. Murphy, he was sure, would try to duck a showdown. Influential people were calling the Ehrlich office. "Don't pounce on him like a seagull on a fish," they pleaded. Jake sat back and listened.

The lumberman had made one move that was interesting. He had hired Harold Faulkner, a criminal lawyer, to stand up with him. Jake grinned. "The man shot *at* gets this kind of lawyer to protect himself!" The grapevine said Murphy had not signed the complaint yet.

"They'll have to subpoena him if they want his testimony," Ehrlich told Roy Sharff. "And they will because they know that if they don't I will stand up and yell: 'Where *is* this man who was hurt so grievously?' " He intended, actually, to take it very easy. Crucifying Murphy would not save Madge Bellamy.

His defense was to be two-pronged: 1) Madge Bellamy had a moral reason for shooting at the millionaire; 2) the criminal act was intended not to hurt, but to humiliate him. Ehrlich pondered one smash question which would accuse Murphy of everything, while admitting nothing. He did not expect it to be answered.

Ehrlich wanted to discuss an issue, the alleged wooing and spurning of a beautiful woman, which had led her to commit a certain act. No woman, he would argue, shoots at a man without justification.

If, by some chance, Murphy was permitted to answer Jake's question, he might be in trouble. If the answer was No, Jake could leap in with startling allegations, perhaps records of trysting places. If Yes, Murphy's position would be worse. Jake would try to force Murphy into an admission that he had promised to marry Miss Bellamy.

The stage was set by January 29. Madge still was singing like an oriole. And Murphy was stolidly silent. The city was primed for a Roman spectacle.

5

When Ehrlich arrived at the Hall of Justice to open the preliminary hearing, he couldn't even get to the front doors. The building was bulging. He had to go to the basement, take the elevator to the fourth floor, come down a stairway and work his way through the spectators. Then he met Madge, the radiant center of a chorusing crowd. She wore a black frock that molded soft curves, flesh-colored stockings and black pumps that accented her celebrated ankles, and a silver fox cape. Only Jake, perhaps, noted that the clothes were inexpensive and that the fox was a little weary.

Other tidings were cheering. The prosecution was unhappy. A. Stanwood Murphy was an uncooperative chief witness. Yet, if the situation got out of hand, they would have to use him to blast Madge. They had had to subpoena him to be certain he would even be present and they could figure that, newly married, he would not be in a blasting mood.

As such times, Ehrlich often had told his young associates, "The top flight guys in the prosecutor's office develop terrible cases of bronchitis. They don't want to face uncle Jake." So it was that Edith Wilson, a matronly woman, was sent by the state to handle its case.

The bailiffs called through the doorway: "Ready in your matter, Mr. Ehrlich." Jake moved slowly through the dense crowd. Halfway to the railing he heard Miss Wilson ask for proceedings to begin immediately. "We are ready, Your Honor." Judge Morris, looking out over the crowd, could see Ehrlich's predicament and replied: "We have to wait for the great mouthpiece." Jake paused to bow to the bench.

A very uncomfortable A. Stanwood Murphy averted his eyes from the actress. His mien was somewhat less cheery than his red, white and blue cravat. He studied the floor as the arresting officers testified. Only the subpoena kept him rooted while Miss Wilson questioned the next prosecution witness, one of the men who had disarmed Miss Bellamy.

Q—Did you ever see the defendant before?

A—I saw her in the vicinity of the Pacific Union Club about 6:00 the night of January 19.

Q—Where were you?

A—In an automobile that was being parked.

Q—What did you see?

A—The woman stepped up to the fence surrounding the parking area of the Pacific Union Club.

Q—Then what did she do?

A—She thrust the revolver partly through the metal fence and fired twice.

Q—What did you do?

A—I jumped out of the car and ran over. In the meantime she had climbed to the top of the fence and was leveling the gun over the fence.

Q—Then what happened?

A—We scuffled and somehow or other we were on the side.

Q—What did the woman do?

A—She was slumped on the ground.

Q—Did she say anything to you?

A—She said, "I'll kill you too."

Ehrlich decided to let the man off lightly. Next came a club barber. He had witnessed approximately what the first man described, but added that he had seen two bulletholes in Murphy's car.

"Did the lady say anything to you?" asked Miss Wilson.

"She said it was all a mistake," he stated, "that it was an impulse. I asked her what she was doing with the gun. She said it was only a toy. The other witness looked at the gun and said: 'That's no toy!' We looked at the hole in the door and at the one in the windshield, and someone said: 'It takes more than a toy to do that.' "

Jake waved him off the stand. A. Stanwood Murphy himself was being called. Judge Morris took the pertinent information for the record. "Your name, please."

A—A. S. Murphy.

Q—What does the *A*. stand for?

A—Albert. (Now *that* was out.)

Miss Wilson addressed the big man deferentially. "On January 19, in San Francisco, did anything unusual happen?"

A—Yes.

Q—What time was it?

A—About 6:10 P.M.

Q—Tell us what happened that night.

A—I had just left the Pacific Union Club and opened the front door of my car to get in when I heard a shot toward the front end of the car. I ducked behind the door and there was another shot. I ran around the end and still another shot was fired.

Q—Did you see Miss Bellamy?

A—Yes.

Q—Did you see her direct the gun at you?

There was a slight hesitation before Murphy glanced at the actress and replied: "No." Madge was weeping.

Ehrlich's turn now, and the courtroom hushed. Bailiffs edged closer. Spectators craned. The attorney fixed the witness with a baleful gaze.

"Isn't it true that you had a relationship for four or five years, and that this act to embarrass or scare you was a result of that association?"

That was *the* question. Murphy squirmed and the explosion of objections followed. Judge Morris upheld them all. Ehrlich tried to argue. "In all cases of assault, a relationship between the parties may be gone into." Judge Morris shook his head. "In some cases that might be relevant, but in this case I cannot see the value." He warned Murphy not to answer any question until the court had had time to rule on it. At one point he leaned close to the witness and appeared to say something more. Jake, facing the judge, suspected that Judge Morris was instructing the lumberman to step down from the stand. Ehrlich edged slowly away, continuing his harangue.

Jake's wide-set brown eyes afford excellent side vision. He saw the big man ease out of the chair, but he kept his own eyes on the bench. Murphy passed close behind him. Jake was glowering fiercely and arguing. At the press table, he was aware, reporters were hissing and gesturing toward the departing witness. So wrought up was Ehrlich, apparently, that he missed their signals.

Privately, Jake was wondering if reporters really are perceptive. They look for blasting counterstrokes, never for subtleties. If Judge Morris wished Murphy saved from a blistering, that would work nicely into the defense plan. It might save Murphy, but it also could save the defendant. Playing it safe, Jake rasped out his arguments and kept the prosecution involved. Miss Wilson knew Murphy was leaving. Everyone in the courtroom knew it.

The flight was slow, though, in the crowded aisle, and Ehrlich couldn't "discover" it until Murphy was safely gone, until it was too late for the judge to recall him. Jake knew there was an airlock on the courtroom door. Until he heard it hiss he must keep up his game of the frustrated defense. As soon as Murphy was clearly gone he could start the hell-raising.

Head down, snorting forensic fire, Ehrlich strode back to the table where Madge sat wide-eyed, amazed by the apparent blindness of the famous attorney. He was pulling papers from his briefcase, patting his pocket as if in search of something, muttering: "Where did I put that? Now where did I put that?" She had no idea what he was searching for. She was, in fact, rather a poor judge of fine acting.

The airlock hissed. Jake turned to face the bench. He spotted the empty witness chair. His mouth gaped and his eyebrows went up. He shook his head with disbelief. "Well, now," he cried, "that's the greatest disappearing act since Harry Houdini! That man's a genius!"

It was safe now. Murphy undoubtedly was scurrying for the biggest, thickest covert of redwood trees on the Pacific slope. Jake hoped Murphy could never be found.

Judge Morris finally gaveled Ehrlich to order. He reminded counsel that this hearing was only to determine the evidence available for Superior Court action. The prosecution had finished with the witness. If the defense wanted him, they would have to subpoena him themselves.

Jake plodded back to his table, an indignant, righteous and impugned defender of innocent womanhood. The press row was making notes with fury, would report with glee how Witness Murphy walked unscathed from the trap laid for him by The Master. Madge patted Jake's hand consolingly. Poker-faced, he hung his head.

The judge obviously had no alternative: Madge Bellamy must be held to answer to the Superior Court. In an instant all chagrin was gone from Ehrlich's face. He leaned quietly back in his chair and stated: "You cannot try my client. There is no charge against her."

Courtroom workers gaped. Edith Wilson, though hesitant, declared: "The charge is, as stated, assault with a deadly weapon.

"Show me the signed complaint."

Miss Wilson caught her breath and the judge frowned. Policemen tactfully covered their faces. There was, of course, no signature on the complaint. As everyone knew, though it had been forgotten, Murphy had never quite got around to that formality. Now, it appeared, fear of Jake Ehrlich had driven him well beyond the reach.

It had been predicted that he would sign no complaint. Jake would have bet his Cadillac on that. The court turned now to Harold Faulkner, the forgotten attorney, and asked if he knew that Murphy wouldn't sign. Faulkner, who had enjoyed the little squeeze play, nodded. "That is correct. My client will not sign a complaint." The prosecution asked for a continuance.

If San Franciscans were disappointed in the Murphy-Ehrlich clash, Police Chief Charles Dullea was furious. "No one," he thundered, "can come into San Francisco and shoot up the town and not be prosecuted." He ordered Frank Lucey, a dutiful inspector who had headed the investigation, to sign the complaint against Little Miss Angelface.

6

In California, as Ehrlich had reminded the court, a complaint charging someone with a crime must be signed. Usually this is done by the aggrieved victim. But there are obviously circumstances, such as murder, in which that would be impossible. In such emergencies, the officer in charge of the case may sign "as the result of investigation, on evidence obtained, and belief." This practice, commonly known as "information and belief," had been a perennial thorn in the side of Jacob W. Ehrlich, Esquire.

On February 5, 1943, when the hearing against Madge
Bellamy reopened, Jake glared up at Inspector Lucey on the
witness stand. "Did you sign the complaint charging this defendant with a felony?"

"That is correct," said Lucey.

"Are you handling the case?"

"Yes."

Ehrlich leaned forward, staring coldly into the officer's
face. "Did you witness the actual shooting? Can you tell us
exactly what happened?"

"No, I can't," Lucey replied honestly. "I wasn't there."

It would satisfy no one if a felony conviction were gained
on hearsay and a district attorney, whose job is elective, cannot be blind to public opinion. The prosecution requested another continuance.

Next day came an announcement: "Having reviewed the
legal aspects of the case, the district attorney's office is of the
opinion that a conviction of the defendant on an assault
charge is very unlikely; that in view of this a Superior Court
trial would only put the city and county to unnecessary and
futile expense." The felony charge was dropped.

In its place was a charge of violating the California laws
by carrying a concealed weapon. A misdemeanor. Lucey
signed it readily; he could testify that Madge had an unlicensed gun. The maximum penalty for that is six months in
jail or a $500 fine. A new hearing was set for February 10.

Overnight, it seemed, Madge Bellamy realized her predicament. Even six months of her life now seemed a terrible
price to pay for emotion. She saw how close she had come to
worse. Worry lines violated the peach fuzz cheeks. Cosmetics
no longer covered the traceries of time. She and San Francisco took a second look at each other.

The hearing was at 10:00 A.M. There wasn't much more
Ehrlich could do. Two men could testify that she had the gun.

They had taken it from her. She had broadcast the fact that she had fired it. Ehrlich looked up at Judge Morris, handsome, calm and kindly, and announced that he would plead Miss Bellamy guilty and submit to the will of the court.

"The court knows the story," he said. "The entire situation is the result of a relationship which resulted in a great hurt to the defendant. Offenses of passion have their mitigating circumstances. I believe the ends of justice would be served if the defendant were placed on probation or given a suspended sentence. The grave concern she has experienced and certainly her acute fear constitute sufficient punishment for anyone. I extend my plea for mercy and consideration."

There were tears in the eyes of Little Miss Angelface. She looked helplessly up to the judge, absently folding the creases in her rumpled black frock. The slightly tattered silver fox rode less smartly on her bowed shoulders.

"In this case, as in others," said the judge, "the matter of punishment is relative. Ten minutes in jail or ten years, one or the other, will serve. This defendant is obviously of a sensitive nature and disposition." He gazed down at her and there was pity in his eyes. "I feel she will not take this gun, nor will she use it again."

For the record he sentenced her to six months—suspended —and placed her on one year's probation with the admonition that she "hold herself in check."

He closed his big ledger and Madge rose impulsively, tears coursing through her rouge. She tripped to the bench to kiss the judge. He averted the act by handing her a pile of letters he said had come from her fans. He turned quickly from the bench.

Jake caught her arm. She planted a kiss on his cheek, then smiled at a handful of older fans who were asking politely for autographs. Cameramen wanted her to meet them in the pressroom for further pictures and, like a good trouper, she hiked down the corridor and obediently sat on a desk with her legs crossed.

She was still talking bravely. "I never wanted to hit him. I have handled all sorts of firearms—I used to handle guns in western pictures, you know—with George O'Brien." Some of the reporters had turned to other matters. Cameramen were calling their city desks for further instructions. "I made *The Great Hotel Murder,* you remember." She smiled self-consciously. "I used to go hunting with Stan, for big game and ducks. . . ."

"Come on, honey," Jake said gruffly. "Don't let the boys take more of your time. They're waiting for you in Hollywood." He escorted her from the drafty little room.

Then Carolyn Anspacher of the *Chronicle* sat down and wrote:

"She drew her shabby cape around her shoulders. The world and the pressroom, both, were cold. She seemed very little and very lonely as she trotted down Kearny, her heels beating a brisk tattoo on the sidewalk. Her crime, one felt, was not in having taken three potshots at A. Stanwood Murphy ('because she wanted to scare him') but in having passed her thirty-ninth birthday."

III

KRUPA BACK

Twice in Jeopardy

By THE time Ehrlich got back to the second phase of the Krupa case, any hope he may have had of shielding the drummer's reputation was gone. The atmosphere in San Francisco was as hot and humid as a summer sky before an electrical storm.

Krupa was completing his ninety-day sentence for the misdemeanor of *letting* the minor Pateakos carry marijuana cigarettes; he had a month more to do in July. He was under sentence of one to six years in San Quentin for the felony of *using* the boy to transport narcotics which, Ehrlich angrily contended, was the same offense warmed over. Knowing he intended to use this contention as the basis for appeal, the newspapers increased their thunder. They wanted Krupa behind bars.

Ehrlich believed Judge Foley had promised that there would be no jail term on the misdemeanor if he brought Krupa back voluntarily. He swore that Ed Leonard, an assistant district attorney, had assured him the felony charge would not be pressed if Krupa came back. Ehrlich felt that both men had forgotten.

Clearly, the second half of the Krupa case was going to get rough. District Attorney Matt Brady, the political institution of a quarter of a century, was willing to stake his tremendous

popularity in a fighting war with Jake Ehrlich, the man he
once had lauded as "an attorney respected for honesty among
his profession." With powerful newspaper backing, Brady was
preparing to turn his heaviest guns on "the criminal lawyer
of the Tenderloin" in the hope that he could destroy Krupa
and return himself to office for a seventh term. Very shortly
Ehrlich would come under vicious personal attack and even
be faced with a criminal indictment.

Immediately after Krupa was sentenced, Ehrlich and Roy
Sharff had started working on the appeals brief. Laboring
painstakingly to perfect every point on which Krupa might
be extricated, Sharff twice got into such a stew that he threw
all the papers off his desk and stalked out to breathe the
foggy air.

Ehrlich also had investigators running a lifetime check on
the missing witness Pateakos, whose performance stuttered
with question marks. Among other things, Jake wanted the
youth's birth certificate; there were rumors that Pateakos
wasn't underage at all, but was hopeful of avoiding the draft.
If true, of course, it would have direct bearing on whether the
Krupa case actually did involve a minor. Although Ehrlich
did not know it, Prosecutor Gillen also had suspicions. As
Jake was flying east to keep a business appointment in New
York, Gillen slipped out of town by train for Los Angeles.

2

On the morning of July 10, while Ehrlich was conferring
with his New York clients, the Krupa case suddenly broke
wide open. Headlines announced that Pateakos had at last
been arrested by the FBI and "loaned" to Prosecutor Gillen.
Pateakos asserted that he had been paid $650 by "Jake Ehr-
lich's assistant"—whom he identified from photos as Roy
Sharff—to "get out of town."

San Francisco was jarred. These charges, if true, could put the city's flamboyant criminal lawyer behind bars himself. Krupa heard them and was stunned. Almost simultaneously, his management heard them in New York and began to call desperately for Jake and an explanation. They did not know he was only a few blocks away.

In San Francisco Sharff came under heavy bombardment. A placid, blue-eyed young man with thinning dark hair and a bristling mustache, he usually managed to avoid the public hurly-burly. His domain was the law library and detail work. Lacking Jake's rough-and-tumble relationship with the press, Sharff could only deny the charge as "utterly false" and wait for developments. It was noon in New York before Ehrlich broke for lunch, saw the headlines, and called his office. He listened carefully to Sharff's summary. Then he exploded.

"What the hell does that Gillen think he's doing? You can tell him and Matt Brady that if they want to make this Krupa case into a war we'll give it to them. I'm flying back!"

Brady and Gillen announced that they were calling a special session of the Grand Jury so Pateakos could repeat his payoff story. The newspapers speculated that Ehrlich and Sharff would be indicted.

"My brothers of the press!" Jake brooded. The worst of it was the frustration of not owning a newspaper to print your own side of the story (an advantage Ehrlich also recognized when the headlines ran in his favor). He knew he had enemies in addition to Matt Brady; every time he won for a client some other client or lawyer lost.

His jolly millionaire pal Lou Lurie tried to josh him and assure him that he would win in the end, as he always had. "Sure," growled Jake, "but in the meantime that guy in the district attorney's office uses me and an innocent defendant to further his political ambitions! I'm going down there tomorrow and hammer some sense into his head."

"Easy, Jake," Lurie said. "You have a reputation in this city for being a gentleman and conducting yourself like one. Those are the strongest weapons in a battle."

Ehrlich listened and in the morning felt better. With an affable smile, he headed down Montgomery Street to call on Matt Brady. Striding into the big inner office, he said pleasantly: "Good morning, Matt. How's the big Irishman?" Brady didn't offer a chair or his hand.

"Look here, Matt, what's all this about paying off this kid in the Krupa case and you taking it to the Grand Jury?"

Brady grunted. His office, he said, had evidence that Sharff had paid Pateakos to disappear. They intended to punish him. Ehrlich shook his head good-naturedly. "Roy's a clean kid, Matt. He wouldn't do that. And me; do you think I would do anything like that?"

Brady glared.

"Look, Matt," Jake insisted. "I'll tell you what happened. We learned Pateakos was going to swear before the Labor Commission that he hadn't collected his salary and expenses from Krupa while he was in jail. We didn't want that publicity in addition to Krupa's other troubles. Rather than go through the commission, Roy simply paid his claim and took a receipt."

"We don't believe him," Brady growled.

He was staring straight through Jake, and Jake knew why. Ehrlich was a friend of Edmund (Pat) Brown, the attorney who was running against Brady and who had been defeated by Brady in the last election by one hundred thousand votes.

"Mr. Gillen," Brady said, "thinks this is a pretty flagrant case."

"Les Gillen thinks any case involving me is flagrant!" Jake retorted. "That's because I beat him in the Ludolph case and got him a jail sentence and fine for his browbeating and contempt in the McDonough hearings."

Ehrlich, by special appointment, had prosecuted the prosecutor himself in one of the outgrowths of the Atherton investigation. Trying to outlaw the McDonough bail license, Gillen had been obstreperous with Judge Twain Michelsen and had been cited for contempt. The judge had named Ehrlich to prosecute. Jake had done such a thorough job that Superior Judge Dooling had fined Gillen $50 with the alternative of twenty-five days in jail. Gillen had appealed to the District Court, but the fine had been upheld.

"If you're going to take someone apart for all this, Matt," Jake said, "take me. Roy is a decent kid."

"We're going to indict him."

"If you do, you'll have to indict me."

"We will."

Ehrlich leaned across the desk. "You are signing your death warrant!"

Brady was on his feet. "You don't like it, Mr. Ehrlich?"

Jake was furious. "Matt, you might as well clear up this desk and start looking for a new job!"

"Would you care to repeat that before the Grand Jury?"

"Matt, if you take me before that Grand Jury I'll make you look sick. I'll lick you so bad you'll never be elected district attorney again." Jake's finger was ticking at Brady's nose. "I am going to see that you are beaten in the next election! Remember that, Matt. I am going to see that you get licked!" He turned and strode to the door.

In San Francisco the Grand Jury meets in a special room at City Hall. Ehrlich had been there many times, as a witness during the Kamokila and Atherton investigations and as an attorney pacing the corridor while his clients testified behind closed doors. He had no fear of the Grand Jury. With reputations being kicked around, he welcomed impartial ears. The Grand Jury wasn't running for office.

The first witness was Barney McDevitt, a Hollywood press

agent. His testimony, as released later to the press, was that
he had received "several calls from Jake Ehrlich's office" and
learned that a man was coming from San Francisco to see
Pateakos. He had arranged the meeting.

There was a stir at the elevator as John Pateakos, the long-
missing star witness of the Krupa case, arrived in a dazzle
of camera flashes. He marched up the hall at the center of a
district attorney's guard, and hesitated as reporters pelted
questions at him.

The guards whisked him into the jury room. He was there
a long time. Then Brady summarized what he wanted the
press to know. Pateakos' payoff story was unchanged. He
said he had asked for $800 and Sharff had told him he would
have to have Ehrlich's okay on that. Later they had refused
to pay that much, he said, and he had settled for $650. Then
he had left California.

The transcript showed that several jurors apparently were
skeptical of the testimony. They seemed to suspect, as Jake
had suspected in the preliminary hearing, that Pateakos was
not *testifying* but repeating a prepared story.

Brady, besieged by the press, carefully avoided direct accusations. "The evidence may direct itself to two prominent
attorneys," he stated.

"Why don't you name them?" demanded the reporters.

"Because the Grand Jury hasn't returned indictments,"
Brady replied. "It would be improper for us to give the names
at this time."

("And damned libelous," snorted Ehrlich when he read
it.)

"The case is one of extreme importance and gravity,"
Brady said. "I am not going to lay myself open to suits by
people who might be as clean as a hound's tooth." He hesitated. "I know what you're thinking: you tread softly when
you tangle with Jake Ehrlich."

When the Grand Jury had recessed, then reconvened, Sharff was called and Gillen attacked. "Why," he demanded, "was a call placed from your office on April 23 to Barney McDevitt in Hollywood?"

Sharff, as usual, spoke softly. "We wished to contact Pateakos through Mr. McDevitt to arrange the meeting. I was going to Los Angeles on other business and decided at the same time to finish some business with Pateakos."

"All right. What was your business with Pateakos?"

Sharff unfolded two pieces of paper. "I will be glad to tell you about that. I paid Pateakos $500—not $650, as I read in the papers. It simply represents settlement of claims against Mr. Krupa."

"Your proof?" demanded Gillen.

Sharff smiled. "I have here two handwritten documents, both in longhand in Pateakos' handwriting. One is a receipt for $500. The other is a statement that the money was being paid purely upon the legal basis of his claim against Gene Krupa for salary and expenses."

Gillen took the documents with unconcealed suspicion. "Why did Pateakos write these in longhand?"

"Because," said Sharff promptly, "I did not want him later to claim he had signed the statements without reading them. I obtained these, as any cautious lawyer would, to avoid any charge of illegality that might arise."

Sharff read the documents aloud. The first said: "Received from J. W. Ehrlich the sum of $500 in full settlement and payment of all my claims against Gene Krupa and Frank Vienere (Krupa's manager). It is understood that this amount is calculated upon the basis of wages unpaid, clothes lost for me, and traveling expenses in accordance with my understanding when joining the Gene Krupa band, and reimbursement for monies laid out, together with all possible claims and demands."

The second paper said: "To whom it may concern: This is my free and voluntary statement that the settlement I have this day made with Gene Krupa and Frank Vienere was made purely upon the legal basis of my claims against them. There was no understanding as part of such settlement that I was to do anything with reference to the case of Gene Krupa in San Francisco, nor that I was to change my testimony in any way. Likewise, no promises were asked of me before settlement was made, and no requests made of me as to my future actions or conduct." Sharff finished reading and was dismissed.

The bailiff called Ehrlich's name.

Out in the corridor, Jake turned slowly, his left arm straight at his side, his fist clenched. Anyone familiar with him would have recognized his fighting walk. Reporters crowded close. "Are you gonna give 'em hell, Jake?"

"I am going to destroy Matt Brady," he replied.

The Grand Jury room is a large hall, laid out much like a courtroom. The foreman sits on the bench like a judge. The jury members sit where the courtroom spectators would be. The witness is placed on a raised dais between the jurors and foreman, with the district attorney directing questions from a desk at the side.

Jake noted that *all* eighteen jurors were present. The overhead lights flashed on his cuff links, gold miniature handcuffs with tiny dangling chains given him by a police captain. Brady himself was at the interrogation table and saw he was confronting a very angry man.

In the heralded first round of the Brady-Ehrlich battle, he asked exactly two questions: "What is your name?" and "Where do you live?" Then he withdrew. "Mr. Gillen will take over."

Gillen appeared to be interested chiefly in a series of telephone calls from the lawyer's office at the time Pateakos disappeared. Jake, Jr., second mate on an ammunition ship, had become seriously ill off Guadalcanal at that time and was hospitalized in Australia. Ehrlich had burned up the telephone wires after the first brief message, trying to get details on his son's condition. Because of wartime restrictions, he had had to obtain special permission from the Navy to call Australia. He had also called Jerry Giesler in Los Angeles, though he couldn't for the life of him remember why. Gillen had a record of all the calls. He accused Jake outright of conniving to get Pateakos out of town. "Perhaps ship him to Australia?" Jake suggested.

He had dropped his usual courtliness. Badgered by the rudest kind of questioning he slashed back with innuendo and insult. First Gillen demanded: "Why, in view of the contact between Roy Sharff and Pateakos, was not the district attorney's office notified, when the Krupa trial had to be postponed three times because of our inability to locate the witness?"

Ehrlich stared contemptuously. "I didn't think it was my duty to keep the district attorney advised of the whereabouts of his key witness."

That didn't discomfit Gillen who seemed to be enjoying Ehrlich's anger. He tried to make Jake contradict the Sharff story and failed. Then he said he was through. Ehrlich asked to be heard.

"I have read," he said, "that the district attorney charges the witness John Pateakos was living outside the state of California during the Krupa trial. I should like to introduce an affidavit from John Pateakos' landlady that he has been living in Los Angeles all during the time it was claimed he was somewhere else." Gillen rejected the document. "I would think," Ehrlich said, "that the prosecution would want the Grand Jury to consider *all* the evidence in an investigation like this. Not just one side." He got up, grim-faced, and went back to the corridor.

Pateakos was recalled. Ehrlich, watching the clock, muttered to Sharff: "He's fighting it all the way to the wire." The weary and almost weeping boy finally came out, and the jury said it would meet for the third time two days later.

Pateakos had been hard-pressed to explain the Sharff version of the money. He fumbled through one unintelligible reply. Gillen demanded: "Why didn't you tell it this way before?" Pateakos crumpled. "Why did you say it was $650, instead of $500?"

The boy tried to explain that he had to pay $150 to the men who arranged the meeting; maybe that was how he got mixed up.

"Why didn't you tell us before that this money was paid on your claim for salary and expenses?"

"You didn't ask me!" the young man said.

In the end, the Grand Jury refused to indict. Brady had urged indictments against both Ehrlich and Sharff for conspiracy to interfere with the administration of justice. "The jurors didn't see it that way," he said ruefully.

The reporters converged on Ehrlich. "The only statement I have," he said wryly, "is that the Grand Jury didn't believe the district attorney, who has now succeeded in adding me to the immortals of law—Bill Fallon, Earl Rogers, J. P. Benjamin, Clarence Darrow—all brought before grand juries and vindicated." He nodded to the jury room. "One red-faced gentleman in there has had his time at bat and struck out. Now he is going to see some heavy hitting. I assure you mine will all be above the belt."

3

On August 9 Krupa completed his county jail term, and Ehrlich posted $5,000 bail to keep him free pending the appeal. He said Krupa had seen the last he ever would see of jail. "You can only punish an innocent man so long, even interpreting law the way our district attorney does in San Francisco."

None of his statements made the papers. The fall campaign was in full swing and the incumbent Brady was the favorite. Ehrlich himself became a target. The *Examiner* fired salvos of editorials, all ignoring the candidate Brown while concentrating on Ehrlich. "It is time," said one, "to lay the cards on the table and expose the men who are trying to take control of the district attorney's office. Two of these men are Pete McDonough, 'the fountainhead of corruption,' and Jake Ehrlich, a lawyer who has been beaten repeatedly by District Attorney Brady in efforts by Ehrlich to free criminals.

"Ehrlich's latest contest with Brady was the notorious Krupa narcotics case in which Gene Krupa, a swing band leader, used an underage boy to hide narcotics when federal agents were searching for the drug. Brady convicted Krupa and sent him to prison despite the fact that the chief witness had decamped and, when caught, testified that a representative of Ehrlich had given him money."

Jake read that one again. "To think," he sighed, "that I starved as a young lawyer because I was *not* McDonough's boy!"

Brady's campaign coupled the names of Ehrlich and McDonough. One paid advertisement demanded: WHO'S AGAINST DISTRICT ATTORNEY BRADY? The answer, in equally black type, was PETE McDONOUGH AND JAKE EHRLICH, CRIMINAL LAWYER FOR THE TENDERLOIN, AND THEIR OBEDIENT CANDIDATE.

Ehrlich picked up the challenge. He went before the Democratic Central Committee and outlined an aggressive program to Bartley Crum, the noted attorney who then was chairman. He took three months off from the practice of law and personally carried on the fight.

There were two immediate results. Jake's friend Lurie, who previously had paid for Brady's advertising billboards, told the district attorney that he would have to make his peace with Ehrlich or forget about Lurie backing. Brady bought his own billboards. Jake went to Paul C. Smith, then executive editor of the *Chronicle* and later president of Crowell-Collier, and persuaded him to give his paper's recommendation to Brown.

Jake also made blood-and-thunder political speeches, carrying a loudspeaker in his automobile and haranguing groups wherever he saw them. He cornered people in bars and on the streets. He rang doorbells.

Brady on the radio was thundering: "Up and down the streets of San Francisco a certain criminal lawyer, Jake Ehrlich, walks announcing that, because I dared to take him before the Grand Jury and ask that he be indicted on evidence which I presented, it would cost me my election."

Almost forgotten was Brown, the opposition candidate who had built his profession, as Jake had, by working days and studying nights. Ehrlich contended that Brown was better qualified than Brady. The papers didn't argue back. They were running Brady against Jake.

The outcome, therefore, was astonishing. Brown the unknown defeated Brady by nearly ten thousand votes. The political institution of a quarter century was shattered by an earthquake he had started himself in the case of Gene Krupa.

4

On February 15, 1944, three months after the elections, Ehrlich went into juvenile court with John Pateakos, now an Army private, with a suit for "perpetuation of testimony." Pateakos now repudiated every story he had told. "I lied," he declared.

The prosecution, expecting to send Krupa on to San Quentin, was taken by surprise. Assistant District Attorney Alden Ames angrily insisted that Judge Theresa Meikle warn Pateakos he could be prosecuted for perjury. The boy nevertheless insisted that his testimony had been false, that Krupa had never asked him to get marijuana from his room. All the drummer had said was: "Johnny, I want you to do something for me."

"I was sure I knew what he wanted me to do and I wanted to help," Pateakos confessed. "So I did it." The narcotics agents, he swore, "told me what to say. They said it would go easier with me if I did." The repudiation went into the official record three months before the District Court of Appeals considered Krupa's appeal.

On May 31, the day a troop-carrying Liberty ship foundered on the Farallon Islands and spewed a thousand men into the tumbling surf, the District Court handed down its ruling. The Krupa story got greater play in the afternoon editions than the shipwreck, for the court by a 2-1 decision upheld Ehrlich's contention that Krupa was being held in double jeopardy.

"The court," said the decision, "by accepting the plea of the defendant to the [misdemeanor] . . . barred a conviction for the felony crime because they are the same act. . . . It is true that the effect of this . . . is that the defendant escapes punishment for the more serious offense . . . [but] it was within the discretion of the law enforcement authorities to prosecute the defendant for either the felony or the misdemeanor. . . . When the state accepts a plea of guilty for the offense which carries the lighter sentence, it is without right thereafter to prosecute for the offense which carries the heavier penalty."

Gene Krupa had to be set free.

State Attorney General Robert Kenny asked the Supreme Court to review the Krupa appeal but it declined. Krupa by then was long gone, happily drumming to greater crowds than ever with the Tommy Dorsey band.

Pat Brown, the new district attorney, was launched on a successful political career; subsequently he became California's State Attorney General and through years of Republican administrations was the only Democrat in an important office.

One day San Franciscans turned out reverently for the funeral of Matthew Brady. "He might have held office to the day of his death," Jake said softly, "if that kid with the drums hadn't started things jumping all around us."

IV

THE CITY EXAMINES MORALS

Including Sally Rand

IT IS characteristic of big American cities that after the still small Puritan voices inside them have sounded long enough they rise up in righteousness and plump overwhelmingly for reform. When that happens, criminal lawyers become very, very busy.

Such a reform movement hit San Francisco in the midforties. In quick succession Jake Ehrlich was asked to represent: a jolly, balding bigamist laughingly dubbed the "Dingdong Daddy of the D Car Line"; a motion picture in which Jane Russell cuddled Billy the Kid in a strawstack; and a West Pointer strangely sworn to destroy anyone who might harm his pretty little wife and who weirdly carried out his vow after he had murdered her himself.

None of these matters might have got more than passing notice if the principals had let well enough alone. For instance, Jane Russell's movie, *The Outlaw,* came to San Francisco first in 1943 without creating much excitement. Then *The Outlaw* went elsewhere looking for patronage and found censors. Howard Huhges took it out of circulation for three years while the squawks of indignation against it built into howls. The picture basically was no tornado.

Neither was Francis Van Wie who, at forty-eight, became a delayed-action Casanova. A jolly chap five feet two inches

189

tall, built like a billiard ball and almost as bald as one,
Francis, tired of pounding a gong on the municipal railway,
settled his silver-rimmed spectacles on his nose and went
looking for women to marry. He acquired twelve wives and
was courting number thirteen in Los Angeles when the law
caught up with him.

Van Wie was such an improbable Romeo that Stanton
Delaplane, a whimsical *Chronicle* columnist, labeled him the
Ding-dong Daddy and hit the public on the funnybone. Delaplane had won a Pulitzer Prize for his coverage of a Chamber
of Commerce publicity stunt in which it was suggested that
several Southern Oregon and Northern California communi-
ties break their existing ties and form the forty-ninth state of
Jefferson. Tongue in cheek, he set out to make Van Wie a
lovable, Santa Clausy little rover and he succeeded.

Bigamy of course was a felony in California and twelve
wives was hardly a laughable number. But overnight, in the
public fancy, Van Wie became a new-found Rip Van Winkle
with goat glands.

Van Wie's case came up for discussion among the Who's
Who gathered around Louis Lurie's famous luncheon table
at Jack's: Ben Swig, owner of the Fairmont Hotel and other
high-class real estate; Bill Kyne, operator of Bay Meadows
race track; George Lewis, a trader in pedigree diamonds; Edward Cahill, city utilities manager; James B. Howell, mayor
of manored Atherton; and Joseph Blumenfeld, owner of a
theatre chain. A blade like Van Wie, they decided, deserved
the finest money could buy. They made up a purse.

Lurie summoned Ehrlich. The millionaire had one of Delaplane's columns before him and was chuckling. "Any man
brave enough to marry twelve women deserves help, Jake,"
he said. "Will you take the case?"

"He needs a defense all right," said Ehrlich.

The next morning, Sunday, he and Delaplane motored to

San Jose to meet the train returning Van Wie. "We've got to see your jolly little man before the crowd gets him at the station," Ehrlich explained.

The *Examiner* had added to the merriment by bringing wives seven and nine to board the train. Both lit into the jug-sized Romeo with tooth and tongue. Inspector Jerry Desmond had to spirit his prisoner to a compartment where Ehrlich found additional counsel in the person of James M. Toner, newly retired chief assistant public defender. Someone else had engaged Toner for the defense.

"I'm ready to face the music," Van Wie stated to both lawyers. He said he did not believe in divorce and had never got one.

At the police station he was ordered to empty his pockets on the desk for checking. He laid out a key chain, $49 in cash, lucky dice and a toothbrush. "For my false teeth," he explained. A little white box held "headache pills." "You'll need 'em," the sergeant predicted. A press agent elbowed in to hand Van Wie thirteen passes to a local movie in which Judy Garland was singing "The Trolley Song." It was all very gay.

"I couldn't help it," Van Wie told the reporters between poses straight ahead and to the left and right for the mugging camera. "My head was split open by an axe when I was a child." He touched a scar on the smooth bald skin. "I was kicked by a mule once when I worked in a mine. Another time I fell off a two-story building I was roofing. Yes, and I fell sixty-five feet from a smokestack I was painting. I couldn't help it, any of it. I even got beat up in an argument over the fare, when I was a conductor." Somehow it sounded funny the way he said it.

"There's one way to handle this," Ehrlich told Toner. "Go into court the first thing Monday morning, waive preliminary examination, plead him guilty and get it through the Superior

Court in a hurry. That way, we might get him off with a county jail term while everyone's so happy."

Toner took it up with Van Wie. "The county jail!" he cried. "But I couldn't help this!" He refused to consider a guilty plea.

Ehrlich thereupon withdrew as counsel and went back to report to Lurie and his friends. "I saw it this way," Jake said. "On Monday morning everyone is still laughing heartily. They are all agreed this is a very funny predicament the little man has gotten into. No one would be vengeful—yet. But when he starts to fight and it begins to drag, we would come again to Saturday. On that day every rabbi would go into his pulpit in the synagogue and demand: 'Why are people laughing at the sacred vows of matrimony?' And on Sunday every priest and minister would cry from his pulpit: 'What's suddenly so humorous about marriage?' By the following Monday, when Van Wie faces a court or a jury, there would be nothing funny about it. They would throw the book at him."

That is precisely what they did. Superior Judge Herbert Kaufman sternly declared: "The Ding-dong Daddy of the D Car Line has reached the end of his line." He sentenced him to San Quentin Prison, from which Van Wie wrote Jake plaintively: "I should have taken your advice. I didn't know people lost their sense of humor so fast." When he got out he continued his marrying ways and reached wife number sixteen before the law caught up again. By then the war was over.

It ended for San Francisco in a V-J Day bacchanalia that just about knocked the city off its pilings, starting prematurely at 11:00 P.M. on August 13, when Tokyo Radio revealed that the Japs were quitting. A blonde climbed a statue at Mason and Market, performed a striptease and remained there for hours, completely nude. A sailor and girl scaled a fire escape seven stories up on the face of a store building and set up light housekeeping on the illuminated sign. Crowds swarmed over streetcars, fire engines and taxis. Bars closed abruptly by agreement with police; the mobs smashed liquor store windows and helped themselves. They started fires in garbage cans, turned over flower stands. All available police officers were called to duty, all leaves canceled. The frenzied celebration roared on.

President Truman's official announcement came at 4:00 P.M. on August 14, but only a handful actually heard it. Chinatown, by then, was sold out of firecrackers. Railroad flares flashed along Market Street. A young lady ran naked into a pool at Civic Center. From 4:00 P.M. to 4:00 A.M., an all-time record 185 fire alarms and 1,250 police calls were rung in. Three hundred revelers were treated at hospitals. The commandant of the 12th Naval District broadcast a cancellation of all shore leaves. When the orgy finally burned itself out damage claims against the city totaled $166,262. Six women had been raped. Licentiousness had had its day.

2

Into this atmosphere galloped *The Outlaw,* clanking noisily in its little reel cans. Particularly Reel Seven. This is the point in the film where the sheriff has shot Billy the Kid in the thigh and he has taken refuge in a barn. Miss Jane Russell finds him there and sets out to nestle him back to health. She is dressed lightly but snugly for the occasion.

Ehrlich had watched the scene at the 1943 premiere without observing any great palpitation on the part of the audience. As a matter of fact, the picture did only a respectable box-office business on that first go-round, and Howard Hughes, who had $2,000,000 invested in it, called on Russell Birdwell, the Hollywood press agent and long-time Ehrlich friend. "Stir up some interest," he commanded.

Birdwell did, concentrating on Reel Seven. He plastered walls, billboards and magazine pages with the lush likeness of Jane Russell in her low-necked frock. It wasn't long before the powerful Legion of Decency issued its seal of disapproval. "The film presents glorification of crime and immoral actions," trumpeted the Legion. "Throughout a very considerable portion of its length it is indecent in costuming."

Other censors joined the chorus, demanding that Reel Seven be cut. Hughes replied: "I am going to fight this battle to the finish and make sure the public sees my picture as I made it." He withdrew it from public showing for three years while Birdwell continued with his promotional duties.

Perhaps the most important of them was to excite public curiosity about Miss Russell, a sulky-looking unknown who until recently had been a receptionist in a doctor's office. By the time Birdwell completed his work there was not a hamlet in America which had not gawked at her Junoesque proportions in still life. Birdwell reported to Hughes that the public now would be eager to see her movie.

Early in April, 1946, Ehrlich got a call from Jerry Giesler saying that *The Outlaw* would make its reappearance in San Francisco as a test showing for the entire country. If it got by there, other censors probably would pass it; but Giesler had information that the San Francisco police were going to close the movie as soon as it opened. Their objection: Reel Seven, which was uncut and unchanged. If the police cracked down on it, Ehrlich told Giesler, it would be the first time San Francisco had ever closed what was technically a first-run movie. He promised to watch and be ready to go into court. Then he strolled down to the Hall of Justice where he learned that the police indeed had been receiving "a flood of advance protests from church and school leaders."

Ehrlich suspected the fine promotional hand of Birdwell but he advised Chief Dullea: "Let the picture alone. If you don't raise a fuss, it will run a week maybe, gross $10,000, and be gone. If you fight it, it will win in court and play to full houses. It's not indecent, Charlie," he insisted. "I saw it the first time. It's the identical film that ran here in 1943, and you didn't touch it then."

The picture opened on the morning of the twenty-third at the United Artists downtown. Two juvenile detail officers sat in and, during the last show of the day, arrested the theatre manager for violation of Section 471 of the Police Code, exhibiting a motion picture "offensive to decency and the moral senses." Ehrlich was ready. When the trial opened on May 15, 1946, he pleaded *The Outlaw* innocent.

The trial opened to the sniffing of blue-nosed puritanism, as everyone knew it would. Judge Twain Michelsen, presiding judge of the municipal court, assigned the case to himself. He was a tough little man with sharp features which resembled the sculpturing of his cousin Gutzon Borglum on the granite hills of North Dakota. He hewed strictly to the form of the law. Once he had issued contempt citations for an entire twenty-man committee of the Chamber of Commerce for criticizing his handling of traffic violations. Ehrlich was delighted to have him as judge. Jake wanted a strict legalist on the trial, since the decision would have national importance as the movie opened in other cities.

He asked for a jury trial so that the decision, when it came, would be the verdict of twelve respectable American jurors, but he didn't intend to have lay opinion kill a $2,000,000 investment. Most of the panel probably would have read the outspoken charges against *The Outlaw,* some would have had a word of admonishment from preacher or priest. Ehrlich intended to slant the case over the jurors' heads to the legal mind of Judge Michelsen.

The first jurors in the box were women. Ehrlich questioned them in his most ministerial manner, the starched cuffs and

pocket handkerchief testifying to his personal purity, hands
clasped clerically to display the cuff links (gold tablets carrying the Ten Commandments in platinum Aramaic symbols).

"If," he asked the first elderly woman, "you came out of
the theatre the same pure woman who went in, you would
find the defendant not guilty, wouldn't you?" She answered
with an emphatic "Yes!" and stayed in the box, as did eleven
others who admitted that they could not be corrupted by
a mere movie.

The prosecution was depending on the film itself, especially
Reel Seven, to convince the jury that *The Outlaw* was "offensive to decency and the moral senses." They made a great
to-do in the courtroom about the female anatomy shown by
the low-cut blouse. Ehrlich had expected that. He brought in
one exhibit—an enlarged photo, six feet square, of the da
Vinci "Madonna and Child," displaying the same approxi-
mate anatomy to which the police had objected.

"Does this work of art, which hangs in the Vatican in
Rome, offend your decency and moral senses?" he demanded.
"Does it—an inanimate painting of a part of the female body
—make you lust? Certainly not!" He knew from the jury's
smiles that he had scored.

On the final morning of the trial the entire court assembled
on Golden Gate Avenue, where movie distributors' offices are
located. There, in a private projection room, Ehrlich ran
through the full film of *The Outlaw*.

Prosecutors wanted to emphasize parts, to give a slow motion repeat of Reel Seven, but Ehrlich argued that that was
not the way an audience viewed it. The judge sustained him.
The jury looked and went thoughtfully back to court. With
the showing of the film, both prosecution and defense rested
and Jake took up his argument and the burden of his case.

The movie, he argued, was educational, depicting people
and customs of pioneer days. He spoke of public morals gen-

erally and American intelligence specifically. He cited the law's tolerance regarding such stage presentations as *Frankie and Johnnie, Mrs. Warren's Profession, Lysistrata* and *Rain,* and court rulings on *Ulysses* and *God's Little Acre,* all of which had been designated as decent.

"Decency," Ehrlich argued, "is a matter of time, place and conditions. Speaking as a family man, I can find no fault with the screen fare in *The Outlaw,* except that it didn't kill enough Indians." The jurors laughed.

"If this is a matter of the nature and form of the star Jane Russell," he continued, "then let my good friends in the police department go down to the opera when it opens here and arrest 95 per cent of the women present, for they will all be wearing low-cut gowns." The jurors laughed again and Jake paused, staring at his enlargement of the da Vinci painting.

"In order to find this defendant guilty, and this movie objectionable, you must be sensually, sensuously and even sexually excited by it," he said. "You must determine whether this picture causes you to become a bad woman or a bad man, instead of the good, moral, upright woman or upright man you are now."

Jake skimmed over the controversial scene in Reel Seven. "The man was lying there in a cold chill with a bullet in his thigh. You would have to stretch your imagination a good deal to see anything immoral in that. I leave it to the tastes of the jurors, tastes that I am sure will find *The Outlaw* and *Billy the Kid* as clean as the driven sands of the New Mexico desert."

Then he turned directly to Judge Michelsen and asked for a directed verdict of acquittal. The judge took the motion under advisement until the next day.

He began his instructions to the jury the following morning without mention of the motion. Instead, he gave an extensive commentary on the law, with quotations covering a

score of similar cases. Finally, though, he veered to a criti-
cism of blue-nose attitudes. He called the new star Jane
Russell "a comely and attractive specimen of American
womanhood."

"There are some fanatical persons," Judge Michelsen said,
"who would object to seeing Miss Russell in a low-necked
dress, but we must consider that the plot of this show was
laid in the desert, which is hardly a place for woolens, high
necks and long sleeves. I must embrace the principle that life
is sordid and obscene only for those who find it so." The judge
concluded that the case did not correctly fall under Section
471 of the Police Code as charged, and directed the jurors
to bring in a verdict of not guilty, which they did.

In thanking them, Judge Michelsen did one final thing to
delight Ehrlich's press-agent pal: he urged everyone in the
courtroom to see *The Outlaw*. The publicity attending the
trial accomplished what a million-dollar campaign and a
world premiere had failed to do. *The Outlaw* reopened at the
United Artists and two other San Francisco theatres simultaneously. It averaged $70,000 a week at *each* theatre in its
first three weeks, played for nearly a year to close to a million
paid admissions, and went on about the country to make
another fortune for Hughes. Everywhere it went, it had the
testimonial of Ehrlich's homespun jury: not guilty of anything but good entertainment.

3

San Francisco, thereupon, settled back until June, when
Sally Rand came to town with her familiar attractions and the
papers recalled her classic homily: "I haven't been out of
work since the day I took off my pants." Six policemen were
on hand to witness her first performance, done as usual in a

"costume" consisting of one coat of talcum powder, one strategically located patch which the officers swore afterward they couldn't see, one war surplus balloon, a smile and the beam from a spotlight described technically as number thirty-seven, or midnight blue.

The blue light dimmed appreciably before Sally came out from behind the balloon, but the officers shouldered into the dusk and handed her a citation for violation of Section 311 of the Police Code of the City and County of San Francisco— for indecent exposure, corrupting the morals of those viewing the act, and conducting an obscene show.

Sally protested that the folks had only seen what by now was as familiar as the Venus de Milo, but the paddy wagon was waiting, news cameras were flashing, and she obviously didn't have any pockets to put the citation in. She dressed and came along, after a call to her old friend and counselor, Jake Ehrlich.

This, after all, was not exactly a new experience for the ex-Kansas farm girl who had been born Helen Gould Beck. She had started as a milliner's model, had been a chorus girl and a cigarette girl in a cabaret where she first noticed how men looked at her; had then danced in a Gus Edwards revue, become a Hollywood Wampus Baby Star (in 1927), and had even been called "an elegant picture actress" by Cecil B. DeMille. One day Sally had caught a full-length glimpse of herself after her bath, had grabbed a stage name from a Rand-McNally map, had taken off her clothes and gone to work.

In the depression year of 1933 Sally got her big break. Chicago had poured $38,000,000 into "A Century of Progress" to stimulate business. It stimulated nothing of the sort; people simply didn't cotton to modern architecture, dioramas illustrating the growth of industry or scale models of old Fort Dearborn.

They did perk up, though, when they hit the midway and

saw the "City of Paris" with Sally Rand. Some authorities say
Sally's skin saved the neck of the Chicago Fair. Overnight
she was a celebrity addressing such learned groups as the
Junior Chamber of Commerce and even classes at Harvard.

"My technique," she explained, with a candor Ehrlich
loved, "is to manipulate the fans so the audience will think
they are seeing things they are not."

In 1939 she had come to San Francisco to install a "Nude
Ranch" on Treasure Island and brighten the Golden Gate
International Exposition. Then she had made a triumphant
return to Hollywood to collect $20,000 for her fan dance in
Bolero. She was needing an attorney more frequently and
Jake was her man.

When he got the call on her arrest at Club Savoy, he
looked over his notes from *The Outlaw*, sighed, and went before Judge Daniel Shoemaker, a fine-looking young jurist, to
plead her not guilty. Sally was almost smothered in a bouquet
of roses provided by a group of naval officers. This encouraged Jake to speak out.

"How times have changed in San Francisco!" he said.
"What has happened to the Paris of the West? Let's either
stop being hypocrites or else hang out a sign at the city limits
saying, 'Don't come to San Francisco!' "

The blonde Miss Rand, smartly tailored under her roses,
was beaming at the judge and he at her, so Jake continued:
"Nudity is not new. The great Greek sculptor Praxiteles made
use of it for his heroic figures. Rodin's masterpieces are ex-
hibited before the public the world over. I can take any person here and show him more nudity among the classics than
he ever saw before."

The judge didn't interrupt.

"Sally Rand's dance is a rhythmic composition. It is done
to Beethoven's *Moonlight Sonata* and a Brahms waltz. Her
dance is a version of ballet."

The prosecution broke in to suggest that Sally Rand's performance had been lewd enough to shock six policemen. Captain Joseph Walsh of Central Station said: "The boys told me all about it. She comes out fully clothed and gyrates around with a bubble. In the course of this her dress slips and one—er—the left—er—is exposed. Then she hikes the dress back up and starts to climb thirteen steps to a raised stage. As she climbs, the dress starts slipping again. By the time she gets to the top it's all the way down and she hasn't got a stitch on except a small, flesh-colored whaddayacallit—patch. And she hid that so we couldn't use it as evidence!"

Jake stormed back to reply: "A person may be undressed, even nude, and not be lewd. It took six big policemen to arrest this lady. Look at her, Your Honor! She doesn't look vicious to me. I say Sally Rand is not indecent. Her dance is immoral only in the minds of a lot of stuffed shirts who ought to go to the laundry.

"Sally has done her dance at theatres and clubs here and at world's fairs all over the country. In all the years I've known this little girl she never has done or said a thing obscene. I think it's an outrage! The police have no excuse except a willful and deliberate attempt to blackball San Francisco in the eyes of the United States! Why I could throw a handful of buckshot out that window and hit twenty-five fan dancers. I think policemen have a lot to do besides this!"

The judge roused himself to announce that he could best determine the nature of Miss Rand's show after he had seen it himself.

"Tomorrow morning?" Ehrlich suggested.

Judge Shoemaker said he would attend.

Ehrlich warned: "She's going to do the same dance tonight and if the police arrest her she and I will probably be back here tomorrow." He asked for and obtained a court order which would release Sally "forthwith" should the police arrest her.

Officers were scattered through the audience a few hours later. They watched grimly as Sally swayed behind her balloon and switched to the fans. Suddenly the blue beam turned to glaring white, and there stood Sally in a breath-catching finale—one white, knee-length French chemise over an 1880 whalebone corset with a placard that read: CENSORED! S.F.P.D. They arrested her anyway but released her when she produced her "forthwith" order from the judge.

Morning brought a scene never to be duplicated in the history of San Francisco courts. At 9:30 A.M. the court convened in a night club. Bailiffs and clerks were there, as were the prosecution, sundry attendants and the complaining officers. Down the street came Attorney Ehrlich and Judge Shoemaker, blinking in the sunshine. They were met at the door by enough newspaper personnel to cover a coronation. This was Sally's famous command performance.

Into the dim night club marched the party, groping for tables in the darkness. Ehrlich, the judge and Assistant District Attorney Frank Brown, brother of the district attorney, were ushered to the best ringside table. Court attachés and press filled all the other tables. The full orchestra took its place and the master of ceremonies opened the regular show. In due time Sally danced, using the same fans, war surplus balloon, talcum and midnight blue spotlight she always used. The applause at the end was deafening.

Back to the courtroom went the assemblage, waiting only for Sally to get into something uncomfortable. The judge took his bench and announced that he was striking out one charge altogether. "Anyone who could find anything lewd in the dance as she puts it on," he exclaimed, "must have a perverted idea of morals!" He pronounced her not guilty on the other charges.

4

Like *The Outlaw,* Sally continued to play nightly to such crowds that Ehrlich could only wonder at the strain protesting San Franciscans were putting on their delicate morals. For himself, he went home to a good book: Lin Yutang's *Importance of Living.*

He was faced with a matter that had disturbed him for eleven years: the strange case of Major Allan Boggs, a big, bluff, white-haired officer who had sworn: "I would kill any person who harmed a hair of my wife's head."

The case had flared briefly in the newspapers and then disappeared. One night Boggs had come home and had seen someone—he thought it was his wife—dash in fright from their bedroom. Someone else was clambering from the twin beds. The room was dark. Major Boggs heard only an outcry. He grabbed his gun and fired at the bed. Then he switched on the lights. The one who had fled from the room as if from an attacker, he saw, was her twelve-year-old son by a previous marriage, who had been asleep in the other twin bed. Boggs had killed his wife.

Ehrlich followed the case with fascination though he wasn't the defense counsel. Here, he thought, was the O. Henry twist he met so often: a man killing the thing he loved most, almost as if he had caused it to happen by saying it so often. Boggs had been sentenced to die, for there had been enough troubles between the man and wife to discredit his "mistake shooting" story, but the Governor had commuted the execution sentence to life imprisonment. Then, eleven years later, Boggs had sent for Ehrlich.

The major had developed cancer of the throat. He wanted one thing of Ehrlich: to get him transferred to "a free-world hospital" so he wouldn't die in prison. Jake tried. He went to

court with a medical record showing that, at most, Boggs
could live six months and pleaded that the doomed man be
permitted "outside hospitalization." The court denied the
plea.

Now Ehrlich had to explain to Boggs. But what do you
tell a man who has killed another human, a man who has paid
with eleven years of mental torture and now months of physical pain? What do you tell a once-proud Army officer who
must grate out his life as a common felon behind bars?

Do you tell him again that he has committed a grave
offense against society and must continue to pay? It would
take a very brave man to stand up under the news Ehrlich
carried.

Warden Clinton Duffy personally accompanied Jake inside
the walls. As kindly men will, they spoke gently of the
doomed man. The cell, as they approached, was still as
death itself. Boggs was on his cot, the covers pulled high
around him. They spoke and he didn't reply. They turned
back the blankets and there, in a great red smear, was the
answer to their quandary. Major Boggs had slashed his wrists
with a razor blade. As he had pledged, he had killed the man
who harmed his wife.

V

ALFRED LEONARD CLINE

Silent Client of the Crematoriums

In the spring of 1944, Mrs. Delora Krebs, elderly widow of a wealthy Chicago manufacturer, met and married Alfred Leonard Cline, a bland, bucolic sort of middle-aged man whose only addictions were to old ladies and travel.

Mrs. Krebs' relatives, mindful of the $250,000 fortune in her name, were not happy with the match and became less happy as months went by. Her canceled annuity checks began to show a weakening hand and when they tried to reach her by telephone Cline always answered. They finally asked a Chicago attorney to investigate. On November 29, 1945, Cline wired them from Portland, Oregon, that Delora had died.

The Chicago attorney already had an interesting lead: this was not Cline's first venture in matrimony or the first of his wives to die. All of Cline's wives had died. Some said there had been a dozen such ill-starred marriages; others said only eight. There was also a hint that the woman who had died in Portland was not Mrs. Krebs—reportedly deceased long before—and that Cline had picked up a poor pensioner in San Francisco to take her place on his books.

Cline, it seemed, had a habit of prescribing buttermilk as a simple home remedy for all ills, perhaps because buttermilk concealed the disagreeable taste of rat poison.

The Chicago attorney presented his grisly file to San Francisco police, who took Cline into custody on December 7, 1945. They discovered that they had in hand the most thoroughgoing enigma in California criminal history. If, as it appeared, Cline had gotten one body behind in his bookkeeping, the police would have to prove that for themselves and they would have to sift the evidence from the ashes of his several wives. Cline was a firm believer in cremation.

Police of a dozen states soon began to uncover clues that Cline was in the marry-for-murder trade on a nationwide scale. However, the only incriminating evidence they could produce was that he had affixed his name illegally to various of his wives' papers. That was merely forgery. Cline said: "Get Jake Ehrlich," and that was almost his final word on the matter. He turned to religious studies and refused to give his lawyer any assistance at all.

Ehrlich interviewed Cline in jail and came away nonplussed. "Here is the most fantastic client I have ever run into or read about," he confided to friends. "His is the strangest criminal mind I have ever encountered."

Alfred Leonard Cline didn't look like a murderer. He looked like a kindly, graying real estate-insurance broker. He was solemn, portly and introverted, and he had a reassuring manner that encouraged lonely widows to trust their affairs to him and to drink the buttermilk he prescribed for all their little ailments.

Though he qualified for hanging, the gas chamber, electric chair or firing squad, Cline never lost his composure. The Cline case was the only one in which Ehrlich used every skill he could muster to get his client *convicted*.

Cline drew up his curtain of silence the evening San Francisco inspectors caught up with him at his hotel. He didn't argue or protest when they said he was wanted for murder. He simply didn't reply. They found a little black book which contained the names of eighty women in eighteen states and diagrams of a house trailer he obviously owned. He wouldn't tell where it was. Neither would he tell how many wives he had had, or where they now reposed.

Thereupon began what probably was the most detailed inventory ever taken of American funeral homes. Ashes of four persons believed to be ex-Mrs. Clines were found in as many different states, but who could determine which was who?

Cline was the errant older son of a large Kansas family. He had married early in life, had a son and lost his first wife, presumably to natural causes, in Denver in 1929. Somehow his signature had got on some wrong lines and he had been confined for a year for embezzlement. Then he was free to travel and attend churches, meeting lonely old ladies with stocks, savings accounts or insurance—sometimes all three— and a desire to travel.

This was the point at which the Krebs family attorney had picked up the trail marked by urns of ashes. In 1939 Cline had persuaded Mrs. Laura Cummings, seventy-five, of Massachusetts, to take a trip to Seattle with him. There she had been hospitalized for food poisoning. Her relatives, discovering that she had changed her will to make Cline beneficiary to $60,000, had persuaded her to redraw the will and come home. Cline traveled on.

In 1931 he was in Reno with Mrs. Carrie May Porter, an elderly Santa Cruz woman who had signed some $20,000 in cash, securities and jewelry to him. She died suddenly—Cline said it appeared to be a heart attack—and he sent the body to California for cremation. When Reno police asked for an autopsy, the crematorium informed them they were too late.

Less than a year later Cline was traveling with the Reverend Ernest Jones, an English evangelist. At Paso Robles Jones made Cline heir to $11,000, and the next day at Bakersfield Jones died.

In 1933 Cline was married to a Mrs. Bessie Van Sickle,

who had a brother Lucias McCreery. One day McCreery complained of the vapors and Cline poured him a glass of the home remedy. "Buttermilk," he declared, "is good for everything."

McCreery drank and died, leaving Cline beneficiary to a $1,000 insurance policy. Bessie died soon after, leaving him $20,000 and the Los Angeles police got interested. They found that Cline had purchased rat poison a few days before each bereavement. Unable to penetrate his reticence and, worse, unable to find anything in the ashes, they had to turn him loose.

It was not until 1934 that a victim's strong constitution and the law of averages caught up with Cline. He poured a beaker of buttermilk for Martin Frame, a Los Angeles businessman, and Frame became violently ill. Cline tried to dose him with coffee, but Frame called a doctor and recovered. Police found poison in Cline's car and sent him to Folsom Prison for drugging and robbing. For nine years thereafter the buttermilk-drinking public was reasonably safe.

Cline came out in February, 1943, and wooed and won Mrs. Elizabeth Hunt Lewis, an elderly Oakland woman. Death came to her in a hotel room at Jacksonville, Florida. Cline ordered her body cremated and two years later still was cashing in on her estate.

The following February found him planning a quick trip with Mrs. Alice W. Carpenter, an Indiana widow, and in a few weeks he was back in Florida cleaning up her estate. Widows were coming a little fast and he was getting behind in his bookkeeping. After his arrest investigators found that Mrs. Carpenter died in Macon, Georgia, and apparently was cremated under the name of "Alma Willa Carter of San Francisco." Mrs. Carter's name was never entered on Cline's books.

No auditor could untangle the entries thereafter. A physician at Dallas, Texas, was called to attend an unconscious, dying woman in October, five months after Cline married Mrs. Krebs. But Cline gave the ill woman's name as Alice W. Carpenter. He had the body cremated and that, police surmised, was when "he got one body behind." Mrs. Krebs apparently had become the standin for the deceased Mrs. Carpenter, who was dead in Georgia. There had to be another "Mrs. Krebs" to keep the records straight.

Apparently Cline found this substitute in the fall of 1945, an old-age pensioner named Elizabeth Van Natta, a San Francisco woman with no money, no insurance and, most important, no relatives to miss her. She told neighbors she was going to Corona del Mar to manage an auto court owned by Cline and was seen by them no more. Authorities could guess that she was the "Mrs. Krebs Cline" who died in Portland.

The death certificates there said someone had died "of cerebral hemorrhage and hypertension." This probably was Cline's own diagnosis, and one for which he had prescribed buttermilk.

Cline's idea of a lawyer-client relationship was unique: do not burden your counsel with information. One day at the jail Ehrlich stepped out of Cline's cell to take a call and two officers sought to question the prisoner. "Hey, Jake!" he screamed. "They're trying to talk to me!" Beyond that, he uttered no sound.

2

By early January, after Cline had been in custody a month, the incriminating reports were coming from near and far, from police chiefs, district attorneys and homicide bureaus, as well as the FBI. It was obvious to Ehrlich that the greatest protection he could afford his client was to keep him in California. The way they were stirring ashes elsewhere, Cline, if he left the San Francisco jurisdiction, might well be tried and executed for murder.

So it was that Ehrlich made his first unusual move for a most unusual client. He went to the district attorney and pleaded with him to indict Cline with all the forgery charges he could generate.

"Put him on ice," Jake urged. "This case is liable to get bigger. Put Cline in Folsom, and maybe you can hook him on a murder complaint later." He realized as he said it that he did not sound very much like a successful trial lawyer.

District Attorney Brown was intrigued, for Cline apparently had forged the name of one of his wives to stock certificates and annuity checks while in San Francisco. The Krebs attorney agreed to come out from Chicago and offer his findings as evidence. On January 15, 1946, the Grand Jury indicted Cline on nine counts of forgery and one of grand theft, the latter involving the property of Mrs. Lewis, which he was liquidating when he was caught.

"It's like trying Hitler for petty theft," Ehrlich acknowledged, "but this Cline isn't like other criminals."

A few days later, it appeared that Ehrlich might be defending Cline on a murder charge after all. Cline's house trailer was found parked in a lot adjoining Central Emergency Hospital. In it were letters and the effects of the old pensioner, Elizabeth Van Natta. The district attorney began to vibrate.

Among Cline's conservative business suits police found women's hats, boxes of women's clothing, cosmetics, a woman's umbrella, a cheap landscape painting that Mrs. Van Natta's friends recognized, and various odds and ends of various homes. Confronted with these objects, Cline only stared stolidly and returned to his reading. His manner seemed to say: "You have some stuff. Do what you will with it."

Other reports were coming in over the teletype. Two Chicago dental experts declared ashes shipped in a cremation urn from Dallas, Texas, to Bloomington, Indiana, and supposed to be Mrs. Carpenter's, probably were not hers at all. They had recovered the artificial teeth of Mrs. Krebs.

Macon, Georgia, reported the ashes which had been stored there since February 21, 1944, were almost certainly those of Mrs. Carpenter. Cline, contentedly reading religious tracts in his cell, merely smiled when they brought him the news. He had a great deal of faith in ashes.

By this time the district attorney had fifteen inspectors on the case, one on a roving assignment to funeral parlors in most of the forty-eight states. He asked and got a special fund of $12,500 to check further on the tangled case and flew to Washington, D.C. to consult with the Department of Justice. Cline's silence was proving expensive to the City and County of San Francisco.

3

Ehrlich was fascinated by the man but in time the fascination palled. With the forgery trial scheduled for April 8, he knew only Cline's name and what the police could add. He warned Cline and pleaded with him. Finally he asked the court to call them both in.

"Your Honor," Ehrlich said, "everything my client has told me could be written on a grain of rice, if the grain was small enough." He asked to withdraw as counsel.

Cline was standing in a characteristic pose, head down and hands in his trouser pockets. "I am not going to agree to Mr. Ehrlich's withdrawal on a few minutes' notice," he said. "I have been very much in the dark about this matter myself."

The judge stared at this defendant with silver-rimmed spectacles and neatly parted gray hair. The court denied Ehrlich's petition. "Okay," said Jake, "I'll be on deck, but I

suspect I won't be in command." Cline smiled his bland smile
and turned back to his studies.

By April 8, the farflung investigations had turned up
enough "almost evidence" to indicate that Alfred Leonard
Cline had murdered a platoon of elderly women. There was
not enough real evidence, however, to convict him of a single
killing. San Francisco had to release him or go ahead with
the forgery trial, which it did that day.

Cline's aplomb was icy when the bailiffs brought him to the
courtroom. He was a man who faced one thing at a time,
and the thing at hand was nine counts of forgery plus one of
grand theft which even he could guess would be dismissed.
He knew better than the prosecutors what evidence they didn't
have. So he lolled back in his chair and listened.

Superior Judge Herbert C. Kaufman, later to move up to
the District Court of Appeals, could see how things were.
Ehrlich had before him only a box of Kleenex, for the gusty
April breezes had brought him a head full of sniffles.

Prosecutor Norman Elkington bulled forth in his opening
statement with a blunt declaration that Cline had been involved in the mystery deaths of at least four women. He described the defendant as "a criminal who blundered despite
his devious machinations, and left a trail of his own handwriting to prove again there is no such thing as a perfect
crime." Cline seemed lost in thought.

By contrast, Ehrlich offered only a fifty-word statement in
which he cautioned the jury against "getting cluttered up by
details not applicable to this case." He gestured futilely and
sat down beside his client.

Suddenly Cline passed him a sheet of paper. Ehrlich
palmed it as Elkington craned. Judge Kaufman leaned over
his bench to watch. If it was the break, Ehrlich decided, he
had better see it privately. He strode to a side door and into
the corridor and read: "Will you please get me four packages

of chewing gum, ten air mail stamps and a subscription to the *Christian Science Monitor?*"

It was that way throughout the strange trial, which occupied the Superior Court for two full weeks. Cline appeared to have relegated the whole matter to counsel while his own thoughts wandered off to some wild blue yonder. He did glance at the jury occasionally, Ehrlich noticed, and particularly at one mild-looking little man in the front row.

The press was intrigued with Cline's aloofness. Irv Kupcinet, columnist for the Chicago *Sun-Times,* informed his readers: "Reporters try without success to get a statement from Cline. Finally Jake confers with Cline in a corner. He comes back to tell us: 'All my client will say is that he does believe in love.' Ehrlich was doubtful even of that."

One day Jake ate a light lunch and strolled back to the judge's chambers to await the opening of the afternoon session. The door was flung open. Captain of Detectives Bernard MacDonald dashed in with a squad of officers. His face was livid. The captain pointed to the courtroom. "He's got a convict pal on the jury!"

Ehrlich almost trampled Judge Kaufman in the rush. There was an officer guarding the meek little man in the front row, the single juror who had interested Cline.

He was George Grissell, forty-four, a forger himself, an ex-convict wanted for bad checks in Oakland. Judge Kaufman was furious.

"Why," he demanded, "did you sign the affidavit stating that you had never been convicted of a crime?"

"Well," said the little man, "my eyesight is poor. I signed it without reading it."

He had, he admitted, been quite interested in the case. He and Cline had served together in Folsom in 1933.

"This is probably the first time this has ever happened in a

California court," the judge declared. He ordered Grissell hustled off to a cell and his place taken by the alternate juror.

Jake smiled. "What a spot for an appeal, if I were in an appealing position!"

The prosecution took no chances on that. It had brought up heavy artillery to make this forgery conviction a lasting one. Clark Sellers, perhaps the nation's top handwriting expert, was called. His testimony had helped convict Winnie Ruth Judd, the Arizona trunk murderess. He had also identified the Lindbergh kidnap notes as the work of Bruno Richard Hauptmann. He testified that all the documents entered as evidence in the Cline matter had been forged with signatures of the ladies involved "crudely fixed after the death." Ehrlich listened attentively but he didn't cross-examine. He dabbed his nose with Kleenex and waved Sellers off the stand. Cline seemed happy.

This was more than Prosecutor Elkington could bear. It was not in the Ehrlich tradition. "Am I doing something wrong?" he demanded of defense counsel. "For God's sake, Jake, are you trying to trick me?" Ehrlich smiled wanly.

By the tenth day of the trial he had become almost as unvocal as his defendant. That morning, suddenly, as Judge Kaufman mounted the bench, Cline rose, indicating that he wanted to confer privately in chambers. Two police inspectors rushed forward. "Your Honor," they said, "this man is dangerous. If you fear for your safety, we'll be right here at the door." Cline pushed past them. The judge, puzzled, nodded to the officers and went in with Cline, closing the door behind them.

They remained together for an hour and ten minutes. The inspectors listening at the keyhole could hear only the low buzz of voices. Prosecutor Elkington asked Ehrlich what the stunt was. Reporters crowded around. Jake swore he was as mystified as they. The door finally swung open and the judge and defendant returned, both solemn. Cline dropped heavily into his seat. The judge announced that he would divulge their conversation only after the jury had brought in its verdict.

Elkington wound up his case with an explanation of Cline's *modus operandi*. "They would register at a hotel or trailer court," he said. "The poor woman would become ill, and Cline would summon a doctor. He would meet the doctor at the door and explain his wife had a bad heart and it was against her religious beliefs to have a doctor. He would request a sedative, and usually the doctor would prescribe one. The next day she would be dead. Invariably death would be attributed to the bad heart he had told the doctor about. Then Cline would have the body cremated, with no post mortem, and would begin to benefit from the estate."

From time to time, Ehrlich objected to the assumed facts— he had to say *something*—arguing that it was forgery, not murder, the jury was to consider.

The prosecutor wound it all up with a finesse calculated to keep Cline in jail for the rest of his days. Ehrlich had no objection to that. He rose to deliver his own closing argument and made the best speech possible in view of his miserable cold and even more miserable lack of evidence.

The *Examiner* reported: "Jake soared to oratorial heights, exuding showmanship even when he disposed of his cleaning tissue . . . with a flourish in the waste basket." It wasn't much more than showmanship, as Elkington seemed suddenly to gather when the jury was filing out. "You let that man get convicted!" he charged. "You weren't even trying."

Ehrlich shrugged. "I guess I must have missed some points along the way," he said. He was sure he hadn't, though, when the jury came back in an hour and thirty minutes with a verdict of guilty. Jake whispered to Cline: "That's about the best

news any lawyer could have gotten for you." The defendant
nodded quietly.

He stood patiently beside Ehrlich as Judge Kaufman prepared to pass sentence. First, the judge said, he wished to explain what had happened in the conference between Cline and
himself. "Upon coming into my chambers," he said, "Cline
asked me if I would advise him to plead guilty. I told him it
was a matter only he and his attorney could decide. I did
advise him, however, that every man has to live with himself
and that his conscience could give him proper advice.

"He offered to plead guilty," the judge continued, "to all
the counts except one if the court would agree to let the sen-
tences run concurrently, rather than consecutively." At that,
Ehrlich's eyebrows went up to a respectful arch.

"Cline indicated to me that he felt the jury would find him
guilty and he expressed surprise over the amount of evidence
uncovered against him. He told me that he felt he had wasted
his life, that he realized that crime does not pay and that there
is no such thing as a perfect crime because all human beings
are imperfect; therefore they must of necessity commit imperfect crimes. He told me he wanted to spend the remaining
years of his life in the study of his religion."

The judge gazed down at the prisoner. "Have you anything
to say before judgment is pronounced?"

Cline glanced up. "Nothing," he said.

The judge's voice became stern. "In my judgment you are
a One Man Crime Incorporated. I do not think it possible
that you can ever take your place again as a member of our
society. The circumstances surrounding the commission of
these crimes indicate a pattern and course of conduct that is
most revolting and shocks the conscience of all decent people."

The sentence he imposed would have stunned a normal
man. It was the maximum possible on each of the nine forgery

counts, a staggering 126 years in prison. Cline nodded, as if that were fair enough, and sat down. Ehrlich made no motion of appeal.

4

Cline was fifty-three years old when they took him off to Folsom. Reports still were coming in on the women he had murdered and authorities still were hoping to pin a capital offense on him. But Cline had had a long and cooperative arrangement with death, and perhaps there is professional courtesy in such things. On August 4, 1948, in the third year of the 126 he was serving, death came and released him.

Did he prove that crime doesn't pay? Not Cline. In his own way he made it pay well. In fact, the Krebs estate paid the fee of the trial lawyer who got him convicted of forgery so that he wouldn't be executed for murder. And there was $5,500 left over to establish that Cline in death was a solvent man.

VI

LAVERNE BORELLI

"If Ever a Man Asked to Be Killed"

THROUGH eighteen long and trying years, LaVerne Borelli, a slim blonde woman of unassuming loyalty, worked, saved and bedded with Gene Borelli in the simple trust that a man and wife cleave one to another, forsaking all others. In the late spring of 1947, she was thirty-eight years of age, a childless housewife. Borelli was two years younger, a handsome man having his small fling on cash from his used-car lot. On the evening of May 8, LaVerne Borelli observed her husband making passionate love to a woman who had been a guest in their home. It was not the first time, but a loyal woman dies hard.

Mrs. Borelli turned in at a neighborhood cocktail lounge. There she remained for hours, forgetfully sipping Manhattans and the deadening medicine a doctor had prescribed for her nerves. In time, she felt only an odd, ethereal fuzziness. No hate, she would recall, no resentment, no jealousy, pity, or love. Just nothing.

At 1:15 A.M., still in a haze, she made her way home and to her bedroom. There, among her husband's clothes, her hand touched his loaded pistol. She had never handled it before. Clutching it now, she went down into the spare bedroom where Gene Borelli lay snoring, still in his shirt and underwear. She fired four shots into him. Then she swallowed

218

from a bottle labeled *Strychnine,* aimed the gun at her breast and fired some more.

This became the famous Borelli case, brought to Jake Ehrlich by her friends while LaVerne lay in a coma. It was the case that tripped the Ehrlich legend and that, some would claim, "Jake lost." This was the one in which his whole detailed defense blew up in his hands at mid-trial—"the sickest feeling a lawyer can experience"—the one in which finally he had to play it through, feeling he had lost.

In this case, disregarding the jury in the box, Jake had to concoct a legal maneuver so revolutionary that it never had been tried before.

LaVerne Borelli killed her cheating spouse at a moment in San Francisco history when someone had to pay the penalty for a guilty woman who didn't. Shortly before the Borelli case broke, the lovely, talented wife of a prominent doctor suspected that his young nurse was taking him from her. The doctor's wife had met the girl at the hospital door and shot her dead. The doctor had killed himself. The jury, in an outburst of compassion, had let the doctor's wife off with manslaughter, then seemingly gasped at its own leniency. The city had gasped with it. No succeeding jury could be so merciful.

When Mrs. Borelli shot her husband, wise observers all said she would have to pay, mitigating though the circumstances had been.

Ehrlich went to the hospital to see her. Pity jogged him as he looked into the troubled blue eyes, still opiate-glazed, and studied the hollow cheeks and tight, twisted lips of a woman who lives long with sadness before she is moved to destroy the thing she has cherished. She couldn't talk. Jake could only drive one idea home: *I am Jake Ehrlich, your friend. Don't talk to anyone else.*

Ehrlich hoped to get a manslaughter verdict. To judge from

what her friends said, Gene Borelli had done more than make love to another woman in a car. He had brought his wife to the end of the road and told her he was dumping her off. She had taken her beating—physical, mental and spiritual—all mitigating factors, but not enough to justify a homicide. Jake patted her hand and hurried off to the coroner's inquest.

He learned there how strong the case was against him. A witness had been in the house when it happened: Borelli's young brother Joe. He had come home with Gene and heard it all. They had his full statement. "A little after one, La-Verne came in through the garage. She came upstairs and walked around a while and patted the dog" (Her pet Pomeranian, Mozzie).

Q—You were in bed, not asleep, and you heard her put the car away and come up the inside stairway?

A—Correct.

Q—What is the next thing you heard after you heard Mrs. Borelli walking around?

A—Next thing I heard was shots downstairs.

Q—How many shots?

A—Four or five. They came fast.

Q—Then what happened?

A—As I ran downstairs I heard my brother call my name.

Q—When you stepped into the downstairs room, what did you see?

A—Well, she had the gun. She was standing right on top of him. He was down. I tried to help him to get up.

Q—What did you do then?

A—I took the gun away and laid it to the side and tried to pick up my brother. Then I heard a couple of shots upstairs so I left my brother and went upstairs.

Q—What did you see?

A—LaVerne was standing by the bulletholes, in the door outside her room, holding the gun. So I took the gun away from her again and I called the police. While I was calling she got away from me. I was holding her and trying to phone. She passed out and dropped on the other side of the telephone.

Q—Did you notice she was shot at the time?

A—Yes, I could see the blood on her.

Inspector Tom Cahill had found a three-page note which conceivably could show a more coherent mind than Ehrlich pictured. It might also be used to demonstrate Mrs. Borelli's specific intent to take a life, which is the very basis of murder. The autopsy surgeon had found four shots, the fatal one entering the *back* of Borelli's right shoulder.

Obviously, the defense position was not good. The prosecution could cry: "Here is a woman who walked in, picked up a gun and shot a man while he slept!" They had one witness. The only other living person who had been on the scene, the defendant, couldn't remember. It might be possible to show that the dulling nerve medicine and Manhattans had deprived her of her mental ability, but that would be mitigating circumstance only. Weighing against it in the jury's mind would be the memory of the woman who didn't pay, Irene Mansfeldt.

2

This was a case, clearly, that demanded painstaking preparation. Jake dispatched a staff of investigators to locate every friend, relative and acquaintance of the Borellis', every tradesman, neighbor and mailman who might know about their daily life. He sent for the brother, knowing Joe Borelli's sympathies were with the prosecution. Joe was the key witness. But he came, as antagonistic witnesses invariably do. Ehrlich satisfied himself that Borelli knew little more than he had told police. He had been half asleep when the shooting started. Of course he defended his brother. Gene had been very considerate about things, he said, very considerate about the divorce. "You start it," Joe quoted Gene as saying, "and we will do it in a friendly way."

"Did LaVerne want that divorce?" demanded Jake.

"Well, no," the brother admitted.

Mrs. Borelli's friends said she had loved Gene desperately. His scornful demand for a divorce had nearly killed her, though she supposedly was the stronger of the two. Borelli was in bad financial shape—no insurance and no cash in the bank. The house was in her name. Immediately after his death, a finance company had repossessed all the cars on his lot. He had put $10,000 into a San Francisco franchise for the radical new Tucker automobile which didn't come out, and had signed a promissory note for another $20,000.

LaVerne was a saver. She had managed a fashionable Los Angeles beauty shop before she and Gene had moved to San Francisco. Now she would have to sell the house to finance her defense.

Newspaper clippings showed something else about Borelli, interesting, though only another mitigating factor. Two years before, he had discovered an OPA investigator about to trap him in an over-the-ceiling car deal. He had assaulted the man with his fists and paid a $100 fine.

A few months before the shooting, LaVerne had gone to great pains to prepare a birthday dinner for him and all the family. Borelli had shown up with two of his lady friends, at which she had protested: "How would you feel if I brought men into our home?" He had hurled a plate of spaghetti at her and the women stayed. Another time he had thrown a lamp at her.

Mrs. Sydney Halliday, a bookkeeper at the car lot and friend of Mrs. Borelli, had been with her on the afternoon of the shooting and again that evening. She said the nerve sedative had affected LaVerne's mind: she had gone shopping for meat although she had $1,500 worth of prime cuts in the freezer at home. LaVerne had been hit terribly by the sight of Gene and the other woman in the car. Mrs. Halliday recalled her words as she started home: "I feel like I'm up in the air and flying."

Jake nodded thoughtfully. That might help a little.

Ten days went by before Mrs. Borelli talked rationally, and even then her mind was foggy. An inherently gentle person, she was also inherently melancholy. The slow-cadenced voice indicated that she had spent considerable time in the south— Texas. She came of stable, divorce-hating people. Telling of her relations with Gene Borelli, she seemed mortified as if she had failed him. The incidents involving the other women, the night she followed and *saw him*, touched raw nerves. What did happen? She shook her head helplessly. "I can't even shoot a gun!"

Here was a woman who probably would break into quivering pieces when the full realization of her act reached her. Jake dreaded the breaking of LaVerne Borelli; it would be devastating.

Ehrlich believed she was "not conscious" when she committed the killing. The snag lay in interpretation of Section 26 of the Criminal Code and the definition of a "person who commits an act without being conscious thereof."

A few nights before, Jake had taken a potent sleeping pill and the next morning Marjorie had scolded him because she had had to crawl over him in the night to answer the telephone. He had not heard it.

Now *if* he had taken the pill so he wouldn't hear the phone, knowing it was going to ring, he of course *had an intent*. But he had taken it only to bring sleep, never expecting the call. How would Section 26 interpret that?

The dulled mental processes of LaVerne Borelli *should* be

valid defense. But what if the judge ruled that, according to that argument, anyone wishing to take a life need only gulp some pills and Manhattans beforehand? It was a real problem, and Ehrlich did something he had never done before. He pleaded LaVerne not guilty, and not guilty by reason of insanity.

He was facing it realistically. The judge in this case, Albert C. Wollenberg, would have been on the bench precisely two months when the trial opened. Wollenberg, though once a U. S. Attorney, had been in the Legislature for the past thirteen years. A just man and a scholar (he had been president of the College of Jewish Studies) Wollenberg would be hearing his first murder case. And a judge, Jake knew very well, needs trial experience too.

The dual plea provides for trial on the homicide charge first. If convicted, the defendant is tried again, by the same jury, to determine if he or she was legally sane at the time of the murder. There is one prescribed test for this: Did the defendant know the difference between right and wrong?

This rule, an inadequate one, was planted in the law before men understood much of psychiatry. It does not consider the other multiple evidences of an unsound mind.

There are other glaring disadvantages in the widely-used dual plea insanity law. Its clear implication is that a crime *has* been committed. Rarely do juries, having convicted the defendant of the crime, then release him on grounds of insanity.

"If they're going to give you a break," Ehrlich always reasoned, "they'll do it when they try the crime." In the Borelli case he was afraid he might need an escape hatch, though he hoped he wouldn't have to go to court with the insanity plea. He hoped to get Mrs. Borelli off the first time with manslaughter.

3

Judge Wollenberg, an alert and physically fit man, called the case on November 24, 1947. He was receiving congratulations that week for capturing a young thug who had strong-armed a woman in his apartment building. The judge had a habit of studying timepieces flashed in his presence, looking for a watch that had been stolen from him thirty years before in high school.

The prosecutor was Assistant District Attorney Alvin Weinberger, later to be a municipal judge, a good lawyer and meticulous grammarian who could prosecute vigorously but without venom. Weinberger, with his dark horn-rimmed glasses and precise banker's dress, was a sharp courtroom opponent, a swordsman rather than slugger.

Inwardly, Ehrlich was stewing when he strode into the packed courtroom with his usual flurry of starched cuffs (the links were gold chihuahua dogs, a gift from George and Anita Vanderbilt). Nodding to friends, he worked his way down to the front and found seats inside the railing for his daughter Dora Jane and her singer husband, Guy Cherney. Cherney had read of the case in New Orleans where he was singing and had flown home to watch his famous father-in-law in action. Privately, the family was worried that this one would take it out of Jake.

Jake appeared to be self-confident, however, smiling and placing a chair for LaVerne when the matrons brought her in. By contrast, she was tense and pale, not fully recovered from her illness and serious injury. She stood rigid, eyes averted, while the clerk read the indictment:

"That Frances LaVerne Borelli, on or about May 9, 1947, in the City and County of San Francisco, did willfully, unlawfully, feloniously and with malice aforethought murder one

Eugene Borelli, a human being, contrary to the form, force
and effect of the statute in such case made and provided for
and against the peace and dignity of the state of California."

Ehrlich went to work on his jury like a horse-race handi-
capper, checking each candidate against a chart that listed
occupation, associations, interests. He directed one question
at them all: Did they understand the difference between a
person who is *un*conscious and one who is *not* conscious? In
other words, did they understand that a person under the
influence of certain opiates might be able to walk, talk and
do various things, yet *not be conscious* of the acts? Six men
and six women stated that they understood, and the jury was
in the box.

Prosecutor Weinberger, in his opening statement, declared
this was a crime of first-degree murder, as he would prove.
Here is a woman, he said, *who took the law into her own
hands. When her husband told her he wanted a divorce, she
picked up a gun and shot him dead as he lay asleep and defenseless. The only defense she offers is that she doesn't remember doing it.*

As the case went on, he made much of the three-page note.
In it, with confounding clarity, she had directed the disposal
of her property and Borelli's. That, declared Weinberger, was
evidence that she had known when and how Borelli was to
die. Then he came on with Joe Borelli, his key witness, and
the brother's story was more damning than it had sounded at
the inquest. He declared now that he had heard LaVerne
threaten to kill Gene Borelli. (She whispered to Ehrlich that
she never had!)

Jake swarmed on him in cross-examination. "Did you ever
tell anyone before that you had heard such a threat?" Borelli
reddened, scowled and squirmed. "I don't remember."

"Uh-huh," snarled Ehrlich. "I didn't think you would."

Weinberger interrupted quietly. "I ask that counsel be confined to cross-examining the witness, and not making comments."

Ehrlich bristled. "The Bible says, '*The wicked fleeth when no man pursueth!*' This man is running and lying!"

He had to destroy Joe Borelli. "Isn't it true," he demanded, "that if you can help to prove Gene Borelli was murdered you will inherit his money? And isn't it true that, if this jury convicts LaVerne Borelli of manslaughter only, you will inherit nothing? You do have a reason for testifying for the prosecution, don't you?" Borelli's denials made little difference. The jury had something to raise reasonable doubts.

Ehrlich built his own defense on Borelli's mistreatment of LaVerne, hoping to indicate her state of mind. Mrs. Halliday told of the birthday party at which he threw the spaghetti plate. Jake nodded and moved to lead her through a recital of other violent acts. Weinberger cut in. "Are you trying to justify this homicide?"

"I am trying a lawsuit," Jake growled. "I think any man who wants to throw a woman out at the end of the road ought to be kicked around a bit." He paused before the box, testing the jurors. "But I'm not the judge."

Weinberger, the swordsman, lanced to the core of it. Ehrlich, he contended, was trying to go into things that had happened two years before. "I object to that as calling for expert testimony. She is two years older and we all change in two years."

"I don't know," Jake retorted. "Outside of getting a little grayer, I am still holding my own." No one laughed. He reframed a question relating to Mrs. Borelli's mistreatment and Weinberger objected again. "I submit that it is incompetent. We are not trying Gene Borelli. He is dead. Let's leave him buried." Judge Wollenberg, staring at a juror's wristwatch, sustained the prosecutor.

"Your Honor," Jake said, "this is an attempt to limit me

in my defense. For all Your Honor knows, or anybody else knows"—he hesitated—"nobody can say what my defense in this case is."

It was no go. Whenever Ehrlich approached the mitigating circumstances and, more vitally, the condition of Mrs. Borelli's mind, Weinberger objected and the judge sustained him. More and more frequently Jake found himself pausing, strolling to counsel table, nibbling his glasses, rephrasing questions and having them blocked. Finally he looked at the clock and asked for a recess. Guy and Dora Jane saw how it was going. There was worry in their eyes.

Ehrlich pushed impatiently through the hangers-on at the doorway. He was in trouble now. If he could not dwell on Mrs. Borelli's mental processes, what did he have? He paced the length of the hall. Then he went back and tried again, through Mrs. Halliday, to build directly on the day in the cocktail lounge when LaVerne Borelli's mind went into a fog. Judge Wollenberg halted him abruptly.

Jake argued angrily, blurting his version of the cocktails and sedative, getting it in essence before the jury. The judge waved him down. *She took the medicine and liquor voluntarily,* he ruled. *If this was allowed, then anyone could take some pills and justify a killing.*

Jake had to ask him to repeat; a street-repair pneumatic gun was firing below the window. The judge sent a bailiff down to quiet the street workers. Meanwhile, he repeated his ruling and ordered the argument stopped.

The rattling gun seemed to hammer in Ehrlich's mind one bludgeoning truth: HE HAS KNOCKED DOWN OUR VERY LAST HOPE. The noise persisted. Jake, who had maintained a smile all through the discourse, offered to go out and stop it. He did, and the cold air helped. He was almost physically sick.

Now he would have to go through with the insanity trial, though he hadn't one legitimate argument with which to prove LaVerne criminally insane. The explicit note indicated that she had had some idea of what she was doing. But he still had to finish this murder trial, even if he had to put Mrs. Borelli on the stand. Maybe some miracle—a good appearance by her, a slip by Weinberger—maybe the jury still could be sold on a manslaughter verdict. *With Irene Mansfeldt smiling in the background?* In his heart, Jake knew better.

He tried, of course. The record will show that Jake Ehrlich tried skillfully. He fenced masterfully with Weinberger, always with a confident smile, the mocking voice of right, the quick retort. He used every device he had learned in twenty-five years of courtroom dueling. He prospected a dozen avenues. He came closest with LaVerne on the witness stand when she told of following her husband and witnessing the love scene in the car. "And did that make you mad enough to kill?"

A—I would liked to have parked the car in back of my husband's place of business and waited until they returned, and ask this girl how she would feel if I was with her husband at that time. She has been in my home several times.

Q—I show you People's Exhibit Number Thirteen [Jake handed up the murder gun, and she asked to borrow his glasses to examine it.] Did you fire this gun at your husband on the night of May 9?

There wasn't a sound in the courtroom. Mrs. Borelli didn't wince. Nothing, apparently, could crack the dead cold composure that suddenly enveloped her. "No," she said.

Q—Do you recall shooting yourself?

A—No, sir.

Ehrlich glanced at the jury.

"At the time your husband told you to get a divorce, he

showed you a diamond ring which he told you he was giving
to another woman?"

"Yes."

Q—It wasn't you who wanted the divorce, was it?

A—No. I don't approve of divorces.

Q—Did you ever threaten to kill your husband?

A—No, sir.

Ehrlich turned, frowning, and paced the green carpet.
Weinberger was sitting patiently. The audience was quiet.
Jake took a deep breath.

Q—Mrs. Borelli, did you kill your husband?

A—No, sir.

Q—Were you in love with your husband?

A—I loved my husband more than anything in the world.

Q—And you didn't kill him, did you?

A—I did not.

Ehrlich rested. No mind in the courtroom had been
changed, and he knew it. Weinberger got up and argued dis-
passionately for a first-degree verdict, though not necessarily
the death penalty.

Jake, in turn, replied with all the heart-tugging fire he could
pour into one oration. He sat down exhausted, certain he was
beaten. His client, sensing it too perhaps and waiting only for
fulfillment of her death wish, listened impassively to the
judge's instructions. The jury filed out at noon and the matrons escorted her down the back hall and over the Bridge
of Sighs to her cell in the county jail.

Two hours went by and Jake knew the jurors were beyond
the manslaughter stage. Dora Jane squeezed his hand. "You
did the best you could, Daddy." He shook his head. "I can't
understand it—a sensitive woman and that stony composure!"
He strode out to pace the corridor. A bailiff hailed him.
"Jury's buzzing for something, Mr. Ehrlich."

Jake went back, tense. The jurors wanted the judge to reread the instruction on malice aforethought. Ehrlich studied their faces; they were keeping their eyes averted. Back they went for more deliberation and the hours dragged on. The afternoon was gone. They sent for a photo of the murder scene. Then for the suicide note. Ehrlich, sitting alone at counsel table, stared into the empty jury box and fretted. After nine hours and forty-one minutes the jurors came back.

Jake steeled his face and held the chair for LaVerne. Her hands were too dry. He whispered encouragement and she answered so quietly he barely heard. She was almost literally not breathing. *Here she goes,* he thought.

"Ladies and gentlemen of the jury, have you reached a verdict?"

"We have, Your Honor."

"You will hand it to the clerk."

Every eye in the courtroom followed the sheet of paper from the foreman to the clerk, who handed it up to the bench. "Mr. Clerk, you will read the verdict."

The clerk cleared his throat self-consciously. "We the jury find the defendant Frances LaVerne Borelli guilty . . . of murder in the first degree . . ." Jake felt her going. ". . . life imprisonment, with no possibility of parole. . . ." He spun and caught her as she toppled, still breathless, rigid as if in death.

Matrons and bailiffs hurriedly carried her to the judge's chambers, and brought smelling salts. Eventually her eyelids fluttered; they took her back to the courtroom. The clerk read the verdict again, for the law says the defendant must be present and know what is going on. *At the time of her punishment,* Jake thought bitterly, *though not at the time of the act.*

Judge Wollenberg instructed the jury to return at 10:00 A.M. December 11 for the sanity hearing. Ehrlich nodded grimly and headed for Cookie's and a drink. There he bought round after round, laughing and taunting the friends who tried to console him, while Dora Jane stared with disbelief. Finally she grabbed his arm. "Daddy! How can you? With that woman just convicted?" Jake gazed fondly on the daughter he had always said "would have made a great lawyer."

"Daughter," he said gruffly, "stop fretting. Your old Uncle Jake's not done yet."

That wasn't what they were saying around town, of course. They were saying that the Ehrlich legend of invincibility had been destroyed. One conviction of murder in the first degree had ended that.

But while Mrs. Borelli tossed, sleepless and dazed, under day-and-night suicide guard at the county jail, Jake locked himself in the big law library in his office and read until his eyes burned. He sampled here and there from the volumes banked against the wall, pondered and searched again. Finally a whole new concept began to take form on his yellow pad. It was revolutionary, but it seemed logical. It would, he knew, stop them cold.

Again the courtroom was crowded, though this time it resembled a meeting of the bar. Jake had promised fellow attorneys a surprise and they were watching skeptically. The testimony itself followed the usual sanity hearing lines, the usual doctor and psychiatrist opinions and counter opinions, but this time Ehrlich brought out every doleful fact of life in the Borelli household. He kept it reasonably interesting for the jury and he cross-examined the state's psychiatrist as if it really mattered. But most of his points were being hammered out on the bright brass rail directly below Judge Wollenberg.

The jury hung, 8-4. Weinberger immediately asked for a new panel to retry the sanity case. Jake got up, clasping a thick legal volume. He smiled.

"At this time, if Your Honor please, we will withdraw the plea of not guilty by reason of insanity. We hereby stand upon the conviction in the first phase of my client's trial."

The judge, studying a watch in the first row of the spectators, turned to Ehrlich as if he hadn't heard aright. Weinberger looked suspicious. Ehrlich flicked his gaze over the august assemblage of attorneys in the room and continued. "Under the dual plea in California, we have excluded the mental processes, and therefore the case is incomplete and a murder conviction cannot stand."

Comprehension and then respect crept into Al Weinberger's eye. It was like a man offering to buy a long-tailed hound from a kennel, permitting the kennel to dock the dog's tail, and then declaring: "I refuse the purchase because you no longer can sell me the long-tailed hound."

But Ehrlich wasn't through. Judge Wollenberg had heard all the mitigating factors now, thanks to the insanity trial. There was a new law on the books—Section 1181—which empowered a judge, if he felt that the jury verdict was too harsh, to reduce it for a fairer one. Jake moved, under Section 1181, to set aside the first-degree conviction of Mrs. Borelli and substitute a verdict of manslaughter. Judge Wollenberg continued the matter for a week.

In chambers, Weinberger admitted that the jury's severity had surprised him. "That Mansfeldt case did it," he said. "I expected a second-degree conviction at most. If ever a man asked to be killed, it was Borelli." He said he would abide by the judge's ruling.

No one expected the first-degree conviction to be set aside when Judge Wollenberg convened court on December 31. Reporters listened indifferently as he reviewed the two trials. "I have been required to exclude all evidence bearing on the defendant's mental condition," the judge was saying, "and therefore the case is incomplete before me for a murder conviction." He nodded to Ehrlich and the press row came to life. "The only evidence of deliberation is the note which was left by Mrs. Borelli before she attempted to kill herself. This is a suicide note and does not show intent to take another life. The jury itself indicated doubt on the question of malice aforethought."

The reporters were scribbling furiously. "I think the evidence shows the homicide was committed in a heat of passion," the judge said. Jake heard LaVerne Borelli draw a deep, slow breath. "It is therefore the judgment of the court that Mrs. Borelli is guilty of manslaughter."

It was almost New Year's Eve. The toot of horns and start of the gaiety carried in through the high old windows. LaVerne Borelli flung herself on Ehrlich and kissed him again and again.

"It was," one newspaper noted, "surprising and dramatic after a brilliant legal maneuver by Jake."

LaVerne Borelli was entered at Tehachapi Prison for Women on January 12, 1948, and served with good behavior until her parole on March 10, 1953. She wrote Ehrlich regularly and said that on her release she would go back to beauty parlor work. Judge Wollenberg continued to watch timepieces in his courtroom until one day he spotted the watch that had been stolen from him in high school. A struggling attorney had picked it up in a pawnshop.

On another New Year's Eve, much later, Ehrlich's wife decided to get a little gift for the girl who had been taking care of her hair for the past six months. She asked her her name, and the slim hairdresser smiled slowly. "My name was LaVerne Borelli, Mrs. Ehrlich. Your husband gave me the greatest New Year's gift I could ever have—my life."

VII

BILLIE HOLIDAY

A Little Opium and Some Big Blues

Leanore holiday was five feet eight and one-half inches tall, and heavy-bodied, with maroon eyes and a moanin' low voice that seemed to well up from a massive and classic case of heartache. Warbling "All of Me" in smoky cellar clubs, she uttered the universal lament of young, unclaimed womanhood. She was herself twenty-nine and unmarried. They called her Billie Holiday, the greatest blues singer in the world.

She had appeared at Carnegie Hall; she had sung with Artie Shaw, Benny Goodman and Count Basie. She flaunted a $10,000 full-length silver-blue mink, a $25,000 diamond-platinum wristwatch made for her at Tiffany's, and somewhere in the background a custom-built, royal blue Lincoln sedan with wine-colored upholstery.

When Billie Holiday arrived in San Francisco early in 1949 for an engagement at Café Society Uptown, she had two reputations, good and bad. Less than two years before, she had spent ten months in the federal reformatory at Alderson "taking the cure" for narcotic addiction. Billie said she was done with the junk after that, but there were people who didn't believe it. She felt their sharp eyes in every crowd she faced. And she still had a cause of much sorrow, a man.

John Levy, forty-one, was the *Lover Man* of whom she

crooned. He was a tall, balding brown man with a quiet, knowing smile. He was owner of the Ebony Club in Harlem, but he traveled with Billie and managed her affairs, principally the $200,000 a year people paid to hear her articulate love's woe.

> Take my arms—
> I'll never use them,
> Take my lips—
> I want to lose them.

Billie lived the lament, for John Levy's sweet talk included no marriage vows. They quarreled frequently, usually about her money, which she didn't want so much as she wanted him. On New Year's Eve they had had a real brawl in a Hollywood restaurant. Sometimes Billie felt that John Levy was trying to get rid of her. She was a big girl, and she carried a torch the size of the Statue of Liberty's.

They were in her suite at a midtown San Francisco hotel on the afternoon of Saturday, January 22, he in pajamas and she in a white satin nightgown, quarreling again about money, when a man called for John Levy on the house phone. A few minutes later there was a rap at the door. John handed Billie a small package and told her to flush it down the toilet.

Billie always tried to do what John told her to do, but as she turned toward the bathroom the hall door was flung open, four men darted in and, as she bent over the toilet bowl, one of them grabbed her. She was under arrest, they told her, for possession of opium.

Billie called for Jake Ehrlich.

On the surface, the Billie Holiday case was an impossible one since all of the cards were stacked against her—a once-confessed addict now accused by the ace investigator of the Federal Narcotics Bureau. Colonel George H. White, who said he had nabbed her with the goods in her hands, was a tough, experienced investigator with a reputation as a fair man and an honest cop.

Against this was the frightened protest of a big, scared girl and her manager who was not always true to her. To acquit her would require a defense so potent that it would shatter the sworn word of Colonel White, and a jury convinced somehow that Billie Holiday could be more truthful than the plain evidence against her. Failure of the defense would destroy her, financially, professionally and emotionally. Ehrlich calculated the odds at 100-1 against him, but he did believe Billie Holiday and he took the case.

Billie Holiday belonged to the half-light world most people never see. At sixteen, already physically mature, she had come out of the Baltimore Negro colony with a sob in her voice that had caught the ear of orchestra leader Red Norvo. Before she was out of her teens she was a headliner at the Hotcha Club in New York, on dancing terms with celebrities like Paul Muni, and on speaking terms with narcotics. A piano player in Harlem had named her "Lady Day."

It was as "Lady Day" that she made her San Francisco entrance, in the grand manner, brown turban, green wool suit, crepe shirt with Barrymore collar—all very expensive—pearl earrings, the Tiffany watch and the flowing mink. A great lady indeed, greeted by the most devoted and vocal set of fans in the city.

Billie poured out her blues in a joint in the heart of San Francisco's Negro district, a dark, smoky basement down a long flight of stairs from the street, without even a stage door for its stars. It was operated by a jowly Hungarian who had appeared in the Folies Bergère, once wrote some non-hit songs and frequently was found in bad company, including that of Mobster Mickey Cohen. Café Society was the kind of place frequented by whites and Negroes of all types, watched closely by city police and narcotics agents.

Although Colonel White was not a man to waste time, he soon became a steady client. The colonel had mixed into and broken up narcotics rings all over the world. He had served O.S.S. with cloak-and-dagger devotion during World War II, but had returned immediately afterward to his junkies.

In 1948, when dope was flooding West Coast ports, he came to San Francisco where he had been a reporter on the old *Bulletin*. He spent many hours at Café Society Uptown.

When Ehrlich got Billie's call that Saturday, he had just come from lunch with Louis Lurie and some of the city's bankers and clergy. One reverend father had mentioned Herb Caen's description of Billie Holiday: "She sings as though her shoes were too tight." "Don't most of us?" the priest had asked. Ehrlich summoned a bail bondsman and went to see the young lady with the "tight-shoe" voice.

She stood by the booking desk, wrapped in her mink, chain-smoking cigarettes and referring all questions to her manager. That gentleman was busy denying to reporters that he was also Billie's husband or that he soon intended to be. If any opium was found in the room, he said brusquely, it must have been "left there by another girl" who had visited Billie the day before.

"They just won't believe Billie has given it up," he said. "They keep trailing her wherever she goes. Billie took it with the needle, anyway. You know you never smoke it after that if you go back."

Colonel White kept judiciously beyond range of the blinking newspaper cameras and told the reporters just enough to carry the story. He had gone to the hotel shortly after noon with two other federal agents and one San Francisco plain-clothes officer—a point of which Ehrlich made note. White had telephoned the room and, when Billie answered, had intentionally mispronounced Levy's name. Levy had informed him that they were just getting up. He had rushed with his squad to the sixth floor suite, in time, he said, to see the nightie-clad singer duck into the bathroom. White had grabbed her as she smashed a dark bottle into the toilet bowl; he had got some of the liquid and mopped some off the floor. Then he had ordered Billie and Levy to dress and come to the station. The liquid recovered was being chemically analyzed. It undoubtedly was opium and White had fragments of the smashed bottle. He was signing a complaint against them both for possession of narcotics. Other details would have to wait for court.

Ehrlich quietly asked whether Colonel White had obtained a warrant before the raid, as federal officers are required to do. He had not. Instead, he had taken the San Francisco plainclothesman with him because a local officer may proceed warrantless "when he believes a felony has been committed."

The $500 bail was posted for each defendant. That night as usual Billie made her flashing entrance at Café Society. "She hugged the mike," the papers reported, "and went through her torrid, throaty songs as if nothing had happened at all."

On February 7 the Grand Jury listened to Colonel White's clipped report of the raid and his recital of Billie Holiday's past troubles. She was indicted for violation of Section 11500 of the Health and Safety Code. The charge against John Levy was dismissed without further discussion.

Jake guessed that the prosecution lacked sufficient evidence to convict both parties, though it appeared to him that if Levy and Billie Holiday were sharing a suite they must also be sharing its contents. She was to be the target. Word came through from New York that her cabaret entertainer's license had been lifted as a result of the San Francisco arrest. It followed too closely the Philadelphia trial which had sent her to Alderson. At that time, admitting her addiction, Billie had complained that because of her prominence dope peddlers charged her $100 for a "fix" that other addicts got for $5 or $10.

When he got his copy of the Grand Jury transcript Ehrlich gave particular attention to Colonel White's testimony, and then he virtually committed it to memory.

A—I knocked on the door and said I was the manager. In about fifteen seconds the door opened and I entered.

Q—Who opened the door?

A—John Levy.

Q—Did you know Levy at that time?

A—No, sir. I knew him by description and reputation, *but not by sight*. (Ehrlich underlined that in red.)

The Colonel related that when he first saw Billie Holiday she was listening at the door. "I told her I was a narcotics agent. She turned and ran toward the bathroom. I followed."

Q—Did you run, walk, or——

A—I ran. She threw herself down over the open toilet bowl, at the same time taking the object she had in her hand, a blackened bottle, and smashing it on the edge. She pulled the flush rod with her left hand. (White was explaining the evidence he had collected.) This represents an improvised opium pipe. It is what we retrieved from the floor of the bathroom. This is a small glass medicine bottle which has been made into an opium pipe and used for the purpose of smoking opium. This is an eye dropper which appears to contain traces of opium.

Q—Did you question Miss Holiday?

A—Aside from admitting her identity, she had nothing to say. Levy said to me: "What do you have on this girl?" I said, "We have possession of opium and an opium pipe." Levy said, "I can't believe it." He asked if he could speak to me alone. I asked the others to leave. Levy then asked me if it couldn't be fixed up and I asked what he meant. He said he meant to pay me some money. I said he couldn't fix it in that fashion. Levy then told me he was acquainted with narcotics agents in New York City and mentioned their names, and said he had cooperated with these agents by furnishing information on previous occasions in years gone by and said he would be able to telephone people and have them deliver a quantity of opium or heroin to San Francisco so I could apprehend them. I declined his offer to do that.

Ehrlich read the conversation, struck by the fact that Levy was escaping prosecution altogether. In all narcotics matters there has to be an informer; addicts simply don't run shouting to the Colonel Whites: "Look! I'm violating the law!"

Jake sent for Billie Holiday. "I'm scared!" she wailed, rolling the maroon eyes. "I never been so scared before!" She insisted she was off the stuff, and rolled up her sleeves to show him. There wasn't a puncture mark on her arms. Ehrlich nodded. Had she noticed Colonel White before the raid? "Every night," she said, "at a table with John Levy." Jake started. Had she ever considered that John Levy might be an informer? She threw up her arms in protest. "He's my man!"

Sure they fought, she said, but it was mostly about her money. Levy took it all. That was all right—"John could have all of me!" She did whatever he said, even when he handed her the package to throw in the toilet. She didn't ask why.

"He said, 'Here, darling, throw this away.' He called me darling and baby and other names." Jake nodded. He saw before him a big, trusting, emotionally immature child who would go to the end of the world for a man without asking a question.

Lawyers normally are reluctant to put defendants in narcotics cases on the witness stand. For one thing, a prosecutor may make them roll up their sleeves—with unpredictable results. Worse, though, is the fact that a narcotics addict lives with a sense of guilt. He or she assumes that the prosecution knows much more than it actually does. Conscience, goaded by skillful cross-examination, acts to destroy them.

However, if a defendant is innocent, the fact tends to come through to a jury. There was a basic honesty in Billie Holiday, Jake decided.

Money matters, he knew, can break up the most intimate partnerships. Suppose Billie Holiday had been framed by the man she loved. She said Levy had handed her the package after he knew someone was coming up. Who? According to Billie, Levy and Colonel White had spent many hours together. Levy had proposed one frameup as a bribe, according to White's own testimony. And White had sworn that he did not know Levy before the raid. There might be an opening there to crack the colonel's austere invincibility.

If Jake figured Levy right, he was the type of man who would leave a standing order to snap his picture with every important person who stopped at his table. Jake sent for Café Society's roving camera girl and ordered a print of every photograph that showed Levy.

The trial opened on May 31, a warm and sultry day in San Francisco. Coming up the basement elevator, Ehrlich heard spectators milling in the corridors. Judge Wollenberg, the scholarly man who had sat on the Borelli case and watched watches, was already on the bench waiting patiently. The prosecution was waiting too—Al Weinberger, the legal swordsman, also from the Borelli case. They were using the "first team" against Billie Holiday.

Ehrlich wore a pale gray suit against the long hot court day, and a necktie that was sky blue. (The cuff links were a gold hat and cane given him by Ted Lewis.) He nudged through the little swinging gate and dropped his hat on the counsel table, surprised to find his client looking somewhat unkempt in a beige suit. He slid his paper briefcase across the table, thanked the bailiff for his pitcher of water, and looked more closely at Billie. She was wearing red- and white-rimmed pixie glasses which did not wholly conceal the evidence of prolonged crying and one eye that was bruised and swollen. Her voice was low as she answered the questions of a woman reporter, and her gold earrings trembled.

"He done it Friday night. It looks better now than what it did. He went off Saturday night—even took my mink— eighteen grand worth of coat. Said he was goin' to give it to his sister to take care of." She looked up to Ehrlich and began to sob. "I got nothing now, and I'm scared."

Ehrlich let her pour it out while the indictment was being read and the first twelve jury candidates took their places. Then he went doggedly at selecting a jury that would believe her.

"Do you believe," he asked each juror, "that because Billie Holiday is of another race, though American and entitled to equal protection of our laws, she is more likely than another person to commit the offense charged?" He dismissed one woman for racial prejudice before he finally accepted a jury of six men and six women. Judge Wollenberg further admonished them: "Under the law you must have no reservations because Miss Holiday is of a different race."

Weinberger's opening statement was a clear and damning indictment. He did not invent a single point or seek to embellish the facts they all now knew about Billie Holiday. Ehrlich waived an opening statement for the defense, concentrating instead on the attack he intended to carry to Colonel White. The Colonel, as the chief witness, told a long, detailed and presumably factual story which he believed warranted conviction of Billie Holiday. If it stood, she was done. Weinberger got it all in the record clearly before he turned, quietly, and told Jake he could have the witness.

Ehrlich began it quietly.

Q—Mr. White, you are in a position with the United States?

A—Yes.

Q—And you are not a police officer in the City and County of San Francisco?

A—No.

Q—Is it your habit and custom to make arrests for the purpose of turning the case over to the state authorities?

"To which we object," said Weinberger. He, too, recognized the direction Ehrlich was taking. The judge sustained him. The issue was not whether Colonel White had employed a San Francisco policeman to expedite the arrest, but whether the defendant was in possession of narcotics when found. Ehrlich listened politely and rephrased his question.

Q—Have you followed the practice of making arrests as a federal agent and turning them over to the state authorities?

"To which we object," declared Weinberger. "The question is incompetent, irrelevant and immaterial." The jury was beginning to get the idea though the judge upheld the objection.

"Did you have a search warrant when you walked in?" persisted Ehrlich. He knew White didn't and he knew the objection, which came immediately, would be sustained. White, however, was beginning to appear not so scrupulously fair as he liked to seem.

Q—How long have you known John Levy?

A—Since January 22, 1949.

Jake didn't change expression. "Did you know him at any other time?"

A—No.

Q—Were you and he friends?

A—No.

Q—Did you and he visit together?

Colonel White was watching the attorney closely. "At what time are you referring to?"

Q—At any time.

The witness frowned. "Subsequent to his arrest I had several conversations with him."

Ehrlich didn't hesitate. He was directly in front of the Colonel. "About what?"

Weinberger objected and was sustained. Ehrlich paused.

Q—Isn't it a fact that, as the result of what Levy told you, you entered the hotel on this particular date?

A—No, it is not a fact!

Q—Isn't it a fact that Levy is the man that got in touch with you and gave you this information and as a result of that you went to this hotel?

Ehrlich's tone implied that he knew something. It was the first overt suggestion of a frameup. He turned grimly and glanced over the audience, waiting.

A—That is not correct.

Q—Well, isn't it a fact that you dismissed the charge against Levy?

"If the court please!" Weinberger objected. Judge Wollenberg ruled the question out.

Q—Let's put it this way (Ehrlich's tone was sarcastic): isn't it a fact that you were in court when the case against Levy was dismissed?

"Mr. Levy is not on trial," snapped Weinberger. Again the judge upheld him.

Ehrlich stood before the rail, angrily buttoning his double-breasted coat, and offered to put into evidence the complaint Colonel White first signed which, he said, led to the arrest of *both* Levy and Miss Holiday. "Both were arrested," he growled, turning accusingly on Colonel White, "but only Billie Holiday is indicted."

He strode to his table. He seized the Grand Jury transcript and brandished it over his head. "Here is a man who swears upon his oath that John Levy and Billie Holiday committed a crime, to wit: that they possessed opium. Now we are in open court and his testimony is not that these two people at this place, on this date, at this time, possessed opium! He says in effect that Levy did not possess opium, but Billie Holiday did!"

The judge was shaking his head. Objection sustained.

"You say you visited with Mr. Levy after the arrest," Ehrlich snapped at the witness. "What did you talk about?"

Weinberger objected that it would be hearsay. "Sustained," droned the judge. Ehrlich unbuttoned his coat with angry movements. He began to search through his cardboard briefcase. The jury was hearing a lot of pointed questions; it was not getting to hear any answers. Finally Jake turned, holding a large glossy photograph. He moved brusquely on Colonel White. "Now I will show you a photograph and ask you whether it is a photograph of you and John Levy."

One of the jurors stretched to look. Colonel White reached for the photograph. Weinberger was on his feet. "I object to it as incompetent, irrelevant and immaterial. It could be a photograph of President Truman and the witness and it still wouldn't be admissible in this case."

Ehrlich and the Colonel were bending over the photo together. There was a chuckle and the judge warned: "Let's not have a conversation between you and the witness."

Ehrlich gazed blandly at the bench. "It so happens this time I am not guilty, Your Honor. I didn't say anything; the witness spoke to me. He merely said that it was not a good picture of him."

The jury laughed and Jake's smile broadened. Weinberger, also smiling wryly, might thereupon have been wiser to ignore the photo. Judge Wollenberg admonished the audience against further demonstrations.

"Does Your Honor want to see this?" Jake asked politely. Judge Wollenberg glanced at the photo and snapped: "It isn't a good picture." Ehrlich used the opening to argue that the witness could be permitted at least to identify himself in the photograph.

"*If* he is in it," corrected Weinberger.

"He's in it!" Ehrlich assured the prosecutor. He handed the photo to White, who nodded and pointed. Jake demanded: "Is the man sitting with you John Levy?"

Weinberger prevented an answer to the question and Ehrlich, sauntering to his table, flipped the photo down. It had served him well. He turned then to attack Colonel White on the whole version of the raid at Billie Holiday's.

"Now isn't it a fact," he demanded, "that you walked in and turned to the left and opened that door?" Here was the outright accusation that the raiders had known in advance where the opium would be planted. White denied it vehemently.

Ehrlich flung the question back at him in a tone that dripped with incredulity.

"I did exactly what I just testified to," White snapped.

Ehrlich pelted the witness with inquiries bluntly phrased to show that every move in the raid had been made with foreknowledge obtained from a well-placed informer. The Colonel could only deny and glare at his tormentor.

"Oh," said Ehrlich, scornfully backing away, "I know you are holy and righteous and never make a mistake."

Weinberger leaped to his feet to demand that counsel be admonished.

"Now, counsel," began Judge Wollenberg.

Ehrlich raised his hands in a gesture of innocence. His voice slowed to a drawl. "I am not going to offend the witness. Mr. White and I have known each other for many years." The judge leaned back and Jake snapped at White: "Isn't it a fact that you walked straight in, whether you showed him your badge or not, and you went immediately to that door?"

Weinberger's angry objection showed he was feeling the blows to his key witness. Ehrlich merely glared at him and addressed the Colonel, his voice biting.

Q—You knew Mr. Levy by reputation?

A—Yes.

Q—And you knew by reputation that he was an informer, *didn't* you?

The question and answer of course were stricken.

Q—And what was the occasion of your knowing him, by *reputation?*

This time Ehrlich balked when Weinberger objected. In the end Judge Wollenberg allowed the question. Colonel White answered, slowly, "I first heard of Levy while I was working in New York in about 1941."

Again Weinberger argued: "We are not trying Mr. Levy."

Ehrlich, who had been putting on his horn-rimmed glasses, snatched them from his face. "Yes," he stormed, "I wish he was here, and we *would* be trying him!" The idea of a frameup was well planted. He didn't even look when Judge Wollenberg sustained the prosecutor. He demanded instead to know more of White's claim that Levy had tried to bribe him. It was time to deliver the coup.

Q—Did you accept the bribe?

A—No.

Q—Did you arrest him for offering you a bribe?

A—No.

Q—Did you ever charge him with offering you a bribe?

A—No.

Ehrlich gazed at the jury. He shook his head with disbelief and turned back to the witness.

Q—Isn't it a fact that you and Levy went into that room and discussed what you wanted Levy to say to Miss Holiday, and you called her in and had him say it to her? Isn't that a fact?

The witness said "No" but Ehrlich didn't heed it.

Q—*Isn't* it a fact that you knew, or that Levy told you, that he was trying to get rid of Billie Holiday because he had promised to marry her?

For the first time in an hour, the courtroom's eyes turned to the singer, quietly crying into her handkerchief.

Q—Didn't he tell you in that conversation he was trying to get rid of Billie Holiday?

The Colonel's response was: "At no time." Ehrlich muffled it with his next question.

Q—Mr. Levy is in New York right now?

A—I don't know.

Jake hesitated.

Q—You know he is not here.

A—I don't know.

Witness White came off the stand a tired, solemn man. Not once had Ehrlich addressed him as "Colonel." Not once had he allowed him a favorable question. Now Jake turned his back on the investigator and gently comforted Billie Holiday. He waved off the last prosecution witness—a chemist who testified that opium was found—without a word of cross-examination. Ehrlich's attitude said plainly that it was no longer important.

Still in her shabby suit, still with her earrings trembling, Billie Holiday took the stand. Ehrlich led her gently back to her humble origins. She had completed only the fifth grade in school because her father, a guitar player, had died of pneumonia when a Dallas hospital refused to admit him, a Negro. She had waited on table in her mother's restaurant, singing for tips when she was only fourteen.

She told of her successes, of the big-name bands that had headlined her and how, after the ten months at Alderson, she had come back to Carnegie Hall and the reviews had hurrahed that "the enchanting voice has again come to life."

"I been in trouble before!" Billie blurted to the jury. "Two years ago, it was. I volunteered for the narcotics cure. It wasn't for opium. But I ain't had no drugs since. I came home and society took me back. Thank God for allowing me this second chance!" On a direct question she declared: "I never *smoked* opium in my life! I don't know those things!"

Ehrlich showed her the photograph he had tried to use with Colonel White. Weinberger was on his feet immediately to object. Jake waited for the storm to quiet and then declared: "I want to show by this photograph, sir, that the man who has tried to bribe Mr. White is visiting with him——" Jake adjusted his glasses and tapped the face of the photo—"sitting and drinking. Apparently, at least—there are glasses there." Judge Wollenberg upheld the prosecution. Ehrlich turned back to Billie.

Q—Do you know Mr. White?

A—Yes. I have seen him in Café Society every night.

Q—And who was he with every night?

A—John Levy.

Jake, hands locked before him, turned to be sure the jury got that. Then he took Billie through her trip from Los Angeles with Levy, continually pleading for an accounting of her annual earnings of $200,000.

"We had been arguing for a couple of months," she said. "I ask him where was the money and what was I making and why didn't he give me some money and what was happening with my money." The argument was still in progress when the raiding party struck, she said, and John Levy was mad at her. Weinberger objected to the whole line of questioning, declaring money was not an issue. Judge Wollenberg sustained.

"Suppose we argued about ten dollars?" insisted Jake. "That wouldn't be important? I remember the days when I was struggling and $10 was a lot of money. I think it just and fair that she be allowed to tell us the amount of money that that man took away from her in a year." The jury, he hoped, felt the same desire for elucidation.

Q—Now you and Mr. Levy were to get married?

A—Yes, we were. We were sweethearts and I turned my whole life over to him. He took every penny I made. He was supposed to marry me. He bought everything, done everything for me. I never handled any money and I can prove it. We were supposed to get married and we didn't and that is why the argument came up that morning.

Q—While you were arguing, did Mr. Levy receive a call?

A—Yes, there was a phone call that came and I answered the phone and it asked for Mr. Levy and it sounded funny to me because it didn't say "Levy." It said it different. And I said: "John, it's for you."

Q—Then what happened?

A—John and I were in my room, room 602. He walked into room 601, his room, and he called me just as the knock came on the door and he handed me a package and said: "Billie, darling, throw this in the toilet." So I just took the package. I went to the bathroom. Somebody grabbed me. A man grabbed me from the back and threw me against the wall and I dropped it. It all happened so quickly.

Q—Why didn't you say anything?

A—What could I say? Everything happened so fast. I didn't expect anything like that. What could I say? And after all I was arguing with John about my money and he takes care of my whole life. What could I say? I didn't know what was goin' on.

Q—Isn't it a fact that Mr. Levy left San Francisco the day before this trial and went to New York?

Weinberger objected, but Billie answered before the ruling could be given. "Yes, he lef' me."

Weinberger was furious. "Let's have a ruling! It is obvious

what counsel is doing. He is making speeches. He isn't interested in the answers!"

Ehrlich turned belligerently. "I want the truth! *I* am only interested in the truth." He turned to Billie again. "Have you used any drug within the past two years?"

Again her response—a firm "No!"—came before Weinberger could get his objection in. "She isn't charged with being a user," he cried. "The charge is possession."

Ehrlich smiled. "You introduced evidence yesterday about how it is used! If it is fair for one side, it is fair for the other. Take the witness."

Weinberger, at that moment, might still have won his case. He chose to quibble with the defendant as to who stood where in the room and to correct the record that she had gone *voluntarily* to Alderson. He made it clear she had gone *after* a narcotics arrest.

Jake was sitting with his chin in his hand, elbow braced on the table, eyes closed. Suddenly he heard Weinberger start a new line of questioning and he leaned back, staring blandly at the ceiling.

Q—How long have you known Mr. Levy?

A—I have been with John for over a year.

Q—Had he been acting more or less as your business manager?

Jake's gaze jerked to the witness. She seemed to be rising from within herself, eyes glowing. *"He's my man!"*

Judge, jury, the entire courtroom erupted with spontaneous laughter. Then Weinberger proceeded to step into the other bucket.

"He has been your man?"

"Yes!"

They still were chuckling, still smiling at the big, simple, dark girl on the witness stand.

Q—You handed the phone to him.

"Why yes!" she blurted. "I never did anything without John telling me!"

Weinberger, intent on the facts of the case, was not watching the jurors. He didn't feel the new undercurrent in the room.

Q—I will ask it again. Was it your intention to throw an object as large as this——

A—I didn't notice how large it was! If your wife asked you to throw something away, would you notice how large it was? You would throw it away, wouldn't you?

Peals of laughter rolled up to the bench. Judge Wollenberg spoke with difficulty. "It is going to be necessary to clear the courtroom if we have any more noise." He regarded the prosecutor with strangely gleaming eyes. "Incidentally, Mr. Weinberger, I notice your wife is in the courtroom listening to you." The laughter burst out again. The prosecutor plodded on.

Q—Were you running from John's room after he handed you the package?

A—How could I run? There is no place to run.

Weinberger scowled. "You didn't ask the officer why you were being arrested?"

A—I did not ask nobody nothing. Listen, I was so mad and so frightened with John when this happened. I was so shocked I couldn't say nothing. Listen, I worked for a whole year and John had taken every dime of my money and we were fighting about my money and when these people come and knocked on the door I didn' know what was happening!

The closing arguments were superfluous. The jurors filed out and the attorneys strolled into the judge's chambers. Judge Wollenberg, who had sustained virtually every prosecution objection during the trial, spoke warmly to Ehrlich. "That was one of the most eloquent and logical cross-examinations of the witness White that I have ever heard in a courtroom. It will acquit Billie Holiday."

The jury was out for two and a half hours. Billie, at Ehrlich's suggestion, changed to a neat apple-green suit. She was still scared, still ready to cry as the foreman reported the verdict: "Not guilty!"

Billie impulsively grabbed Ehrlich's hand in both of hers and covered it with kisses. "I don' know why I'm cryin'," she gasped, "but I kept so much inside me so long, and I been so scared."

Ehrlich left her momentarily with her fans. The jury foreman was talking to the press. They had taken two ballots, he revealed, the first 9-3 for acquittal. The second was unanimous for Billie Holiday. "The jury," he said, "believed the defense contention that she was framed."

Jake turned, smiling, in time to hear Billie Holiday vow to reporters: "John Levy? If he was to walk into this room this minute, I'd melt!"

VIII

GERTRUDE MORRIS

The Woman Who Wanted to be Executed

ON APRIL 10, 1951, the day President Truman fired General MacArthur as Supreme Commander in the Far East, headlines trumpeted that every thoughtful American would be shocked by the event. They weren't quite right. Some people had personal woes that day and didn't even notice the firing. For example, on that day one man and wife in San Francisco were embroiled in the sorriest misunderstanding of their lives. It flared, oddly enough, right there in the Hearst Building on Market Street where the angry presses were thundering out the MacArthur news.

Milton Morris, whose offices were on an upper floor, was a busy man who had just begun to harvest the rewards of diligent work. He was a pleasant little chap, forty-seven, ambitious and alert, an enjoyable after-dinner speaker. In twenty years he had greatly improved his lot. Starting as a clerk in an insurance office, he had become an executive of the Associated Home Builders, and only a week before he had testified before a Congressional committee studying the problems of small business.

His wife Gertrude was forty-four, with streaks of gray beginning to get handholds in her dark hair. But probably she paid little heed to that; inside was where she felt the change. Her childhood had been spent in an orphanage, and it wasn't

until she met Milton Morris that she had known real love—
love and emotional security, vague things, but the substance of
her quiet existence. She had been married twenty-one years
and she was a lonely little person who had made few friends
because she needed only Milton. His friends considered her
odd, subject to spells of self-pity and anxiety. There were no
children.

Probably Gertrude Morris had brooded in the neat cloisters
of her home for some time before she began to unravel. She
fancied her husband was reserving his deeper affections for
his pretty young secretary, Miss Goolo. On the day the President was firing his top general she went to Milton's office and,
in Miss Goolo's presence, poured out all her bitter complaint.
Mr. Morris was shocked and embarrassed.

Hurriedly, he shooed the secretary out to lunch and told
Gertrude she simply could not bring these matters to the
office. More hurt than she had been before, she left. Brood-
ing, she took a streetcar out to the fashionable Lakeside district where they lived. She knew her marriage was doomed.
She knew, too, that she could not face another day if she
didn't have Milton.

She dug out the letters he had written, particularly those
of the war years when he was in Washington and she was selling Victory bonds at a bank. She wept over them as the
afternoon wore on. She got a long-barreled pistol from her
drawer to do away with herself. It had been her brother's gun,
her only brother, who had died in a Navy war plane.

Milton arrived about dinner time. There was no dinner, of
course. He began to pack his things. Her sobbing did not
divert him from his methodical preparation. Perhaps there
had been too many tears, too many moods, too much clinging
and suspecting. He turned from her at last with an armful of
shirts. His empty drawer stood open with a collar button rolling forlornly. She fired the pistol once at his back and he

stumbled, groaning: "Get a doctor." But she couldn't. She was terribly, retchingly sick.

It must have been two in the morning before she recovered her senses enough to change her soiled suit, stagger to a neighbor's and ring the bell. "Will you call the police, please?" she whimpered and stumbled back to her home to be sick again. By then Milton Morris was dead.

There might have been a basis of defense in that—the distraught mind, the heat of passion. But Gertrude Morris, the mousy housewife, was to break under the agony of her act and become a madwoman. Not legally insane, mind you; just obsessed with arranging her own death in the lethal gas chamber. This became the "weirdest murder case" in San Francisco court history, and certainly it was full of paradoxes, with a state alienist helping both prosecution and defense with the same testimony and Ehrlich forced to prove that his star witness was lying. Ehrlich would remember this defense vividly. It almost killed him.

It was unbelievable that Gertrude Morris would destroy a life she had worked so hard to build. For nine years after their marriage, she had remained on a secretarial job to put Milton through night law school. She had helped him start the little collection agency that led to a position of prominence in the building field. No one suspected that she had a gun. But apparently no one really knew Gertrude Morris. The uncle who called Jake—her only living relative—was stunned. "I can't do a thing with her! She refuses to talk to me!"

"That is understandable," Jake assured him. "As a general rule in murder cases there is a sort of guilt complex or shock that lasts for ten days or two weeks."

But this was to be a different kind of case. When Jake went to see his new client she informed him: "Everything will be all right because I will be executed." He thought that was part of the hysteria and that soon she would welcome a friend.

But she didn't. Mrs. Morris went on a hunger strike and had to be fed forcibly to keep her alive for the trial. She tried to slash her wrists. She stabbed herself with metal knitting needles. Finally she refused to see her attorney or even discuss a legal defense.

Ehrlich went searching for threads of the story while waiting for the derangement to pass, as he believed it would. Up to lunch time on the day of the shooting, he learned, she apparently hadn't even been thinking of death. It was just a month before her twenty-first wedding anniversary and she was downtown shopping. She bought a suit at the City of Paris and a hat at Magnin's. Something had triggered her.

The homicide report said that she had shot Morris "after a violent argument over alleged attentions to his secretary . . . as he was packing to leave." But the secretary denied that there had been an office romance. She told reporter Bernie Averbuch: "I can think of no reason . . . why Mrs. Morris would think that Mr. Morris and I were involved. He would give me a ride home occasionally, dropping me at the door. He seemed like a solid family man."

At first, Ehrlich was puzzled by that eight-hour lapse between the shooting and Mrs. Morris' appearance at the neighbor's to seek help. Psychiatry had an answer: the shock of her act had thrown her into a sort of trance. She seemed to bear that out, though unwillingly, in the one rational interview he was to have with her. It was a week after the murder, in her cell. Jake filled a long yellow legal tablet with her rambling statements. He suggested that there might have been a sudden explosion inside her that had caused the fatal shot. She guessed that was right. Ehrlich instructed her to remember it.

At her arraignment she made an unsteady appearance. The matrons had dressed her in a neat wine-colored suit and pale blue blouse, but her hair was disheveled and her eyes were swollen. The judge asked how she wished to plead and Jake had to answer for her, "Not guilty." She seemed beyond the power of speech, even when the judge gently told her that she would have to respond for herself. She finally mumured "Yes" and witnesses in the hushed courtroom wondered if she knew what was going on. "There is no doubt in my mind," Jake told reporters, "that she doesn't comprehend the enormity of her act."

"Why don't you let her die if she wants to?" they asked.

"Because it is my duty to protect her!" he said. He admitted that she had ordered him out of her cell. "Anyone who doesn't want to see me in a beef like this can't be right."

Thereupon Mrs. Morris wrote to the judge and stated that she wished to waive trial and have the court impose sentence. She wanted to be convicted of murder in the first degree. The headlines said: SHE HOPES SHE WILL BE EXECUTED.

Reporters had heard her: "I'm a criminal! I murdered someone! I owe society a life!" That of itself doomed an insanity plea. Gertrude Morris was demonstrating by her own words that she knew the difference between right and wrong.

Demented she was, now, but what was her condition at the time of the slaying? If her mental processes could be shown— if Jake could somehow reverse the plea to read *not guilty by reason of insanity, and therefore not guilty*—he might build a good defense. There was one thing the law did say: a defendant must be competent to defend herself and aid her counsel. He looked in on Mrs. Morris, alternately crying for execution and working jigsaw puzzles. Competent?

Ehrlich made his move, a surprising one, in an affidavit claiming that Gertrude Morris was mentally incapable of standing trial. It was supported by competent alienists. If the district attorney wished to contest it he would have to go to court and prove that she *was* mentally competent. The insanity hearing would have to come first and it would give the defense the opportunity of cross-examining all alienists before a jury. Jake could lay several foundations for a subsequent trial. He would be able to get the whole story of Mrs. Morris' queer behavior into the record and into the newspapers where prospective jurors would read it. Ehrlich wondered why other lawyers hadn't tried this before.

The sanity hearing was held in November before a jury of six men and six women. Mrs. Morris sat through it almost somnolently, bundled in a camel's hair coat, staring at the floor and tearing her handkerchief while Ehrlich interrogated five alienists—two for the defense and three for the state—about normalcy, abnormalcy and subnormalcy. Repeatedly he demanded: "But, Doctor, how do you account for her current condition?" It brought rich response, particularly from the state's experts. Jake was laying broad foundations.

The psychiatrists had studied her background: She was born of an Italian father and a Jewish mother and placed in the orphanage where, she remembered, she was punished often, her hair pulled and face slapped for having candy out of hours. Once, ashamed of orange-colored shoes, she had buried them. As punishment she had been forced to dig them up and wear them. There were two years of high school and two of secretarial school before she met Morris.

"She was determined," one doctor said, "that no other woman should have him and that she would kill him rather than see him devote himself to another. She would make that impossible by death. Now she wants to die because the only person who made life worthwhile is dead."

Once Mrs. Morris perked up when Ehrlich said she heard voices and asked a psychiatrist: "Doctor, you don't hear voices, do you?" The expert smiled. "Sometimes." Mrs. Morris turned to the press seats and pointed at Ehrlich. "Isn't he funny?"

A principal state witness was Dr. Walter Rapaport, California Director of Mental Health and a long-time friend of

Ehrlich's. A sturdy, smiling man with crisply curling brown hair and bright brown eyes, he looked more like a college wrestling coach than an alienist. He had testified in many Ehrlich cases, always for the prosecution, and he came to court with an armful of scientific volumes to support his opinions.

"I feel Mrs. Morris is competent to proceed with the trial," he declared, his gaze level on Jake. "Whether she cooperates with her attorney or not would be a matter of her choice. All we can say is that she does have the capacity to do so if she wishes."

Oddly enough, Ehrlich didn't debate the conclusion. Instead he quietly drew out the doctor for additional opinions. One important one that went into the record was that Mrs. Morris had killed out of love, not malice. When the jury decided 9-3 that Mrs. Morris was capable of standing trial, Ehrlich seemed neither surprised nor displeased.

She received the verdict with a flat, fixed smile. "I will be glad when I can plead guilty and get it over with," she told reporters. To Ehrlich, she sniffed: "If you're such a good lawyer, why can't you get me convicted?"

The strange murder trial of the strange little woman who wanted to die packed the Hall of Justice long before court convened on January 29, 1952. Many housewives slipped in from shopping to stare at the defendant.

Was she, as she appeared, the emotionally unbalanced woman who had been knocked reeling by her dreadful act? Or, as the prosecutor insinuated, was this another desperately clever defense from Ehrlich's crafty repertoire?

Jake jumped on the prosecution with a leather-lunged warning. "I don't want any trouble! I have enough trouble with my client sitting here laughing at me while I'm trying to impanel a jury!"

She did laugh occasionally, a hollow, low-voiced cackle.

Otherwise Mrs. Morris huddled listlessly in the chair beside
Ehrlich. She didn't even raise her eyes when he muttered to
the reporters: "All I can do is hope she will be cooperative."

The district attorney had pitted his deadliest prosecutor
against him, Norman Elkington, a young man who believed in
every letter of every law. He was not afraid of the Ehrlich
reputation, and he came out of his corner bristling.

Somehow they got a jury, nine women and three men. Then
Judge Neubarth announced for the prosecution that the death
penalty would not be asked and applause thundered from the
audience. Ehrlich snorted. There was a purpose in that: to
neutralize any plea the defense might make for mercy. It required a counterstroke, and Ehrlich delivered it forthwith. "I
repeat in open court," he told the jury, "what I have advised
Mrs. Morris: that, despite her desire to plead guilty, she is, in
my opinion, not guilty of first-degree murder. I am going to
put her on the stand, and the Lord only knows what will happen." There was a stir of anticipation in the audience.

Ehrlich promised several sensational days of testimony;
he mentioned a certain incident on a train which he hoped
Mr. Morris' secretary would explain. He neglected, however,
to announce that he would not call the girl; he did not want
to be bound by her testimony. He wanted her only on cross-
examination, and he hoped to raise so many doubts about her
alleged relations with Morris that the prosecution would have
to produce her.

Actually, most of the early Morris murder trial was built
on the promise of bigger things to follow. The prosecution
took only two hours' and thirty-five minutes to offer its case,
with Elkington sticking to the simple facts: Milton Morris had
been slain by his wife and she had confessed.

Mrs. Morris showed little interest. "Weren't you surprised,"
a reporter asked her, "when they announced they wouldn't
ask for the gas chamber?"

She blinked. "To tell you the truth, I wasn't paying much attention."

She appeared even less concerned with the first defense witnesses. She stared into space while a defense alienist described her as "a full-blown case of paranoiac schizophrenia— a woman whose whole life centered on her husband, and she was hurt frequently by his inattention." They might as well have been speaking of someone else.

Prosecutor Elkington had warned of Ehrlich tricks, but even he sat up startled when Jake called Dr. Rapaport for the defense. It had been Rapaport's expert testimony that had indicated she was sane enough to stand trial. The stocky doctor strode to the stand, pulled the bracket microphone in front of him, and settled his big books on his lap.

"Now, Doctor," said Ehrlich. "I am going to ask you for the same testimony you gave for the prosecution in the other hearing." Lawyers in the room were puzzled by this move. "In your opinion," Jake asked, "did Mrs. Morris have the mental ability at the time of the shooting to form the intent to commit murder?"

"No, sir!"

Elkington reacted like a man stabbed. He began scribbling furiously on his yellow pad. Ehrlich was asking a series of involved questions, all stemming from the sanity trial and tending to show that Mrs. Morris could have borne no malice. "Her whole demeanor was . . . that she was extremely devoted to her husband . . . couldn't live without him." Damaging as it was to the prosecution, it came straight from the foundation Ehrlich had laid quietly in the first trial. Dr. Rapaport declared again that there was no malice in the defendant's heart. "She killed because she loved him."

That, thought Ehrlich, should put the prosecution in a deep hole. And it did, as Elkington's cross-examination showed.

How, he scoffed, could a psychiatrist determine Mrs. Morris' love! The answer didn't satisfy him at all.

Q—Is it your testimony that when Mrs. Morris, with a gun in her hand, shot her husband in the back she was performing an act of love?

A—Yes, in her heart, because she couldn't live without him.

Back in his office that evening, Ehrlich re-examined his position. He had scored his first major point with the surprise testimony of Rapaport, but he still felt uneasy. The strain was telling. He was losing weight, with the heaviest going yet to come. The mail, as in all big cases, was tremendous. There were messages imploring him not to let Gertrude Morris destroy herself. There were others, quoting her own words, urging him to give up and spare society the "circus of a trial." Jake felt he must use Mrs. Morris as his star witness, and he knew he couldn't control her. It was going to be a terrific gamble.

The next day he told the jury: "I feel a great concern. I am going to ask this jury to give the matter their undivided attention. I am going to put this woman on the stand regardless of what she testifies."

She came forward hesitantly, obviously provoked with him. She wore no makeup and she was very pale. Her suit was rumpled. She replied tonelessly when the clerk asked her name. Ehrlich swung the microphone close to her face and backed off to begin a slow, patient series of questions.

He had to lead her, as her keepers had to lead her to eat her meals, and Elkington objected endlessly. Once Ehrlich whirled on him. "If the district attorney doesn't stop making these objections we are going to have the greatest brawl this courtroom has ever seen!" A moment later he spun on the prosecutor again. "If you indicate I talked to this woman for the purpose of misleading you or anyone else, you're a common street liar!" The partisan audience cheered.

The threatened brawl, however, did not materialize. Elkington had been studying the witness. He had heard about her desire to plead guilty. Ehrlich had taken a big chance by putting her on. Gertrude Morris, who had waited her opportunity, almost reached out for the prosecutor. The result was devastating.

Q—Did you shoot and kill your husband?

A—Yes.

Q—Did you kill with malice aforethought?

A—Yes.

Jake could only grimace and gesture futilely.

Q—Did you kill with premeditated thought?

A—Yes. (The look in her eyes was wild.)

Q—You did go home with the intent to kill him, didn't you?

A—Yes.

Jake finally got to his feet, addressing the judge. "Your Honor has been a lawyer for many years! You were an assistant district attorney! You have sat on the bench for many years! But, Your Honor, this is the first time in your life you've ever heard anything like this! No man, no lawyer living, ever heard anything like this! Not a soul who ever tried a lawsuit ever saw a witness sit on the stand and say 'Yes' to these questions!"

Elkington only paused momentarily.

Q—And the first opportunity you got when his back was turned, you pointed the gun at him and you shot and killed him, didn't you?

A—Yes.

Q—And you intended to do that, Mrs. Morris, didn't you?

A—Yes!

Q—And the fact is, Mrs. Morris, that you didn't call the

doctor because you intended that he die and you intended to kill yourself? That's right, isn't it?

A—Yes.

Q—It would be fair to say that when you shot and killed Mr. Morris you killed him as a result of an intention on your part to kill him, and to kill yourself? That's right, isn't it?

A—Yes!

The judge mercifully called a recess. Elkington had done his worst.

Mrs. Morris summoned Ehrlich to the prisoners' anteroom and declared she was tired of the whole proceeding and was going to change her plea to guilty. "You will have to do it with some other lawyer!" Jake snapped. He walked out on her. He had to plan something. No other client of his had succeeded quite so thoroughly in destroying himself.

When court convened he approached the bench and asked permission to cross-examine his own witness. "I want to ask, sir, whether it isn't a fact that she told me she was going to change her story so she would be found guilty." The jurors were listening intently and suddenly he realized it might all work to his advantage. They could see what he was up against. "I say that my duty to this woman is more than to an ordinary witness," he argued. "My moral duty to this woman is to see that she gets a fair and just trial." He was asking, in short, to impeach his own chief witness.

The judge nodded. "Considering this witness and the circumstances," he said, "the defense may cross-examine." Ehrlich, turning to counsel table, heard Mrs. Morris address the judge. "What was that?" he demanded. "What did she say?" She was asking to change her plea, and the judge was trying not to listen to her. "You just tell us the story," Judge Neubarth told her gently, "and let the jury decide what should be done." She blinked and retreated into her shell.

Ehrlich pelted his questions at her. *Didn't* you tell me you

never intended to kill your husband? *Didn't* you say you went
home to kill yourself? In our interview a week after that sad
day *didn't* you say you fired that shot on an impulse after you
saw him take his shirts.

She was nodding dully to each query, and Elkington was
objecting furiously. "Mr. Ehrlich is trying to lead the witness! Mr. Ehrlich's questions are improper and suggestive!"

Jake pounded away at his questioning until he thought he
had her story back on the track. Then he asked: *"Did* you intend to kill your husband?" He was turning toward the jury.

"Yes!"

He spun back to her, astonished.

"You did?"

"Yes."

He paused. "Well, then, did you ever make any statement
contrary to that?"

"Yes," she said, "to everybody."

Jake shrugged helplessly to the jury and let her go.

There was one more scene to play. Jake had been charging
from the first day that the prosecution was afraid to produce
the girl secretary. Now Elkington produced her and Miss
Goolo came in with downcast eyes, a demure little lady, dark
and pretty, wearing glasses and no makeup. She certainly did
not appear to be the home-breaking type. Gertrude Morris
stiffened when she recognized the girl. She got up from her
chair like a sleepwalker and stumbled across the room toward a corridor door. It was locked, but she didn't try to
open it. She threw herself against it and fell in a slump.

Miss Goolo denied every allegation Ehrlich had made. His
cross-examination didn't shake her. "All right," he said finally.
"Step down." Then he appeared to change his mind. "Just sit
over here."

He called for Ralph Isaacs, an attorney who had offices in
the Hearst Building. Isaacs, without looking at Miss Goolo,

testified that he had seen Mr. Morris' secretary many times; she was always beautifully dressed, frequently wore orchids, often went to lunch with Morris and seemed quite attached to him "and he to her."

Ehrlich pointed to the girl in the chair. Isaacs said he had never seen her before. Then he gasped and identified her. He said he had *never* seen her wear glasses before. Ehrlich put her back on the stand where he reduced her to sobbing confusion.

Elkington opened his summation with that fact. He said it was part of the "Jake Ehrlich story," just one part of the whole fabricated defense. "There are things," he told the jury confidentially, "that happen whenever Mr. Ehrlich is in a trial that make a good show. I'll say this," he gestured at Ehrlich sitting wooden-faced behind him, "he's a very fine lawyer, a very resourceful lawyer. He is an attorney you can always count on to come up with an unexpected defense.

"In this case," Elkington continued, "it's a very cleverly planned one. He has given the impression he and his client are at loggerheads. If it's successful you'll hear about it in the future as the 'clever defense in the Morris case.'"

Elkington spent the morning explaining the fiction he said Ehrlich had contrived to cover the guilt of Gertrude Morris. Gradually he increased the tempo until at the last he was shouting: "The most eloquent evidence of all is this: she shot him—she saw him fall to the floor—she heard him say 'Get a doctor'—and then she walked away and let him bleed to death!"

The jury looked at Ehrlich.

Jake began his closing argument that afternoon after presiding over the weekly luncheon of Saints and Sinners. He came back down the California Street hill, alone, past Chinatown, Old St. Mary's and the clanging cable cars, swinging his arms and thinking himself into it. He goaded himself to believe the prosecution had him beat at this moment, that they actually could execute the distraught little woman who had sat at his side for weeks if he, Jake Ehrlich, failed in the next few hours. He felt the eighty million bumps rising on his skin.

When he entered the courtroom, he did not look at Gertrude Morris. He had her inside him. Then he began what the papers agreed was "one of the most dramatic and brilliant summations in a San Francisco criminal court." It took him a day and half.

"I have never considered it necessary," he said at the beginning, "to defend myself. But Mr. Elkington, perhaps, thinks my years of experience have deteriorated me, made me a common thief, so that I would make up this pitiful story. I don't have to stoop to that."

He paused to stare coldly at Prosecutor Elkington.

"Mr. Elkington," drawled Jake contemptuously, "the knight on a white horse with a Cromwellian sword of righteousness! Elkington dashes out of his stall, Elkington on his white horse, waving his sword. of righteousness———" Swept up in his phrase, Jake jerked his hand from his pocket. A five-dollar bill came with it and fluttered to the carpet. The courtroom burst into laughter. He didn't pause. "——swords of vengeance rattling—bugles blaring—the white knight of righteousness rides!"

He crouched before the jury. "Sure she answered 'Yes' to all of Elkington's questions! If he had gone on long enough she would have admitted she shot Elkington, shot the judge, and shot me!" Ehrlich had his horn-rimmed glasses clenched in his hand. He pounded the wooden railing of the jury box and the jurors, watching the glasses, leaned away from him.

He smiled and put the glasses away while he discussed the flareups they had witnessed between the prosecutor and himself. None of that, he told the jurors, need concern them. "No one is to be considered but this woman. She is the one to be pitied. She is the one who has been punched in the face, but more punched in the heart!"

Repeatedly he came back to the railing, glasses in his hand. "You must not find her guilty! You must not! You can tell her with your verdict: somewhere in life there is something for you—someone, somewhere, some day—who will put his arms around you and say: 'You're a fine woman!' " He was watching the clock throughout the afternoon. He hammered hard but he avoided the tenderest places. That was for tomorrow. He gave them only enough to sleep on.

The second day was the one they would remember.

San Franciscans woke up mindful of the plight of the little housewife with gray handholds in her dark hair and the dapper attorney now waging a battle for her life. Bailiffs unlocked the courtroom to a floodtide of anxious faces. They poured into all corners of the big room.

Ehrlich rose, his cuffs flashing blue glints. (The cuff links were vaulting horses on finest Wedgewood, given to him by Marjorie.) Mrs. Morris sat huddled in her polo coat.

Ehrlich warmed up with a reminder of the prosecutor's cunning. He recalled the pretty little secretary and his eyebrows arched. What about that? They had accused him of playing tricks on them? What about the prosecution's trick? Dressing pretty Miss Goolo as if she were a drab hen sparrow? Clever, he acknowledged, until good, honest people examined it. But why did they resort to tricks like that against a poor, deranged little woman? He still was saving the best of it.

In the afternoon he appeared the same: fresh linen under his dark suit, his hair carefully combed. It was the look in his wide eyes that was different. He was pleading now, imploring, beseeching. Down the afternoon he went, building to the climax. Sometimes he crouched before the jury, crying for mercy. Perspiration beaded his forehead. His voice grew hoarser. And finally he stopped, braced before them, a trembling finger pointing at Mrs. Morris.

"Look at that woman!"

He advanced to the jury box, slammed his clenched hand on the railing, and shattered his glasses. He scarcely noticed what he had done.

"Look at that woman who saved every dime and dollar to send her husband to law school so they could get somewhere! And when they got to the point where he could eat at the Palace Hotel he didn't want her any more!"

Jake dabbed at his eyes. There were sobs from the body of the court.

He crossed slowly to Mrs. Morris, his face tense, perspiration dripping from his cheekbones. His necktie was twisted. His linen was wilted. He brandished the broken glasses. "What good is a diamond ring," he cried hoarsely, "if, as Mrs. Morris testified, he never put his arms around her?"

A woman juror caught her breath. Another was hiding her eyes. The heads were going down. There was sobbing in the room.

"Here she sits, week in and week out." Ehrlich held up a trembling fist. "Is it because she committed a crime? No! It is because she lost the only thing she loved!" He groped his way along the counsel table, closer to the jury and closer until he almost whispered to them. "Live with your conscience and your God. You cannot convict her."

He backed off. "Set this woman free. Say that she is not guilty. Tell her: 'You may go your way. Build a new life. Maybe you can find a little happiness, a little understanding—'" he faltered—"'and at least a little compassion.'"

He slumped in his chair, his head buried in his arms. Jurors and spectators were weeping unashamedly.

Elkington's argument was anticlimax. Perhaps what he said was never heard. News cameramen were swarming to photograph the complete emotional collapse of Jake Ehrlich. He seemed to have aged forty years. His face was gray and lined; his eyes refused to stay open. The flashbulbs popped and he mumbled, "I feel like a beat dog." He had lost eight pounds.

Gertrude Morris looked at him curiously. "You are a very talented man," she observed. "You missed your vocation, you should have been on the stage. Your oration was a classic." She beckoned for the matron to come for her.

Judge Neubarth instructed the jury ten months to the day after the shooting. They were out for seven hours and thirty-five minutes. When they brought in their verdict they had denied Mrs. Morris the boon she asked. They found her guilty only of manslaughter and she was sentenced to a term of one to ten years in state's prison. She turned to Ehrlich with twisted lips. "Well, Master, I suppose this is one more feather in your cap."

"I suppose it is," he replied wearily. He listened, astonished, as she rambled on: "I am not satisfied. I still believe in a life for a life. I am not paying my debt to society. I have no hopes, no longings—nothing."

She was quite right. Two years later she was in a hospital for the insane.

And Ehrlich had a rare photograph, the most ghastly portrait he had ever seen of himself. He put it in his desk. It was to be part of the legend thereafter. When someone asked his fee for a homicide case now, he could flip it across the desk. "This," he could say, "is why I charge *everything*. This is what a murder case does to me. This was the Morris Murder Case."

Part Four: **THE FRIEND**

I

FRIENDS, ROMANS, COUNTRYMEN

And Lou Lurie

ONE evening Red Skelton, the radio-TV comic, was doing his characterization of a mischievous youngster caught robbing a cookie jar. "I got to get me a lawyer," said Junior to a nationwide audience including thousands of attorneys. Then Skelton added: "I'll get me Jake Ehrlich and beat this spanking rap."

The smiles of the lawyers in the audience probably vanished. "How does that guy get away with it?" many must have asked, referring of course to advertising, the forbidden luxury of the lawyer trade. Some barristers become directors of flower clubs, presidents of debating societies and deacons of churches so as not to escape the public notice. Some make Fourth of July orations. Some run for public office. Many wonder what price Ehrlich had paid to have his name on a coast-to-coast comedy show.

He had paid the price of friendship over many years, including some when Red Skelton was known only to God and his agent.

Skelton had come to San Francisco to do his weekly TV show and, as usual, had had dinner with Jake. "Why don't you hire a press agent," Red spoofed, "and make yourself into a real big-name lawyer?"

Jake clapped hands to his cheeks in mock horror. "It would be unethical!" he cried.

The comedian hooted. "I am going to get you disbarred! Watch me tonight!"

It was no more than that: another short chapter in the Ehrlich legend.

Once Jake appeared against Theresa Meikle, the pretty assistant district attorney who had been the young woman judge in the Dolly Fine case. Theresa thought she had an easy victory and as court adjourned said as much. Ehrlich shook a warning finger. "I'll bet you $20 and I'll give you 2-1 odds," he said. Miss Meikle laughed. "*I'll* give you 2-1 odds you fix the jury!"

Some weeks later Ehrlich advised her that he owed her 10 per cent of $5,000. "Agent's fee," he explained. "A certain gentleman overheard you and retained me for $5,000 because you said I could fix juries."

"The Ehrlich luck!" remarked Miss Meikle.

Perhaps it was, although some people say luck and faith are intertwined. Jake has always had faith in himself and in his friends. And his friends have been legion. They have included George B. Harris who in the early days, as a discouraged and struggling lawyer, almost persuaded Jake to go to Los Angeles with him. Things suddenly broke for both of them and Harris, though younger than Jake, was a federal judge during Jake's boom years.

There were Zsa Zsa Gabor, tripping through San Francisco, and the young Don Steeles, who handled night club publicity and knew almost as many people as Ehrlich. There were: the Shah of Iran, whom Jake took to the boxing matches; Barney Ferguson, once understudy to George M. Cohan; Leo Durocher, Humphrey Bogart, Fire Commissioner Max Sobel, Martha Raye, who used to telephone long distance and get Jake out of court.

There was Al Williams, who had the famous Papagaya Room up at the Fairmont. There was Bob Patterson, the peculiar genius who, as "Freddie Francisco," wrote a trenchant column for the *Examiner*. He sent Jake a hundred-dollar pair of alligator shoes from Mexico and wanted to write the Ehrlich story. He even had a title: *Lawyer for the Lost*. He had faith in Jake and so did "Ropes" McMahon, the tough prosecutor who gentled with time and became a very good judge.

Every one of them would testify that Jake was telling the truth when he declared: "I never forget a friend nor forgive an enemy."

Bill Saroyan could tell of the time Jake said: "If you ever want to have lunch with me, holler and I'll buy." Saroyan sent a telegram to court: "Am expecting to have lunch with you tomorrow, at the Brown Derby in Hollywood."

"I'll be there," Jake wired back. He grabbed a cab from the Hall, then an airplane, flew to Hollywood and bought the lunch, and then flew back to complete his case.

Leo Friedman, who had prosecuted Fatty Arbuckle years before and then become one of San Francisco's great defense lawyers, would remember the case in which he and Ehrlich both had clients though both clients couldn't win. Friedman would remember it because his wife fell into her last illness that week. He might have asked for a continuance but he didn't. He trusted Ehrlich to impanel a jury for them both. Afterward he shook Jake's hand with tears in his eyes because the jury Ehrlich selected was one that would be as favorable toward Friedman's client as his own.

Lawyers who are rich and successful themselves may say of Jake: "He's shrewd and he's an opportunist."

But much of Ehrlich's success stems from simple friendship. Jake is a friendly man; he likes not only people but causes. Among his closest friends is Louis Lurie, and among his favorite causes the Saints and Sinners' Milk Fund.

The Ehrlich legend would not be complete without Lurie and the luncheon table at Jack's, a fine old French restaurant where convivial souls have broken bread for almost a hundred years. And a multitude of individuals have read the little bronze plaque as they walked into Louis Lurie's office to state the particular kindness they wished from "San Francisco's professional rich man."

I shall pass through this world but once. Any good, therefore, that I can do or any kindness I can show to any human being, let me do it now. Let me not defer or neglect it, for I shall not pass this way again.

The free-wheeling gentleman with the pince-nez glasses dispatched many benevolences from his brown-paneled offices on the top floor of the Pacific National Bank Building. His largesse included cash, sponsorship in political campaigns, theatre tickets, introductions to movie producers and to publishers, backing for careers, inventions, gold mines, farm crops, Broadway plays, a world's fair, even letters of recommendation for little bread-and-butter jobs. Louis Lurie was a sort of grand duke to whom people came with their needs.

After his fiftieth birthday a certain group would mill about his office at the peak of the day, drinking his whiskey, smoking his cigars, interrupting his telephone calls and insulting him in the roughest terms. If the gag happened to be particularly good, Lurie would clap jubilant hands and describe it over the telephone to a brother tycoon across the continent, for merrymaking replaced moneymaking after Lurie suffered a heart attack and a wise doctor advised him to make living a more enjoyable game.

Lurie did that by bringing fun-loving friends to his luncheon table. Once it was Jake and Georgie Jessel disputing scripture. Jessel insisted a certain passage was not in the Bible and Ehrlich declared: "You will find it in the New Testament." "The *New* Testament!" Jessel shrieked. "My God, what won't they think of next!"

Lurie would go through the ritual of allowing his guests to study the menu while Henri, his personal waiter for thirty years, waited patiently. When all had decided on their order, Lurie would grab the menus and rip them to shreds. "They haven't printed a new menu here since the Civil War!" he would scold. "Henri, give them the rex sole meunière—the king of fish!"

Herbert Hoover would smile patiently, or Gertrude Lawrence laugh uproariously. During the formation of the United Nations, the ambassadors and foreign ministers of thirty-three countries were Lurie's guests. Occasional invitations reached everyone who might prove interesting but a few such as Bill Wren, the *Examiner* editor, and Jake Ehrlich had standing invitations. Others simply dropped in: theatre folk, artists, writers, scientists, merchants, doctors, lawyers, and probably some thieves.

In the beginning it had been strictly business. Lurie, a one-time Chicago newsboy, was a self-made capitalist, and it took years of pressure work before he signed a famous check for $14,500,000 to buy the Chicago skyscrapers where he had worked as a boy. Until 1939 he ate quickly and hurried his guests on their way. Then one day his heart sputtered.

A month later his doctor told him: "Louis, God certainly was good to you. Because now," said the doctor, "you can live to be as old as you wish to be, provided you change your mode of living. You should try to be cheerful. Let me make a suggestion: Whenever you are feeling down in the dumps, think of some particularly pleasing experience you have had. Your state of being will respond to the thought."

That was where Jake and the gang came in. Jake's office was on the sixteenth floor of Lurie's building. Once Lurie came home from Washington to discover his safe had been tampered with. The gold lettering that had gleamed proudly for forty years was gone. In its place was new gold leaf:

J. W. EHRLICH—70 PER CENT
LOUIS LURIE—30 PER CENT

That was what the doctor wanted.

On another occasion Lurie came into his building to find a huge sign in the lobby. "The name of this building has been changed to the J. W. Ehrlich Building," it said. "After the first of the month all rents will be paid to J. W. Ehrlich."

Lurie retaliated. He spread word about town that Ehrlich wasn't doing too well. "He may not be in my building next month," Lurie said. "Jake never has been able to pay his rent on time. You know how these criminal lawyers are. I've had to carry him."

When Jake demanded satisfaction, Lurie told him he must pay his rent promptly at ten o'clock on the morning of the first. "Not at one minute past ten, but right on the nose at ten o'clock."

Jake had his rent check changed into pennies, five hundred and fifty-nine pounds of them, and armored cars delivered them hard on the stroke of ten. Armed guards trudged into Lurie's private office, pulled the drawstrings on bulging sacks and dumped coins on the floor. Jake also had arranged that no bank would pick up the money. For three days Lurie had to climb over mounds of bright coppers to reach his desk. He finally had to appeal to Jake for mercy.

Strangely, through all their years of friendship, Lurie saw Jake in action in only one trial. The financier read one day of a young Army captain, a doctor from New York, who had held up a drugstore and stolen some morphine. The next morning he had a call from Abe Berman, Irving Berlin's attorney and an old friend. "Get the boy some help," Berman said. "Something's gone wrong with him."

Lurie called Jake, guaranteeing the fee. "Let me look into it," Ehrlich said. He discovered that the doctor-captain had been to a dentist shortly before the holdup and had been given a new type of painkiller that had reacted violently on him. Jake brought in alienists, got a jury and proceeded to prove that it was all a mental mixup. The captain was acquitted.

Lurie, sitting in criminal court for the first time in his life, was fascinated. "Send me the bill," he said. He would gladly have paid a $5,000 fee and was amazed when it was $500, which scarcely covered out-of-pocket expense. "What the hell," Jake growled. "Can't I be a philanthropist too?"

Lurie got an idea from the alienists on this occasion and he subsequently called on Dr. Walter Rapaport, the state mental hygiene director who had testified in the Gertrude Morris case and had known Ehrlich's family in Maryland. Lurie told Rapaport about the practical jokes Jake and the gang had been playing on him. "These fellows seem to take letters from doctors pretty seriously," he suggested. "Now you have testified against Jake in a lot of cases. Haven't you seen how he gets worked up? All those dramatic mannerisms?"

Dr. Rapaport nodded. "I suppose you *could* raise questions about the Ehrlich behavior pattern."

So one day, when Jake was deeply involved in a difficult case, he received a friendly letter from the alienist. Rapaport pointed out little things he had been observing, things Jake's friends had reported, all indicating—and he hated to say it— that perhaps The Master was, well, on shaky ground. He suggested that Ehrlich seek help from a good doctor.

Ehrlich read the letter again. He wasn't exactly alarmed, and yet he did ponder some facets of the diagnosis. He decided to do nothing immediately but locked the letter in his file. When the luncheon gang began to commiserate with him and treat him with suspicious kindness, he breathed easier. Lurie was telling everyone in town he was crazy.

On another occasion Jake was subpoenaed before a congressional committee to describe certain conversations on income tax matters that had engrossed the Lurie Luncheon Table. He used the opportunity to read into the Congressional *Record* a long and glowing account of Lurie's philanthropies and guests. Lurie was delighted.

"I have just ordered the elevator operators to tell anyone who doesn't like Jake Ehrlich that he can't ride up or down," Lurie told Jake later in his office. He also reported a midnight telephone call from Eddie Cantor. Cantor called to complain that Jessel had telephoned him from New York, where it was 3:00 A.M. "Do you know what Jessel wanted? Just to say this: 'Eddie, if you ever eat a sturgeon sandwich on rye bread, don't put any mustard on it. You won't like it.' "

Lurie and Jake were very good for each other.

On Thursday mornings, attorney Ehrlich would show up promptly at nine and go to his work briskly. Opposing counsel could embroil him in no horseplay. At some moment he would rise and ask politely if the noon recess could be extended until 2:30. No judge could readily deny the request, for Thursday was Saints and Sinners' Day in San Francisco.

At the Saints and Sinners' luncheons Jake, the perpetual president, would stand before a dollar alarm clock pounding a massive gavel and assessing strange fines and penalties.

Once he fined Chief Justice Earl Warren $100 "for being too popular." Once he made Artie Samish, the rotund "Secret Boss of California," pungle up $1,000 in cash for refusing to sit down on order. A dignified corporation attorney paid $50 for asking where Ehrlich "gets his jurors." Similar fines have been paid by Prime Minister De Valera, Lefty O'Doul, Lucius Beebe, Warden Clinton Duffy and a host of others.

San Francisco's Saints and Sinners has no connection with the Circus Saints and Sinners of New York. The San Francisco group is dedicated to providing free milk for needy school children, and in the first five years of its uninhibited high jinks raised more than $1,500,000. It had the most successful charity operating in California when the law stepped in.

Technically the organization did violate the gambling laws, for each year it sold chances on various prizes—a new home, automobiles, $1,000 a year for life. But San Franciscans had always regarded charity raffles with official tolerance and the slogan of this group was: "Put more of the milk of human kindness in milk bottles."

Ehrlich has cherished Saints and Sinners dearly from the day in 1948 when it started. It was up at fight promoter Benny Ford's restaurant where a group of men who would never join a Rotary or Kiwanis club met informally for lunch and fined one another for keeping the rest waiting.

Among them were Ehrlich and Ford, attorney Edward Dienstag and Tommy Harris, a radio and stage singer who now operated a tavern. Someone proposed that their accumulating fines be used to help people assisted by no other charity. "Look who's trying to be saints!" scoffed Harris, and the name of the new organization was set. "Always forgive the sinners. None of us are saints."

Later, investigating a lawsuit against the schools, Jake discovered that a surprising number of children were unable to pay for daily milk. He stood before the next Saints and Sinners' luncheon and cut short the horseplay. "With all the millions in our municipal budget," he reported, "there are kids in this city who don't have milk! This is a rich country. If our governments can't get money out of the public for milk I believe Saints and Sinners can!"

He personally led a drive that in ten days raised $50,

176.04—enough for 305,159 free bottles of milk—and the Variety Club singled him out for its Great Heart Award. Five hundred and fifty diners heard the superintendent of schools declare: "The essential of American democracy is regard for the individual. Jake Ehrlich is the sparkplug who got things done when others wondered how to do them."

The next year chances were sold on a $25,000 home, which was won by an officer in the Chinese Nationalist Army. The Saints raised $107,662.29. Someone suggested that this might constitute a lottery. Ehrlich glanced about the dining room, packed with civic leaders and law enforcement officers. "Who," he demanded, "is going to put whom in jail?"

Saints and Sinners started a trust fund to continue the milk project in perpetuity.

In 1952 the grand prize became $1,000 a year for life. It was won by a bride of three months as the Saints and Sinners counted $126,802.92. After the 1953 drive, which netted $139,216.55—enough to buy one million bottles of milk —Jake inserted an ad in the newspapers accounting for all receipts and expenditures.

"Each of you," it said, "is a partner in building healthier children for tomorrow's citizens. *This ad not paid for out of Milk Fund money.*"

He had been hearing rumbles from his old crony Pat Brown, now State Attorney General, to the effect that Saints and Sinners was conducting a lottery and that its overhead was high.

At one o'clock each Thursday, Ehrlich would rise, nod to an associate to sound the big siren and go into his endless gavel pounding while Tommy Harris began the inquisition of honored guests. Harris, with his spontaneous Irish wit, was probably the only man in San Francisco capable of needling all comers without getting murdered on the spot.

Jake was always to be addressed from the floor as "Master,"

even by Governors and Supreme Court Justices. Failure to include this respectful address—no matter how sarcastically intended—would mean an immediate fine for the Milk Fund. However, Jake could be made the butt of any joke.

Saints and Sinners was a source of the fabled cuff links. Jake fined Rod Pohl, proprietor of the Oyster Loaf Restaurant, and Pohl rewarded him with links of pure melted Klondike gold nuggets. Ehrlich asked Tommy Harris once too often what the hour was. Harris gave him links with individual workable watches in them. A Hollywood agent reported that Jake had shown casual interest in a certain bosomy actress, was fined, and retaliated by presenting The Master with links that were magnificent replicas of that star's principal attractions. They were so lifelike, in fact, that Ehrlich could never wear them in public.

There was another reason for his affection for the Saints and Sinners. In the mid-forties, Sophie Tucker had introduced his daughter Dora Jane to Guy Cherney, a young singer, and they were married. As a waif in Chicago, Cherney sang "My Mother's Eyes" so plaintively at a boys' club program that the mother of the Franks boy slain in the Loeb-Leopold kidnaping gave his club $100,000. He became a protégé of Joe E. Lewis and sang in some of the country's best clubs. Then, suddenly, as he was going into the Paul Whiteman Revue, his voice failed. For months he tried unsuccessfully to discover what was wrong. He had just about given up when the Saints and Sinners asked him to lead a song "just among friends." He started it without thinking and his voice returned as suddenly as it had left.

Cherney came back fast and when he returned to open at Bimbo's 365 Club in San Francisco the Saints and Sinners packed the house. Ehrlich was convinced that the challenge and warmth of Saints and Sinners had given his son-in-law his second chance.

When the sniping on the Saints and Sinners' charity began, someone wrote Governor Warren that it was "just a racket." Warren's reply was widely quoted: "Dear Sir: I am now and have been a member of the Saints and Sinners." Later, when he was appointed Chief Justice of the United States, he wrote Jake: "Saints, sinners, Republicans or Democrats, I am grateful to my friends."

Not so Pat Brown, whom Jake had boosted to his first public office as an outgrowth of the Krupa case and the defeat of old Matt Brady.

Brown had been State Attorney General only a few months when three California counties complained that the law forbade their churches to hold charity drawings while million-dollar raffles got by in San Francisco.

In San Francisco, the police department tolerantly looked the other way. In fact, for seventy years it had had its own drawing for the Widows and Orphans' Fund.

Brown was being goaded not only by certain individuals but by some of the newspapers. He indicated that he might challenge the big ticket-selling charities. The reporters flocked to Ehrlich.

Jake patiently pointed out that Saints and Sinners was doing a vital job without paid employees, promoters or salesmen, that all moneys collected were managed by twelve highly respected directors and that all financial transactions were thoroughly reported. "The Attorney General can't mean us," he said. "Our position is legitimate and fine."

"The causes are legitimate," Brown retorted, "but the fundraising methods are illegal." The newspapers hinted that there might be arrests.

Arrests?

Jake's roar could be heard at the Cliff House. "The state would have to arrest every civic leader in San Francisco! All the judges—they're members of Saints and Sinners! They would have to arrest the Attorney General—he's a member! They would have to arrest the superintendent of schools, bank presidents and all the newspaper publishers! They're all Saints and Sinners!

"They would have to arrest the Governor of California and the Mayor of San Francisco. And they'd have to arrest all the men in the streets, the unsung heroes who in selling Saints and Sinners' tickets make their contribution to the sum of human kindness."

It was a panoramic challenge.

Attorney General Brown must have known that he would not escape Ehrlich's ridicule. As a lawyer of the thirties he would remember the time when the San Francisco police department, in a feud with Ehrlich, resurrected two dozen minor traffic citations against Jake and summoned him before a magistrate. The first citation was called and up popped one of Jake's lawyer friends. "Ready in the matter of Mr. Ehrlich," said the lawyer. "We will ask a jury trial." As each succeeding citation was read, another attorney stood up to ask for a trial by jury. Finally, faced by two dozen lawyers demanding two dozen jury trials on minor traffic matters, the authorities admitted defeat.

Ehrlich met Brown privately and tried to convince him that he was fooling with a Pandora's box. Brown was honest about it. "I know you to be outstanding citizens and I think the work you are doing is as worthy as it can be. *But the law says you may not conduct lotteries!*" Other good people, he said, were pressuring him to see that the law was enforced.

One newspaper said Brown was going to seize Saints and Sinners' books and study the charges for overhead. Ehrlich beat him to the punch by sending the books to Brown's office. Expenditures for overhead were very low.

The papers reported next that Brown had his eye on the proposed million-dollar trust fund. They cited a law governing the Community Chest, which ordered that all money must be spent within five years of its collection.

With that Jake went over to the attack. He mobilized his board of directors and marched up to the State Building to confront Pat Brown.

It was an odd position for the state's chief law enforcement officer. He issued a conciliatory statement: "We are making spot checks of all charities in the state. There is absolutely no implication of anything being wrong. The only thing we can do is see that money given for charitable purposes is used for that purpose. Saints and Sinners certainly disburses all its money received—less prizes." Before Ehrlich could gloat, Brown repeated his view that the fund drive violated the lottery laws because it involved tickets, prizes and the element of chance.

As the 1954 drive began, Ehrlich discovered that some of his Saints and Sinners were reluctant to sell tickets. Children's Hospital had given up its annual fund drive until the legal status of charitable projects could be clarified. The Catholic Archdiocese canceled its citywide church raffle.

"You'll never be prosecuted!" Ehrlich stormed. "If any one of you is arrested I will defend you without charge." He once had been general counsel for Bank Night; he knew there were loopholes in the law. "We could ask for contributions," he explained. "No one would *buy* a ticket. Then we could have a Bank Night drawing from the stubs of all the tickets out."

Ehrlich had a statement printed on the backs of all tickets stating they were "receipts" for contributions to the Saints and Sinners' Milk Fund, the receipt to be kept for individual income tax purposes (and incidentally a drawing). "We aren't selling anything," Jake said.

Throughout the city there was a low rumbling of anger. The law was bucking a very popular cause.

Ehrlich, though involved in an $8,000,000 civil suit at the time, prepared for further battle. He had the best people in town on his side. His cause was worthy. His likeliest weapon was ridicule. About town they were saying: "God help Pat Brown!"

The first direct skirmish occurred on a TV panel show, watched with special interest throughout northern California. On one side were Attorney General Brown and San Francisco District Attorney Tom Lynch. "Do you advise us to disregard our oath of office?" Lynch demanded. Would Ehrlich, a reputable attorney, counsel them overtly to disregard the law?

Jake knew that argument well. The State Attorney General was suddenly undergoing cross-examination.

Q—Why is it *not* a sin to go to a horserace track in California and bet money on the outcome of races, but it is a sin—*you* say—to buy tickets that provide school children with free milk? Is it the board wall we build around race tracks that shuts out the sin?

A—(Brown) I don't want to moralize on this issue. The laws says I am sworn to enforce what it states. I would like to point out, though, that no one gets something for nothing.

Ehrlich turned directly to the TV cameras. "And I say someone *does* get something for nothing in the Saints and Sinners' program. All the poor little kids who haven't money to buy a bottle of milk at lunch get one for nothing so they can grow up strong enough to meet the problems of a democracy!"

He glanced at the clock. "I have one more thing to add, if you will allow me thirty seconds. If this method of doing good for your fellow man is a bad thing, then the Bible must be bad because I see they used the system of drawing lots there. I refer you to Acts 1:26. Matthias was picked *by lot* to take Judas' place as one of the Apostles. I don't think the Bible is a very bad book."

If Brown had an answer he didn't get a chance to express it. The time was up.

He was still muttering: "The Attorney General has no right to permit any violation of the law" when the Saints and Sinners went out to sell their 1954 tickets. The quota was $250,000. Every street corner had placards for the drive.

Shortly thereafter Jake was invited to the wedding of Brown's daughter. At the reception he assumed a pixie smile and went down the receiving line asking for "two bucks" and issuing free "receipts" to the Milk Fund drawing. He was doing a brisk business when he paused suddenly before a tall young man who was glaring at him. Jake calmly asked the next person for $2, handed him two tickets and told him to give one "to your companion, the district attorney of San Francisco." There were still no arrests.

Ehrlich has big plans for 1955. He loves to walk slowly up California Street to the Mark, gazing fondly on the newest billboard on which a ranking prelate urges San Franciscans to "give generously" to Saints and Sinners. Jake doesn't believe for a moment that a few saints are going to kill an expression of human kindness by a rollicking band of sinners.

II

MORE VERDICTS

The Legend Intact

Censure has been the lot of all the trial lawyers whose personalities have flowered in American courtrooms— Darrow, Rogers, Leibowitz, Fallon, Benjamin and Giesler. Jake had come to accept disapproval as part of the game. A man engaged in the public defense of criminals cannot be thin-skinned. To sell the good points of bad people to juries of respectable people, he must comprehend the weaknesses and strengths of most people, including himself. Jake constantly repeated: "I never kid me."

If at times he sought to justify himself, he would do so privately. That might be after some such harrowing murder trial as Gertrude Morris', when his skin still flamed with the "eighty million bumps."

By the time of the Morris trial, Ehrlich had the fame and economic security he had set out to achieve. He had multi-million-dollar civil suits to balance his criminal practice. He could relax and accept "one murder case a year, maybe two, just for the challenge."

His home, high on a Marin County hill, looked out in one direction to San Quentin's apple-green gas chamber, which he had contrived to cheat on fifty-some occasions, and off across the bay in the other direction to the skyline of San Francisco, with which he believed he had always played fair and square. If he opened his Bible, as often he did for source

290

material, it spread automatically at Jeremiah, which he admired for its logic, or Isaiah, where he found his theme:

> Seek justice, relieve the oppressed,
> Judge the fatherless, plead for the widow.

The Good Book said: "Add virtue to your faith." But how could a man profess his virtue? Jake recalled the night Walter Winchell was broadcasting his weekly recital. "Flash!" he cried, with a great rattling of the telegraph key. "Inez Norton —she's the former sweetheart of Arnold Rothstein, the slain New York gambler—is going to marry a prominent San Francisco attorney. . . . I have it on good authority that attorney is J. W. Ehrlich!"

Jake telephoned the New York station. "Walter," he said, "Inez Norton is only a client. It so happens that I am married now and have been for many years, and I love my wife and my two children." To him, the home is indeed the pillar of society *and* a reflection of a man's public and private character.

More than any other consideration, Ehrlich's feeling for the home guided his actions in the Walter Wanger-Joan Bennett case in Beverly Hills.

On December 13, 1951, Wanger, the silver-haired producer, saw his beautiful wife, Joan Bennett, enter her Cadillac convertible with her young agent, Jennings Lang. Wanger suspected an affair. He had had private detectives watching them and he had been following them. He caught up with them in a parking lot off Santa Monica Boulevard. Wanger had a .38 caliber revolver and he fired twice, hitting Lang. Miss Bennett and the parking lot attendant carried the wounded agent to a private physician and then to Midway Hospital.

The shooting threatened Hollywood with its biggest scandal in years. Wanger, fifty-seven, had been president of the Academy of Motion Picture Arts and Sciences six times. He was a popular man and a movie pioneer. In 1934 he had dared to try a psychiatric theme, *Private Worlds,* which starred Miss Bennett. He had made the first outdoor technicolor sound picture, *The Trail of the Lonesome Pine.* Wanger was also a trustee of Antioch College and a director of the American Red Cross. He had married Joan Bennett in Phoenix in 1940, and they had two small children.

Recently his star had dimmed. The picture *Joan of Arc,* starring Ingrid Bergman, for which he had borrowed $570,-000, had been a financial flop. He owed more than $200,000. A bank was threatening to foreclose on Miss Bennett's fifteen-room Holmsby Hills home.

Miss Bennett, forty-two, was the youngest of the three famous daughters of Actor Richard Bennett and this was her third marriage. Her face and figure may not have seemed matronly to her fans, but she was a grandmother.

Lang, thirty-nine, was a West Coast television scout for Music Corporation of America. He was a curly-haired young man who had been Miss Bennett's agent for twelve years. At the hospital it was found that he had been shot once in the right thigh and once in the abdomen. Doctors said the damage probably would not be permanent.

Police found a suitcase in Wanger's car containing reports by private detectives on Lang's meetings with the actress. "I did it," Wanger declared angrily, "because he was threatening my home. A year ago Joan's affection for me chilled. I suspected an affair with Lang. Last August I bought a gun from a deputy sheriff. I had to shoot him. It was the only thing I could do."

The Los Angeles *Examiner* went further. It stated that the actress and agent on some occasions had met at the apartment of a well-known actor and "Oscar" winner. The paper said that this information was in two reports by private detectives.

Miss Bennett blamed the entire affair on Wanger's mental state. "I never dreamed a marriage as successful as ours, with a family as lovely as ours, would be involved in so unhappy a situation," she said. She insisted that she and Lang simply were consulting about television roles.

Miss Bennett hired Grant Cooper, a prominent Hollywood attorney; Wanger engaged Jerry Giesler. District Attorney S. Ernest Roll took personal direction of the case. Two days later, Lang revealed that he had called Jake Ehrlich in San Francisco and was going to say nothing. Roll tried for two hours to take a statement from him and came away fuming. "I got the brushoff!" he declared.

The newspapers were licking their lips. Said the *Mirror:* "The lawyers in this case are nearly as prominent as their clients. The entrance of Jake Ehrlich . . . indicates it will become a joust of legal giants." The *Daily News* added: "Promise that the whole matter would wind up in one of Hollywood's most sensational trials was seen in that Lang has retained Jake Ehrlich."

The district attorney telephoned Jake in San Francisco. "Ehrlich," he announced, "is flying here . . . and assured us we will be able to talk to anyone." Jake confirmed this on his arrival. "There will be no difficulty getting the facts when my client is able. Anyone with experience knows it isn't possible to keep a shooting private. When a gun blazes, it is police action at once." He had Roll up to his Beverly-Wilshire suite for a long conference, after which they talked with Lang "until he broke with pain."

On Christmas Day, while the big-name attorneys watched solemnly, Wanger was reunited with his two children. Then Ehrlich okayed a press conference with Lang, who said: "I am bewildered. I can only say Walter Wanger misconstrued what was solely a business relationship." When the reporters pressed the charge that Lang was "breaking up a home,"

Ehrlich interrupted. "I have a gentleman's agreement with the district attorney's office not to go into these matters. Mr. Lang is a witness for the state. He is under their supervision." The battle of the giants was not quite materializing.

Giesler forestalled it entirely. He quietly submitted the case to Superior Judge Harry J. Borde on the basis of the Grand Jury transcript, thereby avoiding testimony on any of the lurid charges. District Attorney Roll consented to this, he said, "to save considerable expense to the taxpayers." The judge found Wanger guilty of assault with a deadly weapon and sentenced him to serve four months in the county jail. The public regarded the three big lawyers as arch conciliators.

Wanger spent three days with Joan in Chicago before surrendering to start his term. The gossip columnists were predicting a swift reconciliation. His first visitor in jail, where he shared a cell with a "phantom sniper" who had killed a housewife, was Gilbert Roland, once his brother-in-law. Wanger already was talking about terrible jail conditions.

He served 102 days, in all, most of it at an honor prison farm, and Joan met him when he was released. He was full of plans for penal reform. "I learned a lot up there," he said. "Freedom is something you don't kid about." He started work immediately on a reform picture, *Riot in Cell Block 11,* which did well at the box office and made him once more the fair-haired boy at Allied Artists. Subsequently he and Miss Bennett spent an evening with Ehrlich in San Francisco and the talk of a broken home subsided. Louella Parsons revealed that Wanger had bought a story to star Joan. The "Hollywood scandal of the century" was dead.

2

There have even been gibes that Ehrlich doesn't know the law he works with and depends solely on the research of Roy

Sharff. A secretary in their office had occasion recently to smile at that. Sharff was sitting gloomily over the newest batch of legislative acts when Ehrlich breezed in from Saints and Sinners. "Here," groaned Sharff, "are 1,220 new laws." Jake waved his hand. "Think nothing of it," he said. "You will find them all in the Bible." He went on to demonstrate that a basis for sanitation laws is in Moses, for farm genetics in Genesis—where Jacob experimented with cattle—and military deferment in Deuteronomy. "The first deferment law," said Jake, "provided that when a man had built a new house he should not be called to war until he had used it."

Jake had pleaded often for justice tempered with mercy, as in the Morris, Borelli and Collins trials, and he had found mercy in amazing places. He was to find it even in Colonel White, the narcotics agent who had fought him so doggedly in the Billie Holiday case. He and White met again in the late forties, in the strange case of John "the Bug" Stoppelli, one of the sorriest clients Ehrlich ever had.

"The Bug" was a member of New York's old Mulberry Gang, a thief, gunman and dope trafficker with a criminal record dating back to 1925. He had bribed federal officers. He was a member of the homicidal Mafia. In the middle of this case, while out on bail, he got into a fracas in Greenwich Village and was shot through the chest. He almost died before it was established that even a hoodlum could be treated justly.

The case started with the narcotics raid in a cheap Oakland hotel. Colonel White, posing as a big-time narcotics buyer, laid $10,000 on a hotel table for twelve envelopes of pure heroin. Then he fired a shot out the window to bring his agents and put four surprised sellers under arrest. His informer said the stuff was coming from the East Coast. White wanted the whole gang. He sent the envelopes to the laboratories of the Bureau of Internal Revenue, where one fingerprint was found, from the ring finger of a man not among the four in custody.

W. Harold (Bucky) Greene, chief of the identification section, thereupon began a laborious search through a massive volume that lists fingerprints and photos of all known narcotics offenders. Eventually he discovered similarities between the lone print and one from the hand of John the Bug. It was the only evidence linking Stoppelli to the case.

Stoppelli denied any part in the dope traffic. On the day of the Oakland raid, he said, he was registering with his parole officer in New York City. But on the basis of the fingerprint, he was taken into custody and indicted with the four other men. When he was brought west for trial in San Francisco Federal Court, he got Ehrlich.

U. S. Attorney Joseph Karesh, an ex-rabbi who had taught Ehrlich's son and daughter, was the prosecutor. Ehrlich was confident that one fingerprint was not enough for conviction. He knew there should be a minimum of five prints, and preferably seven, to make identification positive. A single print could indicate the person to look for, but no more than that. Jake was prepared to attack Greene's identification of the Bug, though he knew that Greene, head of the bureau for ten years, was the acknowledged U. S. expert on identification by single fingerprints.

Greene testified in court that the print from the envelope matched Stoppelli's at fourteen points. He said seven points, sometimes only six, would be sufficient. "Out of six billion fingerprints we have," he explained, "there is only one recorded case of identical prints for two people. That was in the Navy in the 1920s, when a pair of identical twins had identical prints on all fingers."

Ehrlich attacked the expert vigorously, but the jury believed him and found Stoppelli guilty on the first ballot. Crying his innocence, the defendant was sentenced to six years in federal prison. Ehrlich made an unusually impassioned statement.

"Your Honor," he said, "if I thought for a minute that the man sitting here was part of this conspiracy you wouldn't hear me stand and argue. I have never felt so burdened by a case. Something is wrong. I feel a great moral obligation to this defendant because I believe him. I believed him when he told me, 'If I did this I would tell you I did it. I didn't do it.'

"I have made mistakes when I was guided by what I have felt up here (he touched his head). I never make a mistake when I feel down here (his heart). I feel sincerely that this man was not in on this thing. I have no defense of Stoppelli for all the times he has been in the penitentiary. I have every concern for him at a time when I feel in my heart and my soul that this man is not guilty of this crime.

"I say he (Greene) made a mistake. I say he is not the expert that we were led to believe.

"Your Honor, there is something wrong with this case and I don't know where it is, but I am going to stay with it as long as the good Lord lets me."

He obtained affidavits from the four other defendants swearing that Stoppelli was not a partner to the crime. They had no effect. He appealed the case and lost. He spent $700 of his own money to carry an appeal to the United States Supreme Court. The high court refused to consider it. Then he appealed to his old adversary, Colonel White. "Believe me," Jake said earnestly, "he's innocent. I am sure the fingerprint expert was wrong. Talk to the Bug yourself!"

White did, and he became convinced too. He called his boss, Commissioner Harry Anslinger, chief of the Federal Bureau of Narcotics. "I get the same impression Ehrlich did," White told him. "I know the Bug is one of the worst in the business. But still, under our laws, I couldn't be responsible for sending him to jail for something he didn't do, glad as I might be to get him out of circulation."

The lone fingerprint was sent to the FBI laboratory, which found it similar to Stoppelli's in some details, but *not identical*. Ehrlich was jubilant. He asked for a new trial. The answer was no. The FBI report was not, technically, new evidence, but only a modification of the old. The prosecutor opposed a new trial. "This man is innocent!" Jake cried. "Here is the proof!" It was all to no avail. Stoppelli entered prison to start serving his sentence.

Ehrlich hounded Colonel White who again appealed to Anslinger. Months went by with letters flying back and forth. "It's too bad," said White, "if Stoppelli is turned loose on society again, but even a hoodlum has inalienable rights."

Anslinger agreed. "John Stoppelli is no good," he said. "He is a bum, a crook, a racketeer, but I am completely convinced of his innocence. I will recommend that he be freed."

After two years of his sentence had been served, Stoppelli was granted a commutation by President Truman. Ehrlich read the President's terse announcement and looked at the smiling photograph of "HST" floating in a souvenir cigarette lighter on his desk. "People do a lot of yowling these days about Communists and crooks," said Jake, "but there is nothing to fear so long as the whole machinery of the government goes to work to protect the rights of one insignificant hoodlum who didn't get a fair deal."

3

At that moment a young man named Caryl Chessman was sitting out a six-year vigil on San Quentin's condemned row, sentenced to die for two kidnapings with assault involving sex perversion. He had written his version of his crime in a vivid autobiography he called *Cell 2455, Death Row*. Jake had not read the book. He had only read what the newspapers reported as Chessman was granted one stay of execution after another. Now a San Rafael lawyer, Berwyn Rice, was making a last-ditch stand for the boy's life. Public opinion on the case was divided.

A TV panel discussion was arranged on capital punishment and the Chessman case. On one side was Attorney General Pat Brown, and on the other Jake Ehrlich, who abhorred the death penalty. Brown cited Chessman's fourth and most recent stay of execution. He complained that it made a hero of a criminal and a laughing stock of the administration of justice. "If this sort of thing continues," he said, "the death penalty should be abolished. Chessman has attracted such wide notoriety that he has been able to stay in a death cell for six years!" The Attorney General advocated procedures to speed the time between sentence and execution.

The TV lights accentuated the solemn hollows in Ehrlich's cheeks. He spoke earnestly. "A killer is a sick person," he said. "He should be punished, but not killed. I cannot justify killing in defense of society any more than I can justify some poor fool committing murder."

He was not pleading for Chessman so much as reaffirming a lifelong conviction. Less than a month later, however, he was actively defending the doomed author. "Certain San Francisco people," he said, had asked him to appear in support of Justice Carter's decision, which had granted a final stay one day before the execution. It was a desperate move, and Ehrlich worked around the clock to prepare his arguments that the original trial transcript was faulty and the transcriber drunk. He pleaded before the State Supreme Court that he was "interested only in the due processes of law," and that a complete review of the case was needed.

"Little by little they are whittling down the rights of the

American people," Ehrlich argued. "The Los Angeles trial judge actually told the jury to hang this fellow. Justice Carter's order, in my opinion, cannot be set aside by the court without a full hearing on all the evidence and all the issues."

Eventually, the U. S. Supreme Court referred the case back to the district Federal Court, and Ehrlich had gained Chessman a little more time.

Some of his critics said: "Sure, Ehrlich comes in now. Wasn't Chessman's book a best-seller? Now he can pay Jake's fee!" It was more of the old carping, by lawyers Chessman *didn't* send for. Sometimes people said Jake won cases because he was a Mason, which was ridiculous. Ehrlich had saved the lives of Catholics, Protestants, Jews, Negroes and Chinamen, with juries that recognized no fraternity but the brotherhood of man. Jake didn't have time to trade on religious or fraternal affiliation. "There is a time in every trial when I must live inside that defendant," he said. "I must find some bond more universal than a lodge affiliation, and the jury must find it too."

4

There had been a time when Jake would turn out for every celebrity who came to San Francisco, and particularly for old friends like Jimmy Durante and Mae West. But as time went on he became a homebody. He was tired of "being a showpiece." If good friends wished to see him, they could meet him for lunch at Lurie's table, or at his own table in the Palm Court of the Palace.

Home was the spreading redwood house on the knoll in Marin County, where guests could always find the Confederate battle flag flapping from a madrone tree. The sign: "No trespassing . . . on pain of prosecution under Section 602 of the California Penal Code" meant nothing. Any friend was welcome. At home Jake was a throwback to the Southern Colonel of his boyhood, offering bourbon and branch water and endless tale-spinning. An electrically-charged wire circled his eleven-acre estate but only to keep the deer from eating the fuchsias.

At home, Jake was dapperly dressed whether he had guests or not. The starched linen had become almost a part of him; he couldn't tolerate California's traditional sportswear. He owned innumerable white shirts, and he wore them crisp and starched on even the hottest leisure Sunday. And he chose cuff links from his collection of 250 rare pairs as carefully as if he were going to court. (Perhaps the earrings a lady Papagaya Room guest sold to Al Williams when he said that "They would make beautiful links for The Master." Or perhaps the odd, unformed pearls from Governor Knight's son-in-law. Or the single pearls a prominent actress had charged to his hotel bill as a joke.)

A guest curious about the Ehrlich wardrobe would find enough suits in it so that the same suit need not be worn twice in a long trial, but the shoe closet would offer a surprise. Jake never owned more than two pairs at a time, one brown and one black. "A pair of shoes lasts me two years," he liked to boast, "because I never drag my feet. It is with a deep sense of loss that I throw away a pair. It is like discarding an old friend."

All things, it seemed, came back to friendships.

Jimmy Roosevelt's wife called Ehrlich when she decided to get a divorce. Jake remembered the Democratic Convention of 1920, when his own name was little known in San Francisco and he had had a sociable drink with Jimmy's father. Later Jake had several times been a guest at the White House. On one such occasion, Hitler was beginning his rampage

through Europe and had committed his first overt acts against
America.

"Mr. President," Jake had asked, "why don't we declare
war on Germany?"

Roosevelt, Jake recalled, took a long draw on his cigarette
and replied: "I was a father before I became President of the
United States. I do not want my sons to die. I would not want
the sons of others to die."

In the final analysis, Jake wanted no part of the divorce of
one of those sons. He asked Mrs. Roosevelt to arrange for
other counsel.

If friends were very important to him, so were their opinions. Justice Louis H. Ward of the State District Court of
Appeals recommended Jake for duty with the Marines. He
got a copy of the letter and framed it so he could see it often.
"I know him," said the Justice, "to be a keen, shrewd evalua-
tor of character, with a mind well regulated to discern min-
utely the truthfulness and falsity of evidence. I would gamble
on his physical ability in combat service, and I unhesitatingly
commend him as being absolutely loyal to any cause in which
he may be engaged."

Jake beamed like a small boy when he learned that Jean
Hersholt, the venerated "Dr. Christian," had described him as
"a congenial, vital personality, blessed with a rich sense of
humor."

Whenever critics spoke bitingly, he recalled the statement
of Greg Bautzer, a favorite movieland lawyer. "Jake Ehrlich,"
said Bautzer, "is about the best in his field. That's why we
call him The Master."

Others of his profession may have run up a higher score.
What was it Ray Jenkins, counsel for the Mundt Senatorial
Committee in the McCarthy-Army hearings, claimed? Three
hundred homicide cases? Ehrlich shook his head at that.
"When any California lawyer can top that for sheer num-

bers," he said, "the whole damned state will have been depopulated by murder. There won't be enough people left to pick a jury." In a city the size of San Francisco, with the legal work spread among a score of topnotch attorneys, fifty-plus homicides with never a first-degree conviction—Jake's score —would have to stand as a remarkable record. And it did; it was the legend.

But even a legend must include some defeats, and Ehrlich had his share. The most spectacular, perhaps, involved Paul C. Smith, redheaded executive editor of the *Chronicle,* who later became president of the Crowell-Collier Publishing Company. Smith was a combative man, and during the Atherton investigations he had editorial things to say about some of Jake's witnesses. After one attack Jake called Smith "to set him straight." It was one of the most vehement battles of the campaign, with Smith refusing to retreat one pica.

"Okay!" Jake finally shouted. "Say anything you want! Just spell my name right!"

That evening, as usual, Dora Jane went out for the papers. She came back puzzling over a *Chronicle.* "Daddy," she said, "you're all over the first page, but they sure don't know how to spell your name!"

Ehrlich looked and was astounded. Smith had assigned a clever rewrite man to determine how many ways the Ehrlich name could be misspelled. He had come up with just fewer than thirty, from "Earlick" to "Errlack," all crowded into one column. Jake called Smith and said: "Okay, you win."

5

So it was April. Came a crucial moment for the legend: the fifty-sixth homicide defense in the career of J. W. Ehrlich. It was not a big case, and yet for three weeks the courtroom was packed.

In the first days, when the prosecution almost got in an older, experienced jury panel, the legend was on shaky ground. Fighting them, exhausting their panel and getting to the new one dragged the case from April into May. The issues were complicated. Was the accused defending his own property? Or was it torture and robbery? Was he truly of "a malignant and abandoned heart," as the prosecution chose to say? Whatever impression the jury got would decide whether at long last a client of Jake's must sniff the bitter fumes of San Quentin's death chamber.

Tourists crowded in among the spectators. Perhaps they had tired of watching red-bellied ships wallow up from the Orient, had visited Golden Gate Park, the Cliff House, Seals Stadium and the Top of the Mark. Perhaps April's breezes, hounding torn papers off the streets, had chased them into the gray old Hall of Justice. More likely they had heard the legend of the courtroom master, the man of many coats and suits, of whom it was said: "If you're in trouble in Frisco, get Jake."

So here he was, now clutching his lapels like old Abe Lincoln, now standing with hand under his coat like Napoleon —there was a little of both men in him. But mostly it was straight Ehrlich: borrowing the bailiff's pencil, interrupting himself at dramatic moments to pour water, icily castigating the prosecutor, gazing at the judge like a lizard watching the sun half-lidded, constantly coming back to "this unfortunate accident," the alleged crime.

The defense counsel's dress marked the days—first a gray suit, then a brown, then plain blue, charcoal, pinstripe, dark brown, another gray, and finally the funereal "bar mitzvah" black that meant the climax, the denouement, the big day.

Spectators familiar with the legend would recognize faces.

The pretty girl in the front row weighing the evidence was Dora Jane, the daughter. The handsome, smiling woman with the auburn hair near the back of the room was Marjorie, his wife, who had told Jake in his darkest days that he would be a great trial lawyer. The handsome young man sliding a seat up to counsel table—looking exactly like the Jake of thirty years ago—would be Jake, Jr., who had decided not to try to follow in his father's footsteps.

That young prosecutor was watching Ehrlich like a hawk —his father was a pawnshop keeper who used to lend Jake quick twenties to buy rounds of drinks for the gang, back in his struggling days. And there was Willie Kamm, the great old ballplayer, held to the courtroom play even though the baseball season was opening out at the stadium.

Moments stood out above others in the testing of the legend. There was the Tenderloin witness testifying: "It was early in the evening. No tourists are around that early." And Ehrlich replying: "I understand that. I am familiar with San Francisco. I have been around here for some time."

There was the day when he goaded the prosecutor, saying to the jury: "Don't be afraid of Mr. Berman. He can't issue a warrant for your arrest. If he does, I'll defend you free." The jury laughed heartily; it was a favorite Ehrlich quip. And there was the moment in the heat of argument when the judge chided: "You're not impressing anyone."

But he *was* impressing someone. In one way or another, Jake was impressing everyone who watched. His was a unique position in San Francisco courtrooms. That could be seen in the eyes of the jury watching him curiously as he studied his notes, paying strict attention even to routine questions. The young crewcut attorney at his elbow, the press, bailiffs and even the homicide inspector addressed him in all seriousness as "Master." Not impressing anyone? The prosecution automatically agreed to noon recesses on Saints and Sinners' days.

Three additional prosecutors kept constant watch, for Jake was heavy artillery for their young men to oppose alone.

Though the judge might chide, he could not minimize Ehrlich's unique position in the square old courtroom. This was the heart of Jake's San Francisco. He had brought many changes to it in the thirty-odd years since he had stood and sassed a crusty old judge about beardless lawyers and billygoats. There were microphones at the bench and witness chair now, and a machine that reported verbatim the statements of all the principals. And Jake was far more jealous of his precious time.

He had crossed the halfway mark of the century. The fluorescent lights flickered over crests of silver in his wavy hair. There was far more use of the horn-rimmed spectacles; they represented more than an actor's properties now. The glasses might lie at his table for an hour, or be folded neatly into the waistband of his trousers, but eventually he would have to resort to them, with an apology to the jury: "We all get to this sooner or later."

"I suppose," he argued thoughtfully, "there are some people who *never* get excited—people like the atomic scientists over at the university or the man working in a sewer—there being very little real difference between them." Brashness had given way to reflection.

This was the mature Ehrlich defending a life and a legend. Dramatic, humorous, grim, combative, Chesterfieldian and Mephistophelean—this was Ehrlich, thirty-three years of him distilled into one final argument that may have been his greatest. It had to be because the facts were obscure except for that one fact that a man's life depended on his words. The verdict was guilty, but only in the second degree, and Ehrlich nodded. He filed notice of appeal. There still was life and hope, and the fight would go on. The legend of the little ex-cavalryman was intact.